CHINA'S
STRUGGLE TO
MODERNIZE

CHINA'S STRUGGLE TO MODERNIZE

SECOND EDITION

M ichael G asster
Rutgers University

McGraw-Hill, Inc.
New York St. Louis San Francisco Auckland Bogotá
Caracas Lisbon London Madrid Mexico City Milan
Montreal New Delhi San Juan Singapore
Sydney Tokyo Toronto

To my friends in China

 This book is printed on recycled, acid-free paper containing a minimum of 50% recycled de-inked fiber.

Second Edition

8 9 10 11 12 13 14 15 DOH DOH 90987654

CHINA'S STRUGGLE TO MODERNIZE

Library of Congress Cataloging-in-Publication Data ⁻

Gasster, Michael, (date).
    China's struggle to modernize / Michael Gasster. — 2nd
ed.
      p.   cm.
    Includes bibliographical references and index.
    ISBN 0-07-554407-5
    1. China—History—20th century.   I. Title.
DS761.G34   1993
951.05--dc20   93-34052

Cover design by Marsha Cohen.

Cover art, detail from *Ploughing* by Shih Lu, courtesy of the Prints Division, the New York Public Library, Astor, Lenox and Tilden Foundations.

PREFACE

Since 1971, when the first edition of this book was completed, sensational events have been reported in China—an attempt to assassinate Mao Zedong led by his erstwhile "closest comrade-in-arms," a radical clique vaulting into power and creating ten years of havoc all across the country, "a great revolutionary movement" erupting spontaneously in April 1976, a coup d'état six months later, and in 1980 a lurid trial of the old leadership and various alleged conspirators. Although these reports may not be entirely accurate, they require examination. In any case, momentous changes have occurred—new policies that have deeply affected the lives of hundreds of millions of people, earthquakes and floods that have literally changed the configuration of vast areas of the country and inflicted death and suffering on many millions more, the death within the space of eight months in 1976 of three outstanding leaders of Chinese Communism, including Mao. Finally, there has been the unprecedented issuing by the central leadership (after fifteen months of preparation during which thousands of people and many meetings forced six major revisions) of a lengthy document reviewing sixty years of Chinese Communist Party history and reevaluating Mao's role in that history.

All of this would seem to be enough to permit and even require revision and updating of the first edition of this book. But there is yet more. Not the least of the changes in the last decade has been the widening of contacts between China and other countries, including the opportunity for more Chinese to go abroad and for more foreigners to visit China. In particular, relations between China and the United States, after more than twenty years of hot and cold war, shifted course dramatically in 1971–1972 and finally achieved "normalization" in 1979. For American students of Chinese history this meant an opportunity to supplement library scholarship with personal observation and direct human contact.

Beginning in 1976, therefore, I have been able to make three trips to China, spending a total of about fourteen months there and traveling approximately 14,000 miles across the country, mostly by rail but also by boat, bus, and occasionally airplane, plus uncounted miles on foot and by bicycle. In that time I also lived on campuses in three cities in very different parts of the country—Beijing, Wuhan, and Chengdu—for periods ranging from two to six months. So rich were these journeys, so rewarding the sustained contact with Chinese friends and colleagues as well as the chance meetings or brief associations with neighbors, traveling companions, and people with whom I merely shared a table in a crowded noodle shop or small restaurant, that I wish to dedicate this edition to the many people in China who taught me so much. Whether I have been able to transmit some portion of these riches to the reader I cannot know, but having been privileged to be touched by them I feel bound to try to share them. Hence this second edition of my little book.

Another reason for a revised edition is the great volume and high quality of scholarship that has been published in the last decade. I am grateful that for this edition the publisher has agreed to an expanded bibliography, which allows me to acknowledge more fully and explicitly the many colleagues on whose work I have relied. Together with material emerging from political polemics in China, this scholarship suggests reconsideration of many issues in all of modern Chinese history, and particularly the last twenty-five years of it. Some changes have therefore been made throughout the text, especially in the handling of the period since 1956.

In this edition names of people and places are rendered in the Chinese phonetic system (*pin-yin*), which became standard for all Chinese foreign language publications as of 1979. Thus Mao Tse-tung is now Mao Zedong, Peking is now Beijing, Sian is now Xi'an, Canton is now Guangzhou, Yenan is now Yan'an. For personal names, the index lists both new spelling and old. Since *pin-yin* is much closer to correct pronunciation than the old Wade-Giles system, I have eliminated from this edition the footnotes showing how to pronounce Chinese names.

I would like to take this opportunity to underline and amplify one point made in the preface of the first edition. Having now seen different parts of the country and lived among the Chinese people, I am only more deeply convinced that no one book can tell more than a minute fraction of what there is to be known. Not only is there too much ever to be told, but what happens among the people is often related only marginally or very indirectly to what happens at the levels of high policy and leadership. In a small book such as this, full justice cannot be done to both these realms and the relationship between them. Again, therefore, I refer readers to the colleagues whose works are listed in the bibliography and, of course, to the reader's own critical faculties.

Finally, while the substance of the matter must be dealt with mostly in the body of the book, a word is necessary concerning "modernization." Since about 1977, the main thrust of Chinese official policy has been "the four modernizations" or, more recently, "socialist modernization." By one of those peculiar coincidences that crop up occasionally in the history of China and its contacts with the outside world, the term "modernization" became fashionable in China just as it was crumbling under the attack of social scientists abroad, especially in the United States. While the academic battles were by no means without substance, they did depart rapidly from any reality that has much meaning for China, and one has to haul away tons of rubble to find a few breathing wounded underneath. Meanwhile, the Chinese have explained what they mean by "Chinese-type modernization," as I hope this book is able to show. For them too (like American scholars) defining what they meant by "modernization" has been a struggle that sometimes seemed as arduous as achieving modernization. It is *their* struggles that form the subject of this book. Readers who are interested in the academic debates are referred to the appropriate titles in the bibliography. On this matter, as in all else, may the period of polemics end and a new era of irenics begin.

M.G.
New York City

NOVEMBER 1981

. . . According to a general geography by an Englishman, the territory of our China is eight times larger than that of Russia, ten times that of America, one hundred times that of France, and two hundred times that of England. . . . Yet now we are shamefully humiliated by those four nations in the recent treaties—not because our climate, soil, or resources are inferior to theirs, but because our people are really inferior. . . . Why are they small and yet strong? Why are we large and yet weak? We must try to discover some means to become their equal, and that also depends upon human effort. Regarding the present situation there are several major points: in making use of the ability of our manpower, with no one neglected, we are inferior to the barbarians; in securing the benefit of the soil, with nothing wasted, we are inferior to the barbarians; in maintaining a close relationship between the ruler and the people, with no barrier between them, we are inferior to the barbarians; and in the necessary accord of word with deed, we are also inferior to the barbarians. The way to correct these four points lies with ourselves, for they can be changed at once if only our Emperor would set the general policy right. There is no need for outside help in these matters. . . .

What we then have to learn from the barbarians is only the one thing, solid ships and effective guns.

—*Feng Guifen, 1860*

To nourish her own culture China needs to assimilate a good deal of foreign progressive culture, not enough of which was done in the past. We should assimilate whatever is useful to us today not only from the present-day socialist and new-democratic cultures but also from the earlier cultures of other nations, for example, from the culture of the various capitalist countries in the Age of Enlightenment. However, we should not gulp any of this foreign material down uncritically, but must treat it as we do our food—first chewing it, then submitting it to the working of the stomach and intestines with their juices and secretions, and separating it into nutriment to be absorbed and waste matter to be discarded—before it can nourish us. To advocate "wholesale westernization" is wrong. China has suffered a great deal from the mechanical absorption of foreign material. Similarly, in applying Marxism to China, Chinese communists must fully and properly integrate the universal truth of Marxism with the concrete practice of the Chinese revolution, or in other words, the universal truth of Marxism must be combined with specific national characteristics and acquire a definite national form if it is to be useful, and in no circumstances can it be applied subjectively as a mere formula. Marxists who make a fetish of formulas are simply playing the fool with Marxism and the Chinese revolution, and there is no room for them in the ranks of the Chinese revolution. Chinese culture should have its own form, its own national form.

—*Mao Zedong, 1940*

Last year, I was a member of a Chinese economic delegation which visited Switzerland, West Germany, Austria and France. I came away with the impression that the Second World War had greatly damaged Western Europe's economy and that the USA had played an important part in its recovery. But as long as people in those countries rebuilt and developed their national economies by their own efforts, they were able to maintain national traditions and avoid Americanization.

The same holds true for China's modernization. We will surely learn from western countries and further our economic co-operation with the West. However, this by no means amounts to westernizing China.

—*Ma Hong, vice-president of the*
Chinese Academy of Social Sciences, 1981

CONTENTS

xi

1

THE MODERN WORLD AND
NINETEENTH-CENTURY CHINA

ONE DAY in 1945 a team of five Communist cadres* arrived in remote Stone Wall Village. Their mission was to start a revolution among its five hundred residents. They posted proclamations, called a meeting to explain the posters, and tried to speak privately with individual villagers. The cadres found themselves ignored, for the peasants were afraid of the landlord, who dominated the village. Eventually a poor tenant farmer came to talk to two of the cadres. At last they persuaded him that his poverty was not due to his own shortcomings —"I guess I have a bad brain," he would say—but to the high rent exacted by the landlord. The farmer brought his friends to the discussions, and the group grew to thirteen. But news of the meeting reached the landlord, and one of the thirteen was murdered. The terrified peasants promptly ceased coming to meetings; the cadres, themselves shaken, were back where they had begun. But they persisted. Once again they turned to recruiting peasants. When finally the peasants' number grew to thirty, they invaded the landlord's house and took him prisoner. For two days at mass meetings they accused the landlord of crimes and cruelty, and three days later seven hundred

* The term "cadre," sometimes roughly translated "official" or "functionary," refers to someone who has received training in Communist methods of organization and leadership and who is considered qualified to exercise authority and assume tasks requiring initiative and responsibility.

1

people (including visitors from nearby villages) participated in a meeting that ended with the landlord's death.

In the 1940s incidents similar to this one occurred in thousands of Chinese villages. Some peasants who had been brutalized, others who merely saw an opportunity for gain, and still others whose reasons we do not know were roused to deal peremptorily, harshly, and even savagely with landlords and officials. The peasants did not think they were engaged in a nation's "struggle to modernize." They were struggling, not to do anything as abstract as "modernize," but to survive—to eat and to be safe from bandits, undisciplined soldiers, greedy landlords, corrupt officials, and the vagaries of nature. But in their own way the awakened peasants, like the scientists experimenting in laboratories or the workers making steel, were fighting for modernization. Before 1900 peasants had often rebelled and killed, but never had such rebellions been part of a larger movement to change society in fundamental ways. After 1900 such larger movements developed and in the 1920s began to reach out to the peasants. Their struggle for survival became part of China's struggle to modernize; and, in turn, China's struggle to modernize became rooted in the countryside.

In this gradual coalescence of two struggles, a crucial turning point was reached during the war against Japan (1937–1945), when urban intellectuals and workers went into rural areas to organize the resistance. The five cadres who came to Stone Wall Village included two intellectuals (a former teacher and a former student), a waiter, a shop assistant, and a farmer. Thus the cadre team in itself represented a combination of backgrounds and exemplified the new social cohesion that developed in wartime China; but even more important, the cadre team in its relationship to the villagers represented a new conception of politics and a new method of effecting social change.

The overturning of Stone Wall Village thus reveals in microcosm some of the main issues in China's modernization. And it suggests some important questions. What brought thousands of outsiders to isolated villages? What kept them going, sometimes for many weeks, in the face of the peasants' fear and silence? How did the cadres overcome their own fear? What finally made the hesitant peasants act? What happened to the cadres and the villagers and to the relationships between them once the landlords were gone and the villages went through land reform, collectivization, and communization? What does all of this mean for China's modernization? Perhaps we can begin to seek a few answers.

The incident at Stone Wall Village was originally described by correspondent Jack Belden in *China Shakes the World*. When that book was published in 1949, the title must have seemed odd, especially to Westerners, who were accustomed to shaking China rather than being shaken by it. For more than a century, China's weakness had been a fact of life. For several centuries a few Western nations had dominated world history. As Professor R. R. Palmer once wrote to explain why his history of the modern world dealt chiefly with Europe:

> The main reason is that modern civilization has been formed by the expansion of ideas, institutions, and industries that originated in Europe. . . . The last few centuries may in fact be called the European Age, and while this age is probably now closing, it has produced the world as we know it today.

Few scholars in the West would take exception to this distinguished historian's view of the modern world. Indeed, it is by the familiar characteristics of this world that we often decide whether or not a country is "modern." Does the country have enough science, technology, and industry to outweigh traditional forms of knowledge and production? Does it have high-speed means of transportation and electronic communication, a high degree of literacy, and universal education? Do its farmers use chemical fertilizers and machinery, and do they produce for the market instead of only for their own needs? Do its political leaders have close contact with the masses, and do citizens feel a common bond with each other? Do people think that they have a reasonable possibility for having a different and better life than their parents and grandparents? If these characteristics predominate in the society, we regard it as a modern one. The point in time at which these characteristics begin to overshadow traditional ones is said to mark the beginning of a country's modern history. Measurement of such characteristics is difficult, but among the rough yardsticks used are the ratio of inanimate to animate power, per capita productivity, the number of people living close to or using railroads and other relatively high-speed means of transportation, and the number of people occupied in primary industries, such as agriculture, compared with those in manufacturing and service or administrative occupations.

The Chinese, like many other peoples in the last century, have attempted to increase their use of machinery and reduce their dependence on hand tools and human energy, to increase the amount that each person can produce, and to pierce their vast, undernourished interior with life-giving railways, roads, and airlines. But until very recently China seemed unable to effect such changes rapidly and efficiently or, indeed, to perform the most basic functions that a nation should —notably, feeding its people adequately. Despite vast natural resources and the great talents and energy of the Chinese people, change has been painfully slow in China.

One reason that change has been comparatively slow there is that China had a deeply rooted tradition of paternalistic leadership. Relationships between leaders and followers are central to any society, but in China those relationships, and especially the character and outlook of leaders, were the primary concern of the great majority of philosophers and statesmen for some two-and-one-half millennia. Questions of how to exercise leadership were central to thinkers at least as early as Confucius, and his successors grappled endlessly with problems of duty, social obligations, and conflicting loyalties. Eventually an elaborate social code developed that rested firmly on family relationships and therefore reached into the very marrow of every Chinese. Each thought, word, and action was heavily influenced by an idea of what was proper between people of different stations. Just as in the family, so in society at large an elaborate hierarchy developed in which the authority of the older over the younger and men over women was very nearly absolute.

In the society at large the wealthy and the educated few* claimed a status and authority much like a father's in the family. Their claim was bolstered by a wide range of ideological and institutional supports. As the major beneficiaries of the existing system, they tended to be strongly conservative. Change in traditional China was therefore inhibited by the existence of a highly stratified society, a paternalistic hierarchy dominated by a small, wealthy, and educated elite. China's struggle to modernize can be studied by focusing on the emergence of a new generation of leaders that were dedicated to far-reaching change. But our study must give equal attention to the new role of the Chinese masses as a political force and to the new relationships that developed between leaders and the general population.

Modernization in China required conscious, sustained, perservering, dedicated effort against the tide of history. Although modernization

---

* It is estimated that as many as 30 to 40 percent of the male population and 2 to 10 percent of the female population were basically literate in late imperial times, but this may err on the high side, and more than basic literacy was necessary for entrance into the elite.

has occurred nowhere without great effort, the historical obstacles, and therefore the effort required, were probably much greater in China than in Western Europe. But even if the problems were not actually greater, it is clear that in late-modernizing societies the role of leaders would be different. English leaders, if indeed they were conscious that they were engineering "modernization," had no example to study; Chinese leaders could learn from England, Germany, the United States, Russia, and Japan, and they could not avoid being more aware than English leaders of modernization as a conscious goal. Another difference is that China undertook to modernize largely because imperialism threatened its very existence; modernization meant survival as a nation. China's nationalistic leaders therefore felt a special duty to promote modernization. This feeling was particularly strong among intellectuals, heirs to deep traditional obligations both to serve society and to lead it.

Twentieth-century Chinese leaders, especially intellectuals, have been heavily influenced by the West, but to them modernization has not necessarily meant the same as Westernization. Modernization is a process whereby a society *incorporates* the new ideas, practices, and institutions necessary for the mastery of science, technology, and industrial production. For the non-Western world, this process has included a certain amount of Westernization—by which is meant the *transplantation* of distinctively Western ideas, practices, and institutions. But modernization is not mere transplantation; it includes the rejuvenation of some traditional ideas and practices, the modification of what has been taken from the West, and the assimilation of outside borrowings to internal customs and conditions. (An interesting example is Japan, which surely has modernized, but quite a strong case can be made that Japan has not Westernized.) China's leaders, united in their determination to make their country modern, resist policies that tend to make China too Western. Thus Mao Zedong said that China should assimilate foreign culture in order to "nourish her own culture," but he rejected "wholesale Westernization." The Chinese, however, had not always thus distinguished the processes of modernization and Westernization. How they came to do so is a major theme in our story.

IMPERIAL CHINA

China has always been in touch with other peoples and subject to foreign influences. Contact with Central and Southeast Asia was maintained throughout recorded Chinese history. Indirect trade with Rome, by way of the Middle East, began in the second century B.C., and Buddhism came to China from India soon after. Chinese ships, which far surpassed European ships in size and construction, crossed the Indian Ocean to Africa almost a century before the Portuguese sailed to India. Through twenty centuries, China and Europe influenced each other relatively little, but China gave far more to the West than it took; similarly, China changed Buddhism more than Buddhism changed China. What is sometimes referred to as China's "isolation" must be understood as the failure of foreign influence to alter the basic style of Chinese civilization, not the absence of foreign influence.

China knew no civilization higher than its own and had no conception that there could be such a civilization. To the Chinese, all foreign traders and emissaries were barbarians, and almost every contact they had with other peoples, from the nomads of Central Asia to such wide-eyed Europeans as Marco Polo, seemed to confirm their own superiority. Partly as a result of the deference paid to Chinese civilization by nearly all outsiders before the nineteenth century, the Chinese came to believe that the world had only one great culture, China's, and that all people should share in it. Thus China did not develop the idea of a world of nation-states dealing with each other on the basis of equality. As John K. Fairbank has put it, "China was a world in itself, not a nation among nations."

As a world in itself China was thought by its leaders to be self-sufficient. It could supply its own needs in all respects, spiritual and intellectual as well as material. When the British first challenged this notion, sending a mission to China in 1793 aimed at developing trade and establishing diplomatic relations in the Western fashion, the Chinese emperor dismissed the proposal out of hand. Privately referring to the gifts sent by King George III as "commonplace" and "meager," the emperor excused the king for expressing "wild ideas and hopes"; perhaps the British ambassador had exceeded his instructions, or the King himself, living "in a remote and inaccessible region, far across the spaces of ocean," might have been ignorant of China's ways. In any case, "there is nothing we lack," he wrote to London. "We have never set much store on strange or ingenious objects, nor do we need any more of your country's manufactures."

This verbal pat on the head, contained in a lengthy message that oozed condescension in every line, could only have startled, mystified, and perhaps enraged the ruler of the British Empire. But from the

Chinese point of view it was a clear expression of how things stood between China and the rest of the world. As Bertrand Russell once sagely remarked, "No one understands China until this document has ceased to seem absurd."

It is no accident that the tone of the emperor's message was one of a stern but indulgent father addressing a wayward son. The Chinese view of the world, not only of China, has long been rooted in the structure of the family. Much as families embraced elders and youngers unto many generations and to varying degrees of closeness from parents and children to distant cousins, all with clearly defined status, so too all of human society consisted of comparable graded relationships. The emperor could be thought of as "the father and mother of the people." China, the name of which in Chinese literally means "middle country," was at the center of "all under Heaven." The emperor presided over the entire human family. Although there were strong elements of myth in this concept, it reflected a deep and powerful Chinese value, a wish to bring about a world that is organic and harmonious and integrated, along the lines of an ideal family. This wish has frequently influenced Chinese policy and actions, making it intolerable, for example, for China to accept a position in the world comparable to children in a family.

One of the most persistent themes in China's history is the strong effort to create and maintain an effective political unity. Long before China became an empire, the impulse to create a rational political order was already a potent force, and considerable thought was devoted to the best means of creating a viable system of government. As early as the second millennium B.C. the Chinese were beginning to develop an administrative center to which outlying villages were linked in a relatively systematic fashion. During the next thirty centuries, they accumulated a wealth of experience in political administration unparalleled in human history. The solutions they worked out varied according to changing circumstances, of course, but the Chinese have always been faced with certain recurring problems due to the size and diversity of their land and people. Centuries of dealing with these problems produced distinctive patterns of political behavior and organization. Clusters of villages and towns developed relationships among themselves that became increasingly difficult to modify. Individuals became accustomed to dealing with each other according to practiced means: Villages A, B, and C paid taxes to agents sent out from town X and settled disputes according to principles they and their forebears had long since determined were best. There were margins for diversification.

Relationships were not the same in the north as in the south, nor in big cities and their surrounding countryside; but even variations were likely to be deeply rooted in ancient experience. Divergent local patterns sometimes had to be reconciled with the needs of central authority, such as when great armies had to be raised against invading nomads, but the thirty centuries had allowed time for many patterns of reconciliation to be woven.

China's traditional patterns of political unity were far from uniformly harmonious blends, but they had developed out of so much reasoned experimentation that nearly everyone had long since stopped thinking there might be a better alternative. The government was able to perform its essential functions reasonably well, and the people could only give thanks that life was no harder than it was. By late imperial times, according to one authority on the traditional Chinese state, "it was probably the most elaborate and sophisticated governmental system existing in the world in its time." During the Qing dynasty (1644–1912) the system was more elaborate than ever because the rulers were Manchus, descendants of a neighboring tribe that had conquered China. As foreign conquerors who were a small minority in a huge land, they felt insecure and hence added many administrative devices to protect their rule.

Under what has been called imperial China's "centralized authoritarianism," power radiating from the national capital spent itself as it passed through provincial capitals on its way to the nearly 1,500 local administrative districts (or counties). A surprisingly small bureaucracy* functioned with the help of many semiofficial and unofficial aides and supernumeraries to balance but rarely to overcome centrifugal force. At the district level, power administered by bureaucrats gave way to a wide variety of local power relationships. The relationships were worked out, depending on local conditions, among minor employees of the bureaucrats and various members of the local elite, including scholar-gentry, landowners, village elders, and other such prominent or influential people. Wealth was a source of power but so was education, and kinship was so important that a tightly knit clan could have influence that was out of proportion to its wealth and educational level. A shifting and uneasy balance was maintained among what was by 1800 a patchwork of administrative devices and informal local arrangements. Even when sewn as tightly as imperial rulers could manage, the administrative

* In the Qing period there were about 27,000 officials.

system was never all-encompassing. There were always countless communities in which little or no outside authority was felt. Elaborate as it was, imperial autocratic rule remained incomplete. Most people paid scarcely any attention to the central government and only a little more to county officials. They had very few contacts beyond family, clan, and nearby villages.

Administrative voids were filled, where they were filled at all, primarily by the scholar-gentry. These educated men, usually of some wealth, helped to manage local affairs that officials did not handle. Some of them had been officials or would later become officials, and others derived an income from land they owned or from teaching. Their influence, security, and prestige were greatly enhanced by privileges they held (such as exemptions from certain taxes), by their close association with officialdom, and by their stature as learned men. Entry into this class, which constituted the highest social stratum in traditional China, was obtained primarily by success in the civil service examinations. Nearly everyone was eligible for the examinations, but since success required many years of rigorous training, the rich had a considerable advantage. The scholar-gentry was not a hereditary or entirely self-perpetuating group, and there were times when as much as 40 percent or more of its new members came from "commoner" status (that is, from families that had not had a scholar-gentry member for at least several generations). But, on the whole, the scholar-gentry exhibited a remarkably high degree of continuity in its membership, particularly since new members from commoner backgrounds shared or quickly came to share the values and general world view of the elite group. Even prospering merchants, who in Western Europe became an independent force and a major agent of change, in China sought entrance to the existing elite rather than attempting to assert their own class interests. Over the centuries, the scholar-gentry succeeded in virtually monopolizing social status and political power, and therefore a gulf existed between the scholar-gentry and the rest of the Chinese people.

The elite's active participation in local affairs helped to bridge the gap, and so did the power of certain Confucian principles. One principle was that educated men must serve society, and another was that they must set a good moral example. The latter principle strengthened the ties between upper- and lower-class values and institutions. A Chinese family head might feel that he bore the same relationship to his family as the court, officials, and scholar-gentry did to society as a

An upper-class Chinese home, nineteenth century, Guangzhou. © Samuel Wagstaff

whole. Ideally, government and family were based on the same principles.

These shared principles permitted the relatively effective functioning of the society. Although the society was sharply divided between the roughly 1 or 2 percent of the population that had wealth, power, and privilege—the officials, scholar-gentry, their kin, and a few others including some rich merchants and landowners—and the 98 or 99 percent that did not, there were long periods of just rule and acceptable living conditions, to say nothing of the extraordinary achievements of Chinese civilization. Never in the history of the world did so few manage to dominate so many for so long. Hundreds of times, when domination became too oppressive or traditional arrangements failed for some other reason, the peasants rose in revolt, but only three or four times in two thousand years did they succeed in sending great dynasties crashing into oblivion. The old system was always restored, and the changes that were made were always heavily outweighed by the continuities.

By the nineteenth century traditional arrangements were failing more seriously than ever before. Peace, prosperity, and new crops had permitted the population to grow far beyond anything known in the past, and the delicate balance maintained by a resilient but always precarious system was upset. Size of farms shriveled, many had to be sold, hunger and disease spread, and millions existed in suffering, anger, banditry, and revolt. Not coincidentally, the quality of the Chinese leadership likewise declined. A succession of mediocre emperors reigned in Beijing from 1796 on, and the entire administration became riddled with incompetence and corruption. In this forbidding climate the European Age dawned for China.

CHINA AND THE MODERN WORLD

Foreign traders coming to China had long been considered bearers of tribute. From the early sixteenth to the early nineteenth century, European traders were similarly treated. As the Industrial Revolution accelerated, the ideas and economic needs of Westerners in general, and Great Britain in particular, could no longer be satisfied by the Chinese system of dealing with them as tributary states. The British came to regard free trade not merely as an economic necessity but as a law of nature. Government decrees, intoned one English exponent of laissez faire, "are erected against and opposed to the natural tendency of things and are in the end as absurd and ineffective as it would be to direct the winds by Order in Council, or to manage the tides by Act of Parliament." Business interests insisted on official support for their demands that China facilitate Western-style commerce. Meanwhile the British smuggled vast amounts of opium into China, inflaming the trade issue.

China's economic and political system, which had been adequate to manage relations with all preindustrial societies, could no longer accommodate changing British needs. Soon the Chinese belief that China was the entire civilized world also clashed with British national pride. War resulted in 1839, and Britain's victory in 1842 brought its traders most of what they wanted. Hong Kong became British, five ports were opened to trade, and in those "treaty ports" foreigners were allowed to live permanently, trade freely, and be governed by their own laws and courts.

This last provision (called "extraterritoriality"), which many Chinese were later to regard as the most repugnant, was added in an 1844 treaty with the United States. The Americans and French rushed to make treaties with China providing them with the same privileges as those won by the British in war. Eager to avoid further wars, hoping that the foreigners in their greed might fight among themselves and permit China to play one off against another, and seeing no difference between giving all of China's limited foreign trade to Britain alone or dividing it among three countries, the Chinese soon agreed to the additional treaties. The treaty with France added the right to establish Roman Catholic missions. Since the British had had the foresight to specify in their treaty that whatever other powers gained would also be given to Britain, and since the others followed the British example, China was now thrown open to the outside world. A new era, soon to be called by the Chinese the era of the "unequal treaties" and of "semicolonialism," had not so much dawned over China as it had exploded. It would also come to be known as "the century of humiliation." The treaties were not finally abrogated until 1943.

Eventually more than eighty cities were opened to trade. There were also seventeen settlements in which foreigners could live, own property, preach Christianity, and govern by their own laws not only themselves but also the many Chinese who lived in these enclaves. Some of the settlements were sizable. The foreign settlement in Shanghai, for example, by 1928 measured 5,584 acres and had a population of 833,000; the separate French concession added another 2,500 acres and 297,000 people. Thus Shanghai alone had well over a million people living in foreign-controlled territory on nominally Chinese soil, and about 96.5 percent of them were Chinese. It was in such settlements that many Chinese first came into contact with foreigners. Increasing numbers of Westerners also began to travel into the interior of China, introducing their religion and their worldly goods, weaving new threads into China's intellectual, social, and economic fabric. China's tariff became subject to the control of Western powers, and China had to pay heavy indemnities for war damages; these two impositions seriously damaged China's capacity to improve its economy. As defeat followed defeat in major wars and minor clashes throughout the century, Chinese life was affected to an ever widening degree by the presence of growing numbers of foreigners who lived according to their own customs.

In addition to the disturbances connected with foreign relations, China found itself faced with urgent internal problems. Population spurted from about 150 million in 1700 to more than 300 million around 1800, and to 430 million by 1850. This caused a great strain on China's resources, economic system, and government machinery. The strains impaired the efficiency of production and distribution, tax collection, and government services. The cost of wars and defeats added further burdens. As the economy foundered and the government increasingly found its troubles unmanageable, popular protest spread. Outbursts against the government broke out here and there in China toward the end of the eighteenth century and with increasing ferocity and frequency in the first half of the nineteenth century. Rebellions in the middle of the nineteenth century, the most serious of which was the Taiping Rebellion (1850–1864), took perhaps 20 million or more human lives, more than perished on both sides in World War I. Foreign eyewitnesses reported on the destruction, chaos, and human misery: Fields turned into desolate wilderness and cities into rubble, the Taiping capital razed to a degree that it "appeared more like a dense jungle than a city." Wild beasts had come out of their dens in the hills and settled in the ruins of deserted towns, formerly rich plains "were strewn with human skeletons, their rivers polluted with floating carcasses," the survivors in some areas "driven to cannibalism to satisfy the cravings of hunger." Even forty years after the rebellions travelers came upon great walled cities that were empty of human life.

Precisely as these internal troubles engulfed China, the second wave of foreign invasion also struck. Between 1856 and 1860, as the Taipings threatened to overturn the dynasty and forced Beijing to take extreme measures to preserve its rule, the British and French launched new campaigns to expand their positions in China. It was this war that, for the first time, brought foreign power into Beijing itself, sent the court into flight, and forced a handful of people to reexamine China's position.

The wars of 1839–1842 had done virtually nothing to shake Chinese views of the world. A sense of superiority built on so many centuries of genuine achievement, bolstered by girders of philosophical explanation and adorned with myth, did not yield so easily to one demonstration of military strength. The Chinese were no strangers to enemies with superior military skills. For nearly half their history all or part of the territory "within the wall" (i.e., south of the Great Wall), as China's heartland was called, had been under the control of foreigners. The existing dynasty was only the latest example of conquerors who had ridden to power on horseback. Superior military skills were a common trait of barbarians. But the skills of government and the higher arts of civilization were the traits of the Chinese. Even as a high Chinese official negotiated the first humiliating treaties, he referred to Western-ers as "people from outside the bounds of civilization." And while people such as the Americans were to be commended for "their determination to turn toward culture" (the U.S. negotiator had used some polite language about China), there was really no hope for them: "Of all the countries, it [the United States] is the most uncivilized and remote . . . , in an isolated place outside the pale, solitary and ignorant. Not only in the forms of edicts and laws are they entirely unversed, but if the meaning be rather deep they would probably not even be able to comprehend. It would seem that we must follow a rather simple style." There could be no serious consideration of learning from such people. One official who "took the risk," as he put it, of suggesting to the emperor in 1841 that China buy Western ships and guns was silenced and dared not speak again.

Thus in the 1840s China retained its confident belief in its own superiority and self-sufficiency. The foreign threat seemed manageable. The five treaty ports and Hong Kong were all far to the south, on the fringes of the empire, and only a few hundred foreigners were present. Troublesome, to be sure, like gnats and mosquitoes, but controllable with a few swishes of the tail. The real troubles were internal. Still, an old and cardinal principle was that the two combined, "inside disorder and outside calamity," could be fatal to a dynasty.

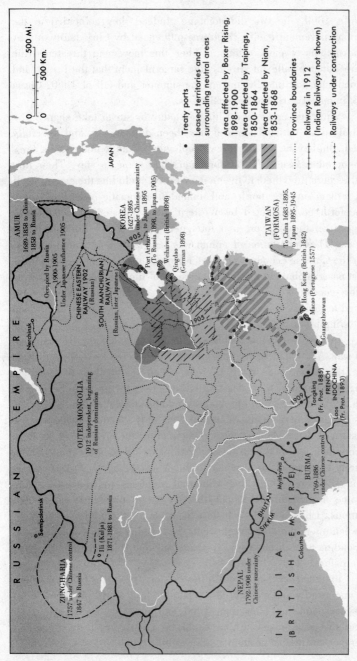

Treaty ports

Leased territories and
surrounding neutral areas

Area affected by Boxer Rising,
1898-1900

Area affected by Taipings,
1850-1864

Area affected by Nian,
1853-1868

Province boundaries

Railways in 1912
(Indian Railways not shown)

Railways under construction

JAPAN

R U S S I A N   E M P I R E

Nerchinsk

AMUR
1689-1858 to China
1858 to Russia

Occupied by Russia
1900-1905

Under Japanese influence 1905

CHINESE EASTERN
RAILWAY 1902
(Russian)

SOUTH MANCHURIAN
RAILWAY
(Russian, later Japanese)

KOREA
1627-1895
under Chinese suzerainty

1905

Port Arthur
To Russia 1898, to Japan 1905

Weihaiwei (British 1898)

Qingdao
(German 1898)

TAIWAN
(FORMOSA)
To China 1683-1895,
to Japan 1895-1945

Hong Kong (British 1842)

Macao (Portuguese 1557)

Guangzhouwan

Semipalatinsk

ZUNGHARIA
1757 under Chinese control
1847 to Russia

Ili (Kulja)
1871-1881 to Russia

OUTER MONGOLIA
1912 independent, beginning
of Russian domination

1902

Tongking
(Fr. Prot. 1885)
FRENCH
INDOCHINA

Laos (Fr. Prot. 1893)

BURMA
1769-1886
under Chinese control

Myitkyina

NEPAL
1792-1908 under
Chinese suzerainty

BHUTAN

SIKKIM

Calcutta

I N D I A
(B R I T I S H   E M P I R E)

The Qing Dynasty, 1644-1912—"Inside Disorder and Outside Calamity"

In 1860, the two did combine. Indeed they coincided in the Taiping movement itself, which was influenced by Christianity and by some notions of modernization. When this movement threatened the entire Yangtze valley at virtually the same moment that the British and French smashed into Beijing, in the summer and fall of 1860, China sank unmistakably into national crisis.

With this crisis, the China of today began to take shape. The central issue, national survival, had been dramatically and forcefully posed. But beyond that, as a few people now began to understand, lay a host of other issues. These foreigners had come to stay. Their new treaties permitted them to live in more cities, including the capital itself and others in the north and inland. Diplomatic relations would henceforth be conducted by Western rules. Missionaries could own property in the interior, and foreigners could travel throughout the empire. The importation of opium was legalized. Foreigners' controls over the Chinese economy were extended. Chinese began to see that the West posed a challenge to their entire way of life and world view. For so history-conscious a people as the Chinese, so lately and wholly committed to their own ideas of self-sufficiency and superiority, this was a shattering blow.

In 1860 only a few people were in a position to view the challenge this way. Many had seen crisis brewing for a long time, but to them it was still primarily an internal crisis, chiefly a rebellion that seemed altogether familiar, to be dealt with as others in the past had been dealt with, after which all other problems would be simple matters. The crisis was a great mix of many elements, some only distantly related to the Western challenge, others affected not at all by the presence of Western imperialism. It would be a mistake to think of nineteenth-century China entirely in terms of its response to the Western impact. Still, between about 1840 and 1900 China's internal problems and domestic affairs became inextricably tied up with its external problems and foreign relations. China's modern history is a story of complex interaction between internal and external events, with China and the outside world responding to each other in ways quite different from anything that had gone before.

In the *modern* period of Chinese history, problems faced by China became rapidly and steadily less separable from world problems, until at some point (no later than 1900 and probably even earlier) no important issue inside China could be clearly understood without reference to China's position in the world.

"Why are they small and yet strong?" asked a Chinese scholar in 1860. "Why are we large and yet weak?"

In 1860 "they" were mainly England and France. Soon Japan was added and others, including countries not so small—Russia, the United States. But the questions have been the same for well over a century, and they have given birth to a quest that is at the center of modern Chinese history: "We must try to discover some means to become their equal," continued the scholar. One generation after another has echoed him, each more urgently, even desperately, than the one before.

The urgency and the desperation are simply explained. The very survival of hundreds of millions of people has been at stake. As Chinese leaders have seen it, the entire heritage of a high and distinctive culture, unique in the scale and glory of its contribution to human civilization, has also been at stake. Our scholar of 1860 was writing no academic treatise, raising no bookish questions. He wrote as British and French troops plundered the capital of his country, laying waste even the palace of the emperor, sending the Chinese court fleeing in terror far into the mountains. Crucial areas of the country were being lost to Chinese rebels and foreign invaders. An immense double-edged crisis, from within and without, had broken across the face of China. Blood was to flow for fully a century before it eased. Tens of millions would die, and countless others would suffer enormous hardship. Discovering some means to become the equal of Western countries has been literally a matter of life or death to many millions in China.

Not surprisingly, the vast majority of those who were in a position to see the Western challenge dug in to defend their way of life. Even our scholar, among the most far-sighted, clear-eyed, and outspoken men of his day, gave a surprisingly simple answer to his own questions: "What we then have to learn from the barbarians is only the one thing, solid ships and effective guns." Nurtured in the crucible of war, China's struggle to modernize has inevitably stressed the tools of war. But as our scholar's analysis of China's inferiority to the "barbarians" makes plain, some Chinese recognized quite early that more than military matters needed to be "corrected":

> In making use of the ability of our manpower, with no one neglected, we are inferior to the barbarians; in securing the benefit of the soil, with nothing wasted, we are inferior to the barbarians; in maintaining a close relationship between the ruler and the people, with no barrier between them, we are inferior to

the barbarians; and in the necessary accord of word with deed, we are also inferior to the barbarians. The way to correct these four points lies with ourselves, for they can be changed at once if only our Emperor would set the general policy right. There is no need for outside help in these matters.

From 1860 to 1900, as the dual crisis deepened, the Chinese undertook many new experiments. They founded schools in which Western languages, mathematics, and science were taught; they studied international law, established a Western-style foreign office, and began to engage in Western-style diplomacy; they built arsenals and shipyards in which they could manufacture modern weapons and introduced new concepts into military training; they sent students abroad; and they began to think about adopting Western methods of transportation and communication. All that they did, however, they considered means of defense. Each step had to be justified on the grounds that it would help to keep the foreigners out; at the same time, each experiment had to be guaranteed not to impinge on the essentials of Chinese life. Thus the founding of new schools had to be justified on the grounds that they would train diplomats who could outwit the Westerners and engineers who could design and build better weapons than the Westerners had; at the same time, the new schools had to enroll only students who already had sound traditional training and who would continue it—the new schools were to offer a supplement to, rather than a substitute for, older learning.

The policy governing such experiments was well expressed by the slogan Chinese learning for the fundamentals, Western learning for practical application. The "practical application," however, was clearly subordinate to the fundamentals, for whenever Western learning intruded too much on Chinese learning, the experiment was terminated. Between 1872 and 1876, for example, after years of proposals and many months of elaborate preparations, about 150 young Chinese were sent to England, France, and the United States to be educated. The 120 boys who came to America, most of them between the ages of twelve and sixteen, were supposed to stay for fifteen years, but they were rather abruptly ordered back to China in the summer of 1881. The chief reason given for terminating the project was that the students were neglecting their Chinese studies (which they were required to continue while abroad) and "indulging in foreign customs."

The Chinese were primarily interested in preserving their own way of life, not in modernization. Most remained confident that their own principles were valid and that Western superiority was confined to such peripheral matters as the manufacture of ships and guns. They would borrow nothing that might fundamentally alter their way of life. This program of moderate, defensive, traditionalist reform has come to be known as the "self-strengthening movement."

Toward the end of the nineteenth century a few Chinese began to look at things differently. One man, Kang Youwei (1858-1927), even went so far as to suggest that the essentials of Chinese life were not incompatible with modernization; imaginatively reinterpreting traditional doctrines—too imaginatively, said critics who accused Kang of distortion—he argued that Confucius himself had been a reformer and that adopting fundamentally new practices need not lead to Westernization. Few would listen to him, and even though the emperor was among the few, the effort to carry out a thorough-going reform program in the summer of 1898 lasted such a short time that the period has come to be known simply as the Hundred Days. The attempt ended when reactionaries led by the Empress Dowager Ci Xi seized power and imprisoned the emperor. Kang's heroic but quixotic foray into reform politics made only a brief ripple in the flow of nineteenth-century traditionalism. The overwhelming sentiment of Chinese leaders was that anything genuinely new would also be Western, and therefore innovation should be confined to peripheral and transient matters.

Traditionalism, however, was not the only massive barrier to modernization in nineteenth-century China. The West itself played a significant role. Chinese in the United States, especially laborers working in mines and railway construction all across the American West, were subjected to severe discrimination and brutality. Chinese students may have suffered much less than laborers, but they were also humiliated. In their case, Western double-dealing and race prejudice contributed to the failure of the experiment. Li Hongzhang (1823-1901), during the last thirty years of his life probably the most influential statesman in China, had expected the United States military and naval academies to accept some of these boys when they completed preparatory school, since an 1868 treaty provided that Chinese and American students could enter each other's government schools. When the Chinese were rejected and when discriminatory immigration legislation and other anti-Chinese policies were adopted in the United States, Li found it difficult to answer the conservatives who demanded termination of the mission.

One possible alternative was to send more boys to Europe, where

Chinese were accepted in military and naval academies. But there too they felt racism. A sensitive Chinese student in France, one of Li Hongzhang's protégés, wrote concerning praise he received from his professors:

> This praise is also caused by the fact that Westerners have had little contact with us Chinese and usually are scornful of us. Thereforefore, whenever there is a Chinese student who knows a little and understands half of what he has studied, he is praised as being extraordinary. This "being extraordinary" [as an individual] is just a sign of being despised [as a race].

It was not only the relative handful of Chinese abroad who encountered this sort of discrimination. Thousands more found it in the treaty ports and, as missionaries spread inland, increasingly in the countryside. A not uncommon reaction was that of the missionary S. Wells Williams, who lived in China for forty-three years and studied his surroundings carefully. He came to the conclusion that although the Chinese "have more virtues than most pagan nations" and although "there is something to commend, there is more to blame." Adding up their shortcomings he concluded that they "form a full unchecked torrent of human depravity, and prove the existence of a kind and degree of moral degradation of which an excessive statement can scarcely be made, or an adequate conception hardly be formed." Many missionaries did not allow their vision of pagan degradation to overshadow their humanitarian desire to bring peace and enlightenment to China, but others agreed with Williams that the Chinese "are among the most craven of people, cruel and selfish as heathenism can make men, so we must be backed by force if we wish them to listen to reason." When men who held such prejudices went among the Chinese people and preached Christianity, all the while claiming the protection of unequal treaties and Western armed might, Western culture could hardly commend itself as a model for China.

In brief, Chinese attitudes toward Western culture were mixtures of resentment and envy. Traces of admiration were heavily outweighed by hostility. These feelings became more ambivalent as Western influence in China spread. Even though Western imperialism paralyzed such efforts as the Chinese made to modernize and Western racism offended them, a few Chinese began to imitate some features of Western life, in business and manufacturing as well as in clothing and religion.

Some also went to work for Western firms, thereby obtaining experience they later put to use in Chinese firms; others began to invest in Western firms, thereby departing from traditional habits of investment in land or moneylending. By the 1890s there seemed to be hardly a feature of Western society that someone or other had not recommended China adopt—a parliament or some other sort of public forum in which to discuss affairs of state, innovations in newspaper publishing to provide information for discussion and a channel for criticism of the government, an alphabetic system to promote greater literacy, jury trials and other legal reforms, and nearly every conceivable type of economic reform, including measures to raise the social status of merchants. The divided feelings that governed such men were recorded by a Chinese educator who recalled his first trip to Shanghai as a teen-ager:

> Shanghai by 1899 was a small city with a few thousand arrogant foreigners. But the city was well governed, with clean, wide streets and electric or gas lights. I thought the foreigners were wonderful. They know the secret of electricity. They had invented the steam engine and built steamboats. They took the place of my old gods who had melted away in the face of my instruction in science, and occupied my mind as new ones. At the same time they served as new devils, too, for their arrogance, coupled with clubs of the policemen, frightened me. In the list of regulations displayed at the entrance of a park on the banks of the Huang-pu River, Chinese as well as dogs were forbidden admission. This said much. The foreigner appeared to my mind half divine and half devilish, double faced and many handed like Vishnu, holding an electric light, a steamboat, and a pretty doll in one set of hands, and a policeman's club, revolver, and a handful of opium in the other. When one looked at his bright side he was an angel; on the dark side he was a demon.

In the nineteenth century the Chinese saw mainly the demonic side of the West. But as the century came to a close they began to feel an ambivalence that was to haunt them for many years to come.

2

THE SWING TOWARD
WESTERNIZATION,
1900–1928

AROUND 1900 China paused at a fork in the road. Looking over its
shoulder along the path of traditionalism, the government could see
forty years of defeat. Ahead, clearly in view, lay almost certain disaster,
for at that very moment China seemed about to be carved into bite-sized
colonial portions. The Beijing authorities decided to explore a new
route, one that seemed to skirt the West by way of Japan. After 1901
Chinese modernization began to follow Japan's example.

Between 1895 and 1905 Japan had defeated China in a brief and
one-sided war, thrown off some of the most obnoxious features of the
unequal treaties that the Western powers had imposed on it, consum-
mated an alliance on a basis of equality with Great Britain, the world's
leading power, and thrashed another prominent imperialist power,
Russia, in a bloody war. It was a decade's work that aroused Chinese
envy, particularly since Japan seemed to have borrowed a great deal
from the West without sacrificing its own unique cultural identity. Japan
had combined industrialism, modern military methods, and at least the
appearance of constitutional-parliamentary government with a strengthening of the emperor's position and the destruction of feudal power.

The Qing government, by contrast, had surrendered much of its
power to provincial governors and military commanders in order to
suppress rebellions. Seeing Japan's success allowed the Qing to dream
once again of restoring central authority. In 1900 it became an urgent

Foreign troops occupy the Imperial Palace, Beijing, following the Boxer Incident, 1900. *Underwood & Underwood*

matter when yet another dual crisis developed. A group of Chinese secret societies* (called "Boxers" by Westerners), loosely organized and ideologically not altogether coherent but with strong anti-imperialist and patriotic elements, struck at both Chinese Christians and foreigners between 1898 and 1900. The conflict escalated with growing brutality by both sides, until an international force of some 18,000 troops landed and defeated the Chinese. Yet another crushing and humiliating settlement was imposed on China, as always far out of proportion to the damage done. Prostrate, the Chinese court now saw no alternative to

---

* See p. 30 for explanation of secret societies.

reform, and so it decided to follow the example of Japan. Ironically, eight thousand of the invading troops had been Japanese, the largest single contingent by far.

Beginning about 1901, therefore, the government intensified its efforts to modernize the armed forces, build railroads and other modern means of transportation and communication, streamline its bureaucracy, promote modern education, and develop industry and mining. Among the most significant measures were the dispatch of thousands of students to Japan and the decision, reached in 1905 and 1906, to adopt a constitution. The students were to provide trained personnel for the government's modernization program. The constitution was a defensive measure undertaken in a spirit resembling nineteenth-century self-strengthening. The Empress Dowager reasoned that "the wealth and strength of other countries are due to their practice of constitutional government, in which public questions are determined by consultation with the people." For her, constitutionalism was not intended to guarantee individual rights or to limit government or to divide power or for any of the other purposes known in Western democracies. Instead, its object was to make China wealthy and powerful. After several months of study the government decided to follow closely the kind of constitution adopted by the Japanese, who had borrowed theirs from Prussia. In the Empress Dowager's eyes, the artful combination of elected representation with strengthened imperial prestige and power was among the most attractive features of the Japanese constitution.

The decision to study foreign governments in order to determine what kind of political system would be best for China represented a remarkable change of attitude. Of their many great achievements, none had given the Chinese greater pride than their form of government, which for lengthy periods had functioned efficiently and justly, despite premodern conditions and problems of immense area and population. For the Chinese now to confess so openly that they had something to learn from foreigners about the art of government was an about-face of the first magnitude.

Thus, as the twentieth century began, the rotting Qing dynasty was moving further than ever toward rejecting Chinese tradition and adopting Western practices. But even as it quickened its pace along the new path, the government was already being overtaken by more radical competitors. To understand the new steps taken by the government and the still newer ones called for by others, we must look into the backgrounds of the new movements.

INTELLECTUAL FOUNDATIONS OF
MODERN CHINA

It is easy now to forget how novel and how enormously revolutionary—in the West as well as in Asia—was the idea that rapid social change is both desirable and possible. That life *should* be very different from what it had always been was an idea that people were beginning to accept in late nineteenth-century China. Still, the conviction persisted that great changes, even if they were desirable, were not really possible; it was difficult to see that life *could* be very different from what it had always been.

Yan Fu and the Idea of Progress

The man who did most to encourage confidence in the possibility of change in China was Yan Fu (1853–1921). Yan came from a family of scholars and received an intensive education in the traditional style. His grounding in the Chinese classics, although solid, was abbreviated due to a reversal in the family fortunes resulting from the death of Yan's father in 1866. The youngster then entered a new shipyard school that offered cash prizes and subsistence allowances as part of its program to recruit able students. He spent five years studying mathematics, science, navigation, and, since it was the language of instruction, English. After graduation he made several training voyages to Japan and Southeast Asia, and in 1876 he was sent to England for advanced training. There his interests blossomed. Like a number of other Chinese in the time of the self-strengthening movement, Yan wanted desperately to know why Western countries were so much stronger than his own. For more than two years he pursued this question relentlessly, studying British society, government, and thought. By the time he sailed for home in 1879 he felt that he had found some answers.

Yan kept his ideas to himself until China's defeat by Japan in 1895. Pained by his country's plight, Yan had to speak out; his countrymen, reeling from their defeat, were at last ready to listen. In a series of newspaper articles Yan compared Chinese and Western societies. The main differences, he found, lay not in technology or military science, but in the values and ideas. Of these, the major difference was that "The Chinese love antiquity but belittle the modern, whereas Westerners struggle to make the present better than the past; Chinese accept the ups and downs of order and disorder, prosperity and decline, as the natural course of the universe, while Westerners consider that daily progress should be endless."

Yan searched more deeply for an explanation of why Chinese and Westerners held such different attitudes, and the search led him into many blind alleys, reversals, and inconsistencies. But some ideas he found struck a responsive chord in many of his readers. One idea was that of competition. The Chinese stressed order, stability, and social harmony, whereas the Westerners believed there were benefits to be derived from struggle and competition. Westerners realized that life was a struggle for existence, that nature selected the fittest for survival, and that fitness was proved by success in competition; indeed, competition furthered fitness by bringing out the potential abilities of each individual. Competition tested people's mettle and toughened them for further struggle and survival. Competition and struggle, therefore, were in Yan's view the keys to progress. Another idea was the utility of individual liberty. People struggle in pursuit of their own individual interests, and, in their determination to satisfy their self-interest, individuals "grind and polish each other. . . . Beginning in mutual antagonism they end by completing each other." The genius of Western society was that it allowed people to exercise freely their abilities: It encouraged them to act and released their energies. Moreover, it did so in such a way that the pursuit of self-interest resulted in the fulfillment of society's interests. Miraculously, Yan thought, Western society was so constructed that each person's struggle to improve his position added up to all improving theirs. In brief, he marveled, "unity and progress result from diversity and competition."

Yan's lasting significance is that he introduced the ideas of Darwin and the classic British liberals to China at a time when the Chinese were ready to receive them. Just when the Hundred Days ended and just when Confucianism seemed to many observers to have failed its last test of adaptability to the modern world, Yan Fu came along to fill the intellectual void. Beginning in 1898 and continuing for about a decade, translations and summaries of works by Thomas Henry Huxley, Herbert Spencer, John Stuart Mill, Adam Smith, and others flowed from Yan's brush. Yan also added mush of his own commentary. Suddenly, within a few years, Chinese intellectuals had within easy reach an immense world of new ideas.

Those new ideas struck China like a thunderclap. The Chinese even began assigning names differently: instead of old standbys like "Admire Mencius," "Virtuous," "Vast Elegance," or "Esteemed Ancestors," names like "Fit" or "Struggle for Existence" were used. The leading reformist newspaper of the time, the name of which might be translated literally as "Current Affairs" or perhaps "The Needs of the Times," came to be known in English as "The Daily Chinese Progress." Its editor and leading writer, Liang Qichao (1873–1929), was also the man who did most to spread and further Yan Fu's work.

Liang Qichao and the "New People"

Liang's skills and temperament overlapped with Yan Fu's in ways that made their work complementary. Until he was about twenty-two, Liang's education and contact with Western learning were not unlike Yan's. At the age when Yan went abroad, however, Liang plunged into reform politics, which Yan always avoided. Liang worked closely with Kang Youwei, usually doing newspaper work or teaching. Like Kang he had to flee for his life when the Hundred Days reform ended. From then on, Liang's thinking departed from Kang's and began to develop along more independent lines. He followed Yan's writing closely and supplemented it with voracious reading in Japan. Liang was deeply impressed by Yan's explanation of struggle, progress, and the importance of individual liberty. He also absorbed Yan's emphasis on the need for changes in people's minds, particularly in the attitudes Chinese held toward social relationships. Yan had reminded his readers of an older saying: "The essence of statecraft is to turn self-interest into public interest." Liang complained that "in China there are duties of individuals to individuals, but there are no duties of individuals to society." Liang set out to do nothing less than transform the Chinese into a "new people." He went at it almost as if he thought he could do it single-handed.

Liang immersed himself in Western writings and flooded one newspaper after another with articles in which he translated, summarized, and compared the Greeks, Luther, Bacon, Descartes, Hobbes, Spinoza, Montesquieu, Voltaire, Rousseau, Tolstoy, Kant, Bluntschli, and many others. In a series called "Discourses on the New People," which appeared in the magazine *New People's Fortnightly*, published by Liang in Japan from 1902 to 1907, he also wrote on Cromwell, Napoleon, Bismarck, Mazzini, Garibaldi, and Cavour. A torrent of Western thought, culture, and history poured from his pen to a generation that thirsted for precisely what Liang offered. The series "opened up a new world for me," wrote one of the most famous Chinese intellectuals of the twentieth century, and so it did for thousands. Liang, elaborating on Yan Fu's work, described a world in which nations and races struggled for existence and only the fit survived. China, to endure, had to renovate its culture. For a time, Liang proposed changes that were thoroughly revolutionary, including the overthrow of the Chinese government. He modified his position between 1903 and 1905, as a result of a trip to the United States and at the urging of Kang Youwei. He no longer called for a revolution but continued to advocate many social changes and to demand the prompt introduction of genuine constitutional government and a democratic system comparable to England's.

It is not likely that the Chinese court was much influenced by Yan Fu and Liang Qichao. The court did agree that China should turn to Western models of constitutionalism in order to make it strong enough to throw off Western domination. However, Yan and Liang went further to stress that constitutional and representative government would strengthen the nation by the sharing of power and the participation of the people in politics. Constitutions and parliaments would allow China to harness to national goals the energies released by clashing opinions. They also emphasized the value of active and direct popular participation in government; they envisioned for China something like the British system, rather than the Japanese or the Prussian. Still, if the area of agreement between the Empress Dowager, Yan, and Liang was smaller than the areas of disagreement, it nevertheless was common ground on which a great many Chinese could meet. Yan and Liang laid the foundations for other conceptions of popular participation and national power.

THE REVOLUTIONARY MOVEMENT

During the same period in which Kang Youwei, Yan Fu, and Liang Qichao produced their reform ideas, a more radical current of thought also materialized. Like Yan, Liang, and the Qing court of the 1900s, the radical movement looked to a foreign model of constitutional government, but its inspiration was United States-style republicanism, and its methods were uncompromisingly revolutionary.

Sun Yatsen (1866–1925), the founder and moving spirit of the revolutionary movement, came to his calling by a peculiarly winding route. His early life was scarcely different from that of tens of thousands of other farmers' sons. But in 1879 Sun joined an older brother who had migrated to Hawaii. The next fifteen years included education in American and British schools in Hawaii, a return to his home village during which he offended the villagers by destroying some wooden idols, further British education in Hong Kong culminating in graduation from a medical school, and medical practice in Macao. Throughout the fifteen years Sun's professional education was his major concern, but his interest in social and political problems followed closely behind. He soon abandoned his medical career and spent the last thirty-one years of his life as a full-time professional revolutionary.

Sun tended to think in terms of contemporary Western (especially American) standards of nationhood and government. He usually emphasized the need for China to achieve full national sovereignty, to be independent of all foreign control, and especially to develop a sense of national community. He was later to stress that the Chinese people were "scattered sand," granules of families and clans with no cement of national spirit. Sun's education and temperament did not equip him to formulate a coherent or profound political philosophy, nor was his career as a revolutionary conducive to the development of systematic ideas; but to the extent that he was able to think out a program, it was one of nationalism, democracy, republicanism, and economic modernization.

Nationalism meant to Sun driving out the Manchu rulers and creating a Chinese-controlled nation-state; democracy meant a representative system with a strong executive branch and a system of checks and balances much like that of the United States; and economic modernization meant a dimly perceived compromise between socialism and capitalism that he hoped would avoid the evils of both. Only to a relatively small extent did he attempt to explain the relevance of his program to Chinese needs and conditions. Sun's idea for adapting democracy, for example, was simply to add to the legislative, executive, and judicial branches two other branches of government that had functioned in traditional China: One was to administer the civil service bureaucracy and the other, to be known as the "control" branch, was intended to inspect the entire government for signs of malfunctioning.

On the basis of this program Sun regularly appealed to foreign governments to support his movement, and in his anxiety to obtain foreign aid he occasionally made rather extravagant promises of economic concessions in return. For a long time he remained convinced that the Western democracies would welcome and help a Chinese democratic movement. With only a few modifications, his followers,

although resentful of Western imperialism, allowed their admiration for
Western strength and prosperity to outweigh their resentment.

Sun's ideas were influenced not only by his Western education
but also by his early home life and, probably more profoundly, by the
overseas Chinese with whom he lived and among whom he traveled for
much of his later life. The Chinese in Hawaii, Hong Kong, Japan,
Southeast Asia, and all over the world lived in tight communities of their
own, islands of industrious immigrants struggling to maintain themselves and at the same time earn something extra to send home. Their
settlements remained largely isolated within the countries in which they
lived; and without the protection of family and clan, a Chinese who lived
overseas relied on the secret society organizations that had protected
commoners in China for centuries. Hence Chinese secret societies,
which were essentially mutual aid and mutual protection organizations
with mystical-religious ideologies, had active branches in the overseas
Chinese communities.

Sun's early revolutionary organizations depended heavily on
money contributed by Chinese who lived abroad, especially businessmen. Many of Sun's earliest political associates and most trusted allies
were secret society men, often from societies that had branches
overseas. His own organizations had initiation rituals, oaths, slogans,
sworn brotherhood, and other secret society characteristics. Indeed, one
of Sun's recurring problems was that, like a secret society leader, he
often insisted on the unquestioning obedience of his followers. He
exercised a very personal, cabalistic, almost occult kind of leadership.

Sun's style of leadership found few followers. A poor organizer
and an inept tactician, Sun spent an unhappy decade fruitlessly
promoting revolution. In the summer of 1905, however, his fortunes
changed. And so did the course of modern Chinese history. Sun now
became caught up in a swelling tide of revolution that was already
changing China more than anyone could see at the time.

Several currents intersected to produce this tide. One was the
reform program of the Qing government, which in 1905 not only charted
a new political course for China, but also initiated fundamental social
changes. Its most important measure was the abolition of the traditional
civil service examination system. This measure opened the way for the
destruction of the elite group of scholar-gentry, whose social status and
privileges had sharply distinguished them from everyone else in China.
Similarly, the old educational system, which had been designed to
prepare students for the civil service, received a crippling blow, and so

did the entire body of Confucian principles that the old education had taught.

The major beneficiaries of these changes were the thousands of students who were sent abroad, mostly to Japan, to receive a new education. From a few hundred in 1902, the number grew to fifteen thousand in 1906. The government hoped they would return to employ their new skills in the service of a modernized Qing state and of the new army it was also attempting to create. But the students, sensitive to the changing intellectual climate in 1901 and 1902, were already listening more to Yan Fu and Liang Qichao than to the Empress Dowager. When they arrived in Japan the students were dazzled by what they discovered. Japan was on the march. The country bustled with confidence. A militant nationalism spun the wheels of social and economic change, producing goods, weapons, and national pride. Relations with Russia happened to be worsening at the time, and war fever swept the land. When Japan's victory came in 1905, thousands of Chinese students participated vicariously. An Asian nation had demonstrated that it could quickly develop a modern army, navy, economy, and government and thereby subdue a major Western imperialist power. Reasoning that if Japan could do it, so could China, the students decided that the time had come to dedicate themselves to China's future and to organize for concerted revolutionary action on a large scale.

By 1905 the students' ideas had outraced those of Liang Qichao, who was lowering his sights precisely when the students were raising theirs. In the absence of other attractive leadership, the students decided to unite behind Sun Yatsen. But this was not entirely a decision by default. Sun had great personal magnetism, and in ten years of devoted revolutionary work he had cultivated a wide range of very useful contacts, including secret societies, overseas businessmen, and foreign adventurers and politicians. Some of his exploits had earned him a considerable reputation abroad. A persuasive speaker (and fluent in English), a medical doctor, and at least a nominal Christian, he favorably impressed many foreigners. The students felt he might be effective in future negotiations with the imperialist powers. Meanwhile, he could raise money among overseas Chinese and seek foreign support for the movement. All in all, he had qualities no other Chinese leader could match, and there was nothing he wanted more than to overthrow the Qing dynasty and make China a republic, aims that suited the students.

The revolutionary alliance that was forged in the summer of 1905 toiled mightily for six years in behalf of anti-Manchu republicanism, and in that time it grew into a broad coalition of discontented groups. Between October 1911 and February 1912 this rather loose coalition saw its efforts rewarded at last. A revolution overthrew the Qing government and ended the Chinese empire. The alliance between Sun and the students contributed a good deal to the fall of the Qing dynasty and the founding of the Republic of China. Most important, it infiltrated the imperial army and weakened the soldiers' will to fight in behalf of the dynasty, and it effectively spread ideas of democracy and republicanism.

Still, the alliance was not solely responsible for the momentous events of 1911 and 1912. Among the several other forces that combined to terminate the ancient imperial system, two must be mentioned here. Ironically, both played their roles after being called on stage by the Qing court. The government created the first when, as part of its plan to introduce a limited form of constitutionalism, it decided also to permit elections. Held for the first time in 1909, the elections produced assemblies in each of twenty-one provinces. Few members of the assemblies were revolutionaries, but many were highly critical of the central government, and their vocal demands put added pressure on Beijing. Then a national assembly, initiated in 1910, harassed the court still more. But in addition to undermining the authority of the central government, the assemblies provided rallying points for many protesters. Through the assemblies it became possible for landowners, businessmen, educators, journalists, and even some ordinary citizens to become active in politics and to make their voices heard. These people found both their nationalist sensibilities and their economic aspirations outraged by a government railway nationalization plan that favored foreign investors. The assemblies protested but were unheeded, and the members' loyalty to the government evaporated. Thus, new interest groups and new instruments of power, which had been allowed to exist by the Qing court in the hope that they would modernize the government, appease its critics, and strengthen its claim to rule and its ability to enforce that claim, now decided they could better promote their interests by throwing off Qing rule and creating a republic. When the opportunity came in the autumn of 1911, fifteen provincial assemblies declared their independence, and China began to break up into provincial regimes.

In a last-ditch effort to stave off disaster, the Qing court called upon General Yuan Shikai (1875–1916), whose help had been decisive in the Empress Dowager's coup of 1898. He had been in retirement since her death in 1908, but his army, which was the best-equipped and best-trained army in China, had remained intact. Yuan negotiated terms with the court that were favorable to himself, entered the fray, fought until a stalemate was created among the revolutionaries, the various provincial regimes, and himself, and then maneuvered adroitly until he managed to obtain the Manchus' abdication. Thus the Qing government committed unintentional suicide by sending students abroad, initiating constitutional and representative government, and inviting back into power the very man who finally forced it to step down.

Yuan Shikai, by compelling the Manchus to abdicate, persuaded his other rivals for power to accept a compromise. In exchange for ending the empire, he was to become president of the Republic of China, but he in turn was to permit free elections, a parliament, and a system of constitutional government providing for checks and balances and a sharing of powder. Sun Yatsen and his allies accepted a compromise with Yuan because they feared division in the country. Inexperienced, disorganized, woefully lacking in mass support, and afraid that continued disorder might lead the foreign powers to intervene, the republicans chose not to prolong the struggle by military means. They agreed to recognize as president a military man they distrusted and to count on a constitution and their strength in the parliament to control him. Perhaps a bit intoxicated by their own propaganda about the merits of republicanism, they were unduly optimistic that democratic institutions were taking root in China. They lost the gamble. Yuan outmaneuvered them, used the parliament and constitution for his own purposes, and moved rapidly toward making himself a dictator and even emperor. Before Yuan could take this final step, he died in 1916. Meanwhile, although a courageous few rose to resist Yuan, many others who had fought for republicanism until 1913 simply renounced political activity in disgust. Some even left the country. Speaking for his generation, one émigré explained in a letter to a friend: "Politics is in such confusion that I am at a loss to know what to talk about."

NEW CULTURE AND NATIONALISM

Governing authority after 1912, and increasingly so between 1916 and 1926, devolved upon "warlords"—military men of narrow vision, limited objectives, and, with few exceptions, mediocre abilities. Each warlord controlled as much territory as he could without taking great risks, taxed as heavily as the people could bear, governed minimally, expanded his army, and maneuvered cautiously to maintain his security vis-à-vis other warlords. All relied heavily on armies whose numbers fluctuated due to the soldiers' unreliability but which were intended to be personally loyal to an individual warlord. Some had small forces of no more than a few thousand men, but major warlords had armies that occasionally numbered more than a quarter of a million. Some controlled small areas no larger than a county; others controlled several provinces. Some nourished vague ambitions of greater glory, perhaps even a throne; many sought and some obtained aid from foreign powers; a few carried out, usually on a modest scale, social reforms such as attempts to discourage vice or promote education and public works. Some warlords even paid attention to national problems, but for the most part they were concerned only with their own immediate welfare and security.

After the death of Yuan Shikai in 1916, China had no political leader of national stature. The republic, crippled from the very first, now almost ceased to exist. Its officers and agencies functioned at the whim of whichever warlord managed to hold Beijing. That warlord handled China's diplomacy in the name of the republic, but in China his writ extended only to the territory of the neighboring warlord. China was divided among countless satrapies and for a long time after the republican revolution had anything but a modern government. Intellectuals began to think that little had changed despite the fall of the monarchy. They felt that the introduction of reforms over the last fifty years in the armed forces, schools, government, and economy had brought China no closer to being a strong and prosperous nation.

When Japan in 1915 presented to China a set of Twenty-one Demands, the intellectuals' frustration turned to rage. The demands were so far-reaching that it was humiliating merely to be presented with them; only to a country held in utter contempt could Japan have dared to present so naked a claim for virtual colonization. China managed only narrowly to avert full accession to the Japanese demands, and the entire incident provoked immense anger among patriotic Chinese. The day Japan delivered her final ultimatum (May 7) became National Humiliation Day, almost a day of mourning, but also a day of commemoration and rededication. It was in this atmosphere—the failure of republicanism, the renewal of foreign imperialism, and the frustration engendered by failure and weakness—that a handful of Chinese intellectuals undertook to reexamine the problem of modernizing their country.

The intellectuals who surveyed the wreckage of the 1911 revolution were led by men who had not played an important part in it and who felt no stake in justifying it or rationalizing it. They evaluated the revolution coolly and ruthlessly, judging it to have produced a "pseudo-republicanism" under which

> we have experienced every kind of suffering known to those who are not free. These sufferings remain the same regardless of political changes or the substitution of one political party in power for another. When politics brings us to such a dead end, we have to arouse ourselves and realize that genuine republicanism can never be achieved until politics is initiated by the people. In order to get the people to initiate politics, we must have as a prerequisite an atmosphere wherein a genuine spirit of free thought and free criticism can be nurtured.

With this ringing denunciation of the republic and call for more popular initiative in politics, China's struggle to modernize entered a new phase. Intellectuals retained continuity with Yan Fu by reaffirming the doctrines of struggle for existence, natural selection, and survival of the fittest, and they demanded a "new culture" much as Liang Qichao had called for a new people; but the leaders of the New Culture Movement went further than Yan and Liang by condemning all of Chinese tradition. Liang had criticized "those who are infatuated with Western ways and . . . throw away our morals, learning, and customs of several thousand years' standing"; to Chen Duxiu (1879–1942), who by 1915 was on his way to becoming the most influential writer in China, Chinese tradition resided in an antiquated Confucianism that "did not go beyond the privilege and prestige of a few rulers and aristocrats and had nothing to do with the happiness of the great masses." Evaluation of the 1911 revolution led men like Chen to conclude that Chinese tradition accounted for the republic's failure. In particular, Confucianism, with its subordination of the young to the old and the individual to the family, stifled the freedom of thought that the people needed in order to bring about true republicanism. Thus New Culture Movement leaders not only continued to uphold ideals of Western democracy and science, but they also promoted those ideals even more fervently and uncompromisingly than earlier modernizing movements, and they went beyond earlier movements in their antitraditionalism and in their appeal for mass participation and even for popular initiative in political action.

In 1915 Chen Duxiu founded a magazine called *Youth*, which for the next five years was probably the most widely read and influential publication in China. For the first issue Chen wrote a "Call to Youth," in which he urged young people to assume responsibility for eliminating "the old and the rotten" from Chinese life and replacing it with science and democracy. Chen's theme was this: "If we expect to establish a Western type of modern nation then the most basic step is to import the foundation of modern Western society—the faith in the equality of men."

Chen's "Call to Youth" was heard, and the response was immediate and powerful. Within a few months many of the men who soon dominated Chinese intellectual life were writing tributes to Darwin, the scientific method, the experimental spirit, and liberty, equality, and fraternity. Chen's magazine changed its name to *The New Youth* and, symbolically, later adopted a French title, *La Jeunesse*. To the English and American influences fostered by Yan Fu, Liang Qichao, and Sun Yatsen, China's new youth had added the scientific and French revolutions.

The young people's burgeoning activism was furthered early in 1919 by developments at the Paris Peace Conference. China had entered World War I after much debate. One of the most convincing arguments for participation in the war was that a contribution to victory would entitle China to share in the rewards. The Chinese hoped that at the very least they would regain from the losing powers whatever holdings the losers had in China. Thus the Chinese negotiators at Paris were confident of obtaining the return of Germany's concessions, and, hearing the worldwide proclamations of "territorial integrity" and "national self-determination," they had hopes of obtaining much more. Perhaps even the Twenty-one Demands would be reversed. These hopes were shattered by the revelation at Versailles of secret agreements Japan had made years before with Britain, France, and the warlord government of China. Germany's holdings were not to be returned to China; they had been promised to Japan. Japan's position in China was not to be weakened, but strengthened.

Details of these agreements had trickled into public view during 1918 but at first aroused only small and scattered protests. The protests grew in size and frequency and were supported by new social and economic groups as well as by the intellectuals. The Chinese economy expanded considerably due to the war, and embryonic classes of merchants, industrialists, and workers began to grow. Demonstrations against foreign domination began to bring them into contact with each other and with students and teachers. The minor outbursts of 1918 and early 1919 turned out to be rehearsals for the volcanic political eruption of May 4, 1919.

On May 1 reports from the Chinese delegates revealing that they had lost the diplomatic contest began to appear in the Beijing press. Readers were dumbfounded, unbelieving, outraged. Despite all signs to the contrary the public had not been able to believe that the effort to secure China's rights would end in failure. Wilson and others had spoken too well; the world could not ignore the truth and beauty of such noble principles. The disappointment was cataclysmic. One student recalled:

> when the news of the Paris Peace Conference finally reached us we were greatly shocked. We at once awoke to the fact that foreign nations were still selfish and militaristic and that they were all great liars. I remember that the night of May 2 very few of us slept. A group of my friends and I talked almost the whole night. We came to the conclusion that a greater world war would be coming sooner or later, and that this great war would be fought in the East. . . . Looking at our people and at the pitiful ignorant masses, we couldn't help but feel that we must struggle!

The struggle burst forth almost at once. The students had planned a demonstration for May 7, National Humiliation Day, but government repression made them decide to move more quickly. Student leaders hurriedly called a meeting for the evening of May 3 and passed a number of resolutions, including one for a mass demonstration the next day. On Sunday morning, May 4, some three thousand students met, drew up manifestoes, and marched. Spectators cheered, some wept, and even Western observers were impressed. John Dewey and his wife, who had arrived only a few days earlier to begin a visit that was to last more than two years, wrote home in wonder: "To think of kids in our country from fourteen on, taking the lead in starting a big cleanup reform politics movement and shaming merchants and professional men into joining them. This is sure some country."

As Dewey observantly noted, this was not merely a student demonstration in Beijing. It became nationwide, both geographically and socially. A sixteen-year-old high school boy in Sichuan, 1,000 miles from Beijing, recalled the day he heard the news:

> Only a month was left before my graduation. We were having our examination period. And suddenly, like a black Japanese bomb, the Fourth of May exploded over our heads.

Busy with our noisy studying we did not see the teachers
running hurriedly to the office of the director. The servants who
carried tea to the conference whispered in our inattentive ears: "A
letter. . . . Important. From Peking [Beijing]. They don't know
whether or not to show the students."

. . . The secretary pasted a long letter on the black
announcement board. A thick crowd of students, panting with
excitement, gathered quickly around the board. Our best orator,
who had a ringing voice and clear enunciation, read every
sentence of that remarkable letter. . . .

The letter upset us completely: Boycott . . . Union . . .
Constitution . . . Organization . . . Collections . . . All these
were strange words. The weight of important political action was
laid upon our narrow boyish shoulders.

. . . That night we could not sleep. Our meeting rumbled
loudly in the light of oil lamps, and the timid sparrow-like twitter
of the younger boys mingled with the harsh breaking voices of the
sixteen-year-olds.

. . . Noise, exciting speeches. One student after another
came up on the platform. When had they learned to speak? When
had they found these ardent gestures—these boys who only
yesterday were engaged in childish scuffles. Where did they learn
to make those exalted, convincing speeches, to which teachers,
directors, and the representatives of merchants now listened so
attentively, nodding their heavy heads in time to the angry shouts
of their sons and pupils?

The three boys' high schools dedicated themselves, down to
the last person, to the anti-Japanese boycott.

. . . Every word of every orator fell into the crackling fire
of applause. The treasurer reported the rapid growth of Union
funds. I, the secretary, waving over my head a blueprint map of
the town, announced how we were going to carry out the boycott.

"All Japanese merchandise must be destroyed," I shouted.
"Not a single Japanese object must be hidden. The Peking
comrades summon us to join the strike!"

"The strike!"

The May Fourth incident created an unprecedented wave of
patriotism in China. Boycotts, strikes, and demonstrations erupted all
over the country and continued for more than a month. Government
attempts at repression failed. Rumors circulated that police and soldiers
were going to side with the students, merchants, and workers. Several
cabinet members resigned. And finally, on June 28, under pressure

from Chinese students and workers in France who surrounded its headquarters, the Chinese delegation at Versailles defied its government's instructions and refused to sign the treaty.

But the May Fourth incident was only a partial victory. The secret treaties were not abrogated, and China still had to confront the militant and aggressive Japanese. The confrontation, however, was now on a different basis. The masses were far from mobilized, but nationwide political organization and action had taken place on a scale never before seen in China. A new intelligentsia that had been developing at least since the early 1900s, when thousands of students had gone abroad, had become a major force in Chinese life. Their own organization spanned the country. They had discovered that organized propaganda and demonstrations could bring results. They had tasted the excitement of political activity and some fruits of success. They had made contact with big industrialists and clerks, merchants and laborers, college presidents and janitors, university professors and professional politicians. They had created a pattern for future action and a basis for a new feeling of national commitment, a beginning of a national community and a sense of nationalism. In future confrontations with outside powers China would stand more as a nation than ever before. The combination of freedom and cohesion sought by Yan Fu, the devotion to the public interest called for by Liang Qichao, the cement of national spirit yearned for by Sun Yatsen—this common goal of the last twenty years seemed attainable in 1919. The question was whether the new sense of nationhood could be harnessed to the cause of building a new culture. The answer, soon given, was that cultural change was to be subordinated to political action.

THE GUOMINDANG REVOLUTION

Following the May Fourth Movement, political activists struggled to organize themselves. The only existing party that seemed to offer any immediate promise was the Guomindang, also known as the Nationalist party. Led by Sun Yatsen, it had grown out of the 1905–1911 revolutionary movement. Since that time Sun had been struggling with only minimal success to keep the party together as a potent political force. From 1920 to 1923 he was nominal head of a nominal Guomindang government in Guangzhou; in actuality he was little more than an appendage of the local warlord regime, and his position was extremely precarious. Thus he was again looking for firmer sources of support precisely at a time when many Chinese were bent on political action. Guomindang ranks began to grow accordingly.

Sun, as usual, was anxious for foreign help. It turned out that the only place from which help was forthcoming was the Soviet Union. At the same time, Chinese intellectuals were also beginning to pay closer attention to the Soviet Union. Their interest in Russia, which had grown slowly after the Bolshevik Revolution of 1917, snowballed in the post-May Fourth atmosphere. The Bolsheviks helped to encourage this interest (with policies we shall explain later), but equally important encouragement came inadvertently from the West and Japan. The imperialist powers had already alienated the Chinese at Versailles. Then they created a bond of sympathy between China and Russia by invading Russia and supporting anti-bolshevik forces and regimes. As the West turned its demonic side to China once again, Chinese ambivalence shifted away from its admiration for Western-style democracy and toward anti-imperialism. The availability of an alternate foreign model doubtless facilitated the renewal of Chinese anti-Westernism. Scores of Soviet-oriented groups of many kinds sprouted in 1920 and 1921. In July 1921 the Chinese Communist Party (CCP) was formally organized, and Chen Duxiu became its head. In 1923, thanks to the tireless efforts and adroit maneuvering of the Soviet Union, a Guomindang–CCP united front was set up.

The Emergence of a New
Guomindang, 1923–1924

Like the Communists, the Guomindang entered upon the united front because its leaders thought the benefits it would bring in the short run outweighed the long-run risks. Indeed, the appeal of a united front to both sides was precisely that both were concerned chiefly with immediate problems and only marginally with future ones. Most of all, the leaders of both the Guomindang and the CCP came to the conclusion that their movements were stymied unless they could mobilize enough power to eliminate the warlords and take a strong stand against Western and Japanese imperialism. Each was too weak to do this alone, and so they were logical allies.

The Guomindang had several more specific reasons for agreeing to collaborate with the CCP. After nearly thirty years of unstinting effort, Sun Yatsen had obtained only sporadic and sparing foreign help. He had scarce financial reserves and no reliable sources of funds. He had built no effective party organization. The party, in addition to being loosely organized, had a small membership that was not broadly representative of Chinese society. Among its most numerous and influential members were intellectuals whose education was obtained mostly overseas, businessmen whose orientation was toward Western commerce, and Chinese scattered over numerous overseas communities. Many Guomindang leaders, and most of all Sun, believed that with the help of the Soviet Union and the CCP their party could strengthen its organization and broaden its membership.

Sun Yatsen was therefore highly receptive to overtures made by the Soviet Union in 1922. After negotations lasting into the next year, a declaration was issued jointly by Sun and a Soviet emissary named Adolf Joffe. In a statement that he soon qualified, Sun stipulated, "the Communistic order or even the Soviet system cannot actually be introduced into China, because there do not exist here the conditions for the successful establishment of either Communism or Sovietism." Joffe added: "China's paramount and most pressing problem is to achieve national unification and attain full national independence"; to these ends Joffe promised Russian "sympathy" and "support." The most concrete evidence of Russian sympathy and support was the arrival in China of advisers, money, and weapons. All three began pouring in after further discussions, some of which were held in the Soviet Union between Russian leaders and a Chinese delegation headed by Jiang Kaishek (1887–1975).

Sun Yatsen had meanwhile to counter doubts in his own sharply divided party. In its influential right wing were many who questioned the wisdom of accepting Soviet support and cooperating with the Chinese Communists. There was great concern about the possibility of excessive Russian influence, and there was fear that the Communists would prove to be unreliable and excessively radical allies. The vigor with which Sun attempted to persuade his followers suggests that the opposition among them was great. It was finally agreed that the Communists would be allowed to join the Guomindang but could retain their own separate party. Many of Sun's followers remained disturbed about the dangers of subversion, and they were only partly reassured when Sun bluntly told the Soviet emissary that the Communists "must submit to discipline and not criticize the Guomindang openly. If the Communists do not submit to the Guomindang, I shall expel them; and if Soviet Russia should give them secret protection, I shall oppose Soviet Russia." Sun also tried to persuade his followers that they needed outside help and could obtain it nowhere else, that the Chinese Communists were too small and weak a group to carry out a revolution, that the Russians had no choice but to work with the Guomindang if they wanted to "collaborate with China," and most of all that the outlook, needs, and interests of the Russians and the Guomindang coincided.

Sun invoked both ideology and tactical considerations to justify his policy. On the one hand, Sun argued that Communist doctrine was not significantly different from his own Three People's Principles of nationalism, democracy, and people's livelihood. His last two principles were less congruent with Soviet doctrine than nationalism was, but, in Sun's opinion, the gap had been narrowed ever since the Soviet Union had adopted the New Economic Policy. Furthermore, Sun held, the Russians were increasingly emphasizing nationalism, where their agreement with the Chinese was greatest. Sun insisted that too many of his followers were exaggerating the ideological differences between the Guomindang and the Soviet Union.

Sun also took pains to explain how the Russians' experience could be immensely valuable in curing what had been the Guomindang's most persistent ailment: its inability to become a popular mass movement. In December 1923 the Soviet foreign minister wrote to Sun that propaganda and organization were the first necessities in building a powerful movement. He added: "Our example was significant: our military activities were successful because a long series of years had elapsed during which we organized and instructed our following, building up in this way a great organized party throughout the whole land, a party capable of vanquishing all its adversaries." Virtually as this letter was being written, Sun was telling a party meeting that the party had relied too heavily on military force.

> What was the power that we lacked? It was the support of the people. . . .
>   . . . Why has not our Party engaged in organized, systematic, and disciplined struggle before? It was because we lacked the model and the precedent. . . . If we wish our revolution to succeed, we must learn the methods, organization, and training of the Russians; then there can be hope of success. . . . The reason behind the Communist Party's success is that it suits the desires of the majority of the Russian people, so all the Russian people support it.

Sun immediately launched a sustained effort to spell out his own ideas. In a series of sixteen lectures to top party representatives between January and August 1924, Sun developed anew his Three People's Principles and gave them significantly new emphases. His principle of nationalism now stressed anti-imperialism in a way that fitted the new pro-Soviet orientation of his party; his principle of democracy stressed more than ever before the weaknesses of representative systems and the need for strong government; and his principle of people's livelihood attached a new importance to its similarity to socialism and its opposition to capitalism. Furthermore, while Sun spelled out his ideas, the manifesto of the first Guomindang Party Congress stressed the importance of party power, party centralization, and the mobilization of the masses for action.

The pillars of Guomindang policy came to be admission of the Communists into the Guomindang, alliance with the Soviet Union, creation of a party army, and mobilization of the masses of workers and peasants. With Russian guidance and financial backing and Chinese Communist assistance in organization and propaganda, the Guomindang became a more disciplined, Communist-style party with growing support among the masses and the nucleus of a party army.

The Rise of Jiang Kaishek

The leader of the new Guomindang army, Jiang Kaishek, was among those followers of Sun who remained unreconciled to the reorientation of the party. As late as 1926, however, Jiang was supporting the united front enough to ask an American reporter indignantly, "Why does she [the United States] preach fine sermons, but in the end tag along with the others [imperialist powers]? Why does she not, like Russia, prove her friendliness by acts?" (Questions such as these earned for Jiang the now ludicrous sobriquet "Red general.") But he soon struck fiercely at the Communists and reoriented once again the Guomindang and the Chinese revolution.

After a visit to the Soviet Union Jiang recalled:

From my observations and from my conversations I became convinced that Soviet political institutions were instruments of tyranny and terror, and basically incompatible with the Kuomintang's [Guomindang's] political ideals. . . . I came to the conclusion that the possibility of a revival of Czarist ambitions against China could not be ruled out. . . . I felt strongly that Russia's stratagem and program of World Revolution could constitute an even greater menace to our national independence than had Western colonialism.

Jiang relates that he served Sun in the united front because Sun appealed so persuasively to his party loyalty. But Sun Yatsen died in March 1925; maneuvering for leadership in the party began soon thereafter.

Within a year after Sun's death, Jiang had gone far toward resolving the succession crisis and consolidating his leadership in the party. In March 1926 he felt strong enough to move against the Communists. By a series of bold political and military strokes, Jiang reduced the power of Russian and Chinese Communists in the Guomindang, strengthened his own position in the party and as commander-in-chief of the National Revolutionary Army, and launched the Northern Expedition. His armies swept rapidly over much of southeast China; by March 1927 Jiang had established a new base for the Guomindang in the lower Yangtze River valley, anchored in Shanghai and in Nanjing, which became the Guomindang capital. A month later he moved against the Communists again, this time even more boldly, decisively, and viciously than in 1926; now the Communists were not merely checked but crushed in a bloody coup that nearly wiped them out.

Jiang Kaishek's victories over the Communists did not place him in an entirely secure position. There were other old enemies yet to be confronted, particularly some of the major warlords; there was also Japan, which watched with growing anxiety the rise of a new nationalistic movement backed by a substantial army. Even in his own party, moreover, Jiang had exacerbated old tensions and created new ones, especially among those who opposed abrogating Sun's united front policy so summarily. These problems continued to plague Jiang and the government he founded in 1928. Most of all, Japan's anxiety grew quickly into outright military aggression; and by the time it did, the Communists were reorganizing themselves and beginning to worry Jiang.

In brief, Jiang Kaishek's rise was rapid, but his power was severely limited. Nevertheless, the Guomindang had been transformed, and its position in the country had changed radically between 1923 and 1928. Instead of its narrow and shaky base in Guangzhou, the

Guomindang now controlled most of two provinces in the lower Yangtze area and substantial parts of several other provinces; it possessed the most powerful single military force in China; it had become a better organized and more disciplined party; it had broadened its support by making inroads into the laboring classes, rural as well as urban; and it had produced a daring and decisive new leader. With considerable help from the Soviet Union and the Chinese Communists, the Guomindang had done more to unify the country than any leaders for at least sixty years, thereby earning more respect from the foreign powers than China had received within anyone's memory. A strong, united, and prosperous China was not yet around the corner, but in 1928 there was hope again.

At the beginning of the twentieth century China's leaders had chosen to begin systematically to import foreign ideas and institutions. The imports came in rapid succession from Prussia and Japan, England and the United States, the France of Robespierre and Danton, the Russia of Lenin, and scientists and philosophers the world over. In 1928, with the prospects for effective government better than they had been for many years, the time had come to see whether the new ideas and practices could help solve problems that had long been neglected.

In the thirty years that preceded the founding of the Guomindang government, China had experienced an intellectual revolution of massive proportions. Education had been transformed, and the old scholar-bureaucrats had been replaced by a new intellectual elite. The new intelligentsia was militantly antitraditional, increasingly radical, and inclined primarily toward Marxist and positivist assumptions and values; but it was still a far from unified group of people. Intellectuals could come closest to unanimity when they discussed the scientific method, the epistemology of science, the inevitability of some form of socialism, and the need for industrialization, all of which were widely accepted. All else was ruthlessly questioned, and a lively diversity made the air crackle with ideas. In universities and new research organizations intellectuals pursued their work with imagination and fervor. In the realm of ideas China's revolution proceeded apace.

In the same period changes also touched other parts of Chinese society, but not as deeply or widely. Industry and trade began to grow, the traditional family system began to break down, women gained considerable independence, and business and labor classes expanded and organized. But the growth of new ideas far outstripped social changes, and in the countryside the lag was greater still. In the major cities a few thousand intellectuals were discussing in sophisticated terms the ideas of the world's greatest thinkers; elsewhere, old beliefs and an antiquated institutional structure held sway over the lives of 500 million people. The new ideas had to be translated into solutions for problems of hunger, disease, overpopulation, and underproduction, and political life had to be fundamentally reorganized at the same time. China once again arrived at a fork in the road. A "new culture" had to be broadened beyond a small urban intellectual elite.

3

MODERNIZATION UNDER THE GUOMINDANG GOVERNMENT, 1928–1949

A GUOMINDANG administration still survives on Taiwan; however, it is generally recognized to have been the official government of China only from 1928 to 1949. During the entire twenty years of Guomindang rule, hardly a day passed that a frightful number of Chinese did not die in civil war or in fighting against Japan. Against these conditions of prolonged strife, the hopes of 1928 were dashed.

From 1928 to 1937 the Guomindang government had its best opportunity to function. Although its authority extended to only a fraction of China's area (and even in that fraction its rule was not unchallenged), the Guomindang had momentum and considerable popular support, and it could call on a substantial pool of administrative and technical talent. Even though that pool was much too shallow to supply all the country's needs, the party was able to make a start toward solving some major problems.

From 1937 to 1945 China was at war with Japan. For a young government, newly emerging from decades of foreign oppression and internal disorder, the demands of a prolonged war against a major mechanized military power were excessive. The war brought to the Chinese people destruction, deprivation, and suffering that can scarcely be imagined. Casualties among Chinese regular troops are estimated at 10 million. There were at least another 3.5 million dead, wounded, and injured among guerrilla troops, militia, and civilians. One hint of the human cost is the fact that between 1938 and 1944 nearly 50 million refugees are said to have received relief aid. Since we may be sure that at least an equal number went unaided, it would be conservative to guess that 100 million human lives were shattered by the war. Suffering on so gigantic a scale, enough in itself to demoralize a society, created huge problems for the government, which were aggravated because the Japanese invasion forced it to move inland from the coastal areas and abandoned the most highly developed sectors of the country. Such harsh circumstances have led many scholars to conclude that it was above all the accidents of war that caused the Guomindang to be defeated.

Compelling though this argument is, it may also be said that the Guomindang did not make the most of the opportunities it had. In 1928 the Guomindang controlled only a small area in parts of Zhejiang and Jiangsu. By about 1934 it controlled most of those two provinces, at least four others, and parts of three more. It also had considerable influence in six additional provinces. Pursuit of the Communists in 1934 and 1935 extended Guomindang power to at least four other provinces, and during the war three more moved closer to the Guomindang government. The outbreak of war with Japan in 1937 produced a new surge of patriotism, of which Jiang Kaishek was the major symbol, and the country closed ranks as it had not done at least since 1919. Even the Communists, who had an opportunity to eliminate him at the end of 1936, were forced to admit that Jiang offered China its best chance for unity, and indeed perhaps its only chance at that time. Thus the war was not entirely without its positive side for Guomindang rule and Jiang Kaishek's personal leadership. The challenge was to convert such opportunity into a reality that could withstand the arduous tests of the 1940s. The Guomindang was unable to build on the unity of 1937, however, and by the end of the war Jiang was no longer the country's unquestioned leader. Instead of being in a position where he could claim to have led the nation successfully through one of the greatest crises it had ever faced, Jiang found that his government had lost ground to the Communists. Although the Guomindang had been at least the nominal leader of the wartime resistance, in 1945 the CCP controlled about one-fifth of the country and was prepared to challenge the Guomindang for control of the rest.

In the last period of Jiang's rule on the mainland, following a brief effort (under United States pressure) to negotiate a settlement in 1945 and 1946, the Guomindang and Communists fought a civil war. As long as a Guomindang regime exists on Taiwan, the civil war cannot be considered to have ended formally, but for most practical purposes its outcome was decided by the end of 1948. Offensives in Manchuria in May and June 1947 turned the military tide in favor of the Communists; support for the Guomindang, waning steadily for some years, was almost totally eliminated because of Jiang's political, economic, and military blunders. In 1949 Jiang, his government, and his army fled to Taiwan. The Communists founded a new government in Beijing, and in their turn confronted problems very similar to those the Guomindang had faced. The two governments' approaches to those problems show some notable parallels but far sharper contrasts.

POLITICAL UNITY

Early twentieth-century revolutionaries thought that republicanism and constitutional government provided relatively simple and very nearly complete answers to China's political problems. The Guomindang inherited this spirit of uncritical imitation of Western political institutions. Later, when Sun Yatsen became more critical of the West, his party followed his example. This change of policy created an ambivalence that the Guomindang was never able to resolve.

Sun had never been an entirely uncritical admirer of the West, but his praise of Western institutions, his belief in the need for Western aid, and his confidence in the value of Western models for a long time outweighed his occasional reservations. He had been the earliest and most insistent advocate of United States-style republicanism, but after 1911 he began to criticize the opportunities it offered for what he called a "congressional absolutism" that weakened the authority of the executive branch, and he objected to the federal principle insofar as it contributed to disunity. Eventually he came around to a position resembling that of the nineteenth-century reformers.

> As soon as we learn Western machinery we can use it anytime, anywhere. . . . But Western social customs and sentiments are different from ours in innumerable points; . . . Hence this difference: in ways of controlling physical objects and forces we should learn from the West, but in ways of controlling men, we should not learn only from the West.

The last part of Sun's statement still assigned to Western models a partial role in guiding Chinese social change, but it also opened up the possibility of a compromise with tradition, which the Guomindang was soon to pursue further. This compromise took the form of the five-power constitution Sun had been calling for since about 1905. In this scheme, the executive, legislative, and judicial branches known in the West would be supplemented by the civil service and control powers taken from traditional China. Sun regarded his conception of constitutional government as "a new discovery" in political theory and "a fundamental solution" to the problem of establishing democracy in China.

Sun claimed that his solution would give the government enough power to govern and yet enable the people to control their government as efficiently as they could turn on a water faucet or flick an electric switch. (Sun's choice of metaphor is typical of his propensity to think in Western terms, and it also reveals his tendency to view government as a machine or gadget.) "We who have vision and foresight," Sun said, would first build an "all-powerful" government administrative machinery based on the five-power constitution. The five administrative powers would be controlled by four "political powers" held by the people—suffrage, recall, initiative, and referendum. "Then we will have a completely democratic government organ, and the strength of the people and of the government will be well balanced. . . . With these nine powers in operation and preserving a balance, the problem of democracy will truly be solved and the government will have a definite course to follow."

To bring constitutional government into existence, Sun provided for a revolution in three stages. In 1905 he had prescribed that the first step would be unification of the country by military action. Then a military government would rule for about three years. As old evils were eradicated and order restored, military law would be replaced by local self-government under a provisional constitution. Sun believed that, because the Chinese people were politically inert, they needed a gradual initiation into democracy. A period of tutelage was required as an interim step. This stage would last about six years, after which there would be a final stage in which military government and tutelage would be eliminated and full constitutional government introduced. This formulation was later modified a good deal, but the basic idea of three stages remained. The most important modification, clearly stated in the 1914 regulations of the Guomindang, was the proviso that in the period between the outbreak of military action and the promulgation of the constitution the responsibility for all policy would be borne by the party. For the first time the concept of party tutelage was explicitly enunciated.

By 1924 Sun was urging that China follow the Russian example of "placing the party above the state." The idea of party tutelage was a natural corollary to his concept that certain people (of whom Sun was one) "have vision and foresight" and that it is they who should have responsibility for building the machinery of the state. Sun was a highly inconsistent thinker, and he did not hold steadily to the idea of party tutelage. It was, however, one of his more important ideas, and it became a pillar of Guomindang policy.

When the Guomindang turned to the task of political unification in 1928, it enshrined Sun's ideas as holy writ, above criticism, fostering an almost mystical cult of Sun. But in more mundane practice, too, the government followed much of Sun's blueprint. Even as early as 1925, less than four months after Sun died and a full year before the Northern Expedition carried the party's flag out of Guangzhou, the Guomindang Central Executive Committee had promulgated a law that provided for party direction of national affairs. In 1928, virtually simultaneous with the conclusion of the Northern Expedition, the party proclaimed the beginning of tutelage and the establishment of a five-branch structure of government corresponding to Sun's ideas of a five-power constitution. In subsequent years the party spent much of its time either debating the nature and duration of tutelage and the propriety of having a constitution during the tutelage period or writing constitutions and other legal documents. There was a constant tinkering with one or another foreign-style mechanism or device. The party's preoccupation with such matters is symptomatic of its failure to come to grips with the central problems of political unification.

An elaborate traditional administrative system had been shattered by more than a century of dynastic decline, revolution, and foreign wars. Decades of social change and political experimentation had further eroded the old system. This erosion had permitted the development of even more local autonomy and administrative variations than had been customary. Thus the fundamental political problems centered on how to integrate a changing polity that included old-fashioned warlord satrapies, new parties and independent political clubs, modern and traditional political interest groups, and a vast range in between. Furthermore, political integration had to be attempted in the face of armed challenges from the Chinese Communists, Russia, and Japan, and amid a host of other foreign pressures.

The party's solutions to these problems were shaped by its own history at least as much as they were by Sun Yatsen's ideas. Its revolutionary heritage was not suddenly erased when the party came to power. But during the 1920s membership multiplied many times, and the party came to be led by military and merchant groups. Many of its leaders had been educated abroad, especially in Japan, the United States, and Western Europe, and they came from the coastal areas of China that had been most exposed to treaty-port influence. The result was that policies were reversed in rapid succession. The military, for example, which had been built along Soviet lines, now hired German advisers and adopted a system modeled on Germany and Japan. China's models remained foreign and modern, but they now came from the political right instead of the left.

The sudden growth of the party, coinciding with the acquisition of power, created new internal stresses and aggravated old ones. Competition for the fruits of victory split the Guomindang into many factions, and Jiang Kaishek had to maneuver adroitly to consolidate his leadership. Divisions within the party demanded so much of the leadership's attention that little time was available for dealing with the country's problems. More important, almost every decision required a massive effort at coalition-building. The resulting policies rested on flimsy ad hoc agreements, and the policy makers became laden with a double burden—political debts to their allies and the enmity of those they had outmaneuvered.

Alliances among party factions, warlords, and other groups shifted bewilderingly, and the maneuverings continued for years. While jousting of this sort prevailed at the level of national politics, the problem of local administration festered. Vast areas of the country lay beyond the Guomindang's reach. Tens of millions of people neither contributed taxes needed by the government nor received the services they needed in order to improve their lives and feel that they were citizens of a nation. The faction-ridden government attempted to concentrate power in its own hands. Strict surveillance of local authorities by the provincial government and of provincial authorities by the central government thwarted local officials. They lacked autonomy and training needed to adapt general policies to varying local conditions; at the same time the central government failed to supplement its general directives with special instructions for particular localities. As a torrent of legislation, procedural rules, governing principles, administrative regulations, and action programs poured out of Nanjing, a huge but top-heavy apparatus of party and government workers struggled to implement them.

The laws and action programs were often reasonably well designed by knowledgeable political practitioners and theorists, and party and government workers were frequently educated, experienced, and dedicated men. But the designers, especially the large proportion who had been educated abroad and returned to live in the large modernizing cities like Shanghai, could not take into account the diverse problems of 1,500 to 2,000 far-flung districts; and the county staffs were too small (the average size was about eighty people who governed an area and population about the size of Delaware) and generally not familiar with the details of their districts to adapt the directives from the central government to local circumstances, even when they had the will and motivation. There were too many programs on paper that had little relationship to what the population needed and wanted, and the men charged with the awesome burden of translating directives into action hardly knew where to begin. Government and party offices, mapped out neatly on rational organization charts as befits a modern state and political party, failed to carry out their functions at the local level.

In the county capital, a government-appointed magistrate and his small staff tried to deal with the crucial day-to-day problems that touched people's lives most directly—land administration, education, elections, public works, tax collection, health and sanitation, relief, law enforcement, military conscription. The magistrate had to produce the results that Nanjing wanted, and since he could not do everything he had to assign priorities according to those of the central government. Those priorities stressed tax collection, police work, and conscription. One county, for example, allotted approximately 90 percent of its budget to the salaries of administrative officials. But so few resources went into education, welfare, and development projects that only about 30 percent of the school-age children attended school, and the administration of the government's model land reform law remained so underdeveloped that the entire county Department of Land Administration was finally abolished and replaced by two officials. Without land reform and educational opportunities, farmers remained poor and their children remained uneducated.

The problem of political unity remained unsolved. Twenty years after its founding Jiang Kaishek's political apparatus had still failed to unite the people. In 1948 a Sichuan farmer named Lin, living about fifty miles from his county capital, which in turn was about 12 miles from China's wartime national capital of Chongqing, commented that he had heard of the Guomindang but had never had any personal contact with

baojia

it. The government had placed Lin and his family in a group with thirteen other families, who were convened for a meeting whenever instructions had to be passed along. Instructions filtered down intermittently through several tiers before reaching the fourteen families. These tiers were the heart of the relatively informal apparatus through which the government attempted to supplement its more formal government and party structure.

The group of fourteen families made up a ward; together with nine other wards of approximately the same size (a total of 150 families, about 850 people, living in an area roughly a mile square), it belonged to an administrative unit called a borough; thirty-one boroughs made up a township, and seventy-one townships a county. Through these tiers the county administration attempted to govern the 800,000 people in its district. Heads of families constituted a ward assembly, which was to elect a borough assembly, which in turn would elect the township assembly, which was to elect a county political council. According to theory, this system was to result eventually in the end of Guomindang one-party tutelage and its replacement by free popular exercise of the rights of suffrage, recall, initiative, and referendum. Theory, in other words, called for a thoroughly democratic process of local self-government. But elections for borough and township assemblies and for the county political council only formalized, institutionalized, and perpetuated the power that the wealthy had exercised for generations over people like farmer Lin. "There isn't a single tenant in the whole Council," observed a high county official in 1948. "Many of the Council members are able men, but they are all men of wealth, education, and leisure. They are conservative and aren't interested in changing the *status quo*. The *status quo* is not bad at all from their own personal point of view, which is the only point of view most of them have."

SOCIAL AND CULTURAL CHANGE

Political integration was inseparable from social problems. Class consciousness and differing living styles, attitudes, and customs divided not only the wealthy and educated from the poor and illiterate, but also the modern-educated from the traditionally educated and the city poor from the rural poor. Divisions cut many other ways as well. A single family might include illiterate peasant parents, a son who was a struggling urban worker, a son who was a returned student from America (and perhaps a Christian) and employed by a Western firm in Shanghai, and a daughter who insisted on choosing her own husband.

Of the many divisive stresses felt by individuals and families, two have particularly troubled political leaders in modern China. One has been the conflict between loyalty to the family and loyalty to the nation. The other has been the clash between traditional culture and modern culture, accentuated by the prevalent belief that change from traditional to modern could only occur if it were also change from Chinese to Western: To modernize was to Westernize and therefore to cut off one's cultural roots. This was liberating and therefore satisfying, but it also left an aftertaste of guilt. Young Chinese, still sensitive to their deep tradition and lengthy history, felt a disquieting suspicion that the uprooting might have been premature and therefore a form of cultural murder. As one writer put it, China had come to "worship all foreigners" and had become their pupil; "the result is material improvement, but spiritual degeneration." Many felt alone and adrift on a foreign sea.

As antiforeign patriotism swept the country, the intellectuals who had taken the lead in the Westernization movement of the early twentieth century felt guilty at having rejected their ancestors in favor of foreign ways. Many of them took refuge in nationalist movements as a way of resolving their internal conflicts; rejection of their families could be justified in the name of loyalty to the nation, and Westernization could be explained as a movement to establish the universal values of equality and justice and to build a greater China. Thus nationalism seemed capable of resolving both major conflicts by placing nation above family and by concurrently serving to replace the old cultural tradition with something else that was distinctively Chinese—the nation.

The masses were affected differently, although no less seriously. We know less about what happened to so-called ordinary people, but we do know that the impact of Western ideas faded quickly as it passed beyond the walls of major cities. Vast areas of the country were hardly touched by changes such as the rise of nationalism. Early in 1936 patriotic students marched into villages near Beijing and attempted to arouse the peasants against Japanese invaders who were virtually at the villagers' doorstep. One farmer's response was typical: "The present governor seems all right. Our taxes are lower than before. Why bother us?" Further inland, William Hinton has reported, peasants were even more isolated but so wretchedly preoccupied with survival that they resembled men standing in a well up to their necks in water—the slightest ripple would be enough to drown them, and yet they could no more envision new possibilities than they could survey the sky.

For political leaders seeking to reintegrate the society and mobilize its resources, this many-faceted and amorphous cultural crisis posed a variety of concrete challenges. One of the most persistent was to bridge the widening gap between the city and the countryside. Life in major cities was turning toward Western styles and becoming dominated by businessmen, intellectuals, politicians, and soldiers who looked to the West. Foreign enclaves, having been regarded in the nineteenth century primarily as centers of foreign pollution, had become in the twentieth century not only objects of anti-imperialist agitation, but also havens for revolutionaries and examples of new ways of living. Shanghai, Nanjing, and other large cities contained only a small proportion of China's half-billion people, but at least 15 million people lived in the twelve largest cities and many more millions lived in sizable cities. China's urban inhabitants were numerous, potentially influential, and coming to believe in the possibility of a very different life than their fathers had known.

In the countryside, by contrast, changes were only beginning to touch a handful of wealthy people, some of whom served in the new organs of local government or received some modern education. Three-quarters or more of the parents in China continued to arrange their children's marriages, and three-quarters or more of the children continued to consider it their highest duty to follow their parents' wishes. Three-quarters or more of the people continued to conceive of life as offering the same possibilities it had offered to their fathers and grandfathers.

To those who saw the new possibilities, a Western education was becoming the surest route to status, influence, and prosperity, especially in the fields of government service, business, and the professions. The opportunity to be educated abroad, however, came no more easily to the poor under the republic than it had before. While the number of Chinese students increased markedly, the proportion of those who received government support dipped. Students going abroad had to support themselves, and few besides the wealthy urbanites could do so.

The Guomindang government was unable to solve this problem. It could not sufficiently extend and improve Chinese education; it could not make foreign education more widely available; and it could not free itself from relying heavily on men who had Western training. Indeed, between 1932 and 1947, perhaps as many as 70 or 80 percent of high government officials were men who had been educated abroad. This was not necessarily harmful, but it turned out to have some baleful effects on Chinese modernization. A United States mining engineer, working in China as an adviser on mineral resources in the early 1940s, complained that all the Western-trained geologists he met excelled at making maps and charts but would not dirty their hands in the field. He claimed that none of them had discovered a single mineral deposit and that all the mines and oil and salt wells he visited had been worked by local peasants for centuries. His comment may have been somewhat unfair, but in general it cannot be said that the Western-educated elite dug their hands very deeply into the morass of China's needs. Many, for example, studied agricultural subjects abroad but returned to teach Western-style scientific agriculture in college or work in other occupations; their prescriptions for rural China slighted problems such as high rents, insecurity, usury, and absentee landlordism. Many returned engineers worked for foreign firms in large cities and contributed little to Chinese development. A high proportion of business students returned to work in Western or Western-style banks in large cities. Of the many who returned to China to take up teaching careers, most did so at the highest levels of education, which also kept them in the larger cities.

In short, modern education deepened the gulf between city and country, between educated elite and uneducated masses, and between those oriented toward Western life and those oriented toward traditional Chinese life. The Guomindang did not create this situation, but once in power the party perpetuated and even worsened it. The modern elite, now rapidly increasing in numbers, staffed the new universities, banks, trading companies, and the party and government bureaucracies, but their training did not equip them to deal with the problems that lay beyond the city walls. They expanded the system of higher education, managed the growing trade, worked wonders in currency reform, restructured the party and the government, and improved services such as the postal and transportation networks. Meanwhile, remnants of the old elite, whose forebears had bitterly resisted modernization in the nineteenth century but accepted limited constitutionalism in the twentieth, continued to dominate the countryside from small villages right up to county level.

The Guomindang allowed several experiments in rural reconstruction that revealed both the potential power of innovation and some of the pitfalls. Its own Rural Service sent students to the countryside during their vacations, but this was more a strictly limited economic effort to help bring in the harvest than it was an attempt to bridge the gap between urban and rural society. Perhaps the most famous experiment was the Mass Education Movement directed by James Y. C. Yen (Yen Yang-ch'u). Educated at Yale and Princeton, Yen had worked with the Chinese Labor Corps in France during World War I and had developed a system for quickly teaching basic literacy. In 1930, with financial support from American missionaries and the backing of local leaders and the Nanjing government, Yen launched a pilot project in a northern county. The project was aimed at a wide range of rural needs, including improved agricultural production and sanitation, but it began with an attempt to wipe out illiteracy in the hope that other problems could then be solved primarily by means of education. Yen also believed in starting at the village level and working up to the county.

The program was successful enough to warrant further experimentation along the same lines. But of greater interest than a balance sheet of success or failure is Yen's estimate of the obstacles to social change and their historical background. Reflecting on how matters stood in rural reconstruction in 1937, he discerned a historical pattern into which his movement and others of the 1930s fit. Two movements that had been essentially destructive and had relied primarily on force of arms (the Taiping Rebellion in the nineteenth century and the 1911 revolution) had each been followed by a movement that was more constructive and peaceful (the Taipings by late nineteenth-century reforms such as those of 1898, and 1911 by the May Fourth Movement). These constructive movements, he implied, had not touched the rural masses. Now the revolution of 1926 was being followed by rural reconstruction. History had at last produced a national and cultural "self-awareness" that had in turn promoted rural reform.

Yen's approach to rural change resembled much of what the Communists later said and did. He wrote: "In the solution of rural problems, the first thing is to rely on rural people as the main force; secondly, it is also necessary to rely on people who have knowledge, vision, new methods and new techniques (which rural people do not have) to unite with them." In the preceding ten years, Yen found, this dawning awareness of common purpose was reflected in the intellectuals' slogan, Go to the people. He continued: "Formerly, educated Chinese only read books and wrote essays; they left practical work to farmers, artisans, and merchants. But today's intellectuals realize that if learning is not related to real life it is bound to be empty and sterile."

The task was now to work from the roots outward, as he had tried to do in his pilot project, and this could be done only if intellectuals "went down to the countryside (*xiaxiang*) and if the worlds of politics and learning intermingled. In his model county, he said, all had "realized the need to make scholarship politicized and to have politics become scholarly." Elsewhere he spoke of "the unity of politics and study."

Yen's experiment suffered from weaknesses that included excessive paperwork and top-heavy structure. Nevertheless, it showed that Western-educated Chinese could dedicate themselves to solving the elemental problems faced by the millions in the countryside. James Yen's experiment was not a panacea, and it was not the only experiment. There were others that resembled his in the rural areas, still others in small urban communities, and yet others that concentrated on vocational education or emphasized something other than education. But the government provided only marginal support for all of them.

Jiang Kaishek had his own ideas about social change, and, to the relatively limited extent that the Guomindang government engaged in social reform at all, it followed Jiang's ideas. He believed that the Confucian virtues should be rejuvenated and made the basis of modern reforms. This approach to social change was embodied in the New Life Movement, which he initiated with a speech in Jiangxi in February 1934. The time and place suggest that Jiang's interest in social reform had immediate and specific political ramifications that in his mind outweighed social reform as a worthy goal in itself. Jiang's speech came in the midst of his fifth massive campaign to smash the Communist forces that had settled in Jiangxi; Nanchang, which was headquarters for the campaigns, also housed the Central Association of the New Life Movement and was the site of its various model projects. Not until about a year after the Communists abandoned Jiangxi and marched north was the Central Association transferred to Nanjing.

The New Life Movement functioned quite differently in Jiangxi than it did elsewhere. In Jiangxi it was designed to gain popular support in the struggle against the Communists and to win back for the Guomindang the loyalty of those who had lived under the Chinese soviet regime. Thus the Guomindang actively promoted the New Life Movement in the Jiangxi countryside, where it was aimed chiefly at physical rehabilitation of recaptured areas. Elsewhere the New Life Movement was an urban program, and it was aimed at a kind of moral rearmament rather than at economic problems. Jiang Kaishek, however, tried to refute the notion that he was neglecting the country's material needs. China's major problems were spiritual and ethical, Jiang replied to his critics.

> The four virtues are the basic elements of man. If one cannot be a man, what is the use of having an abundance of food and clothing? . . . The four virtues, which rectify the misconduct of men, are the proper methods of achieving abundance. . . . People become traitors, Communists and corrupt officials, not because they are driven by hunger and cold, but because they have neglected the cultivation of virtue.

The virtues Jiang had in mind were the traditional Chinese principles usually translated as "decorum," "righteousness," "integrity," and "sense of shame." Thus the New Life Movement has generally been considered a prime example of Jiang's essential traditionalism. But this and other perversions of Chinese tradition should not be allowed to obscure the kind of conservatism Jiang and his government stood for, which was not simply traditionalism. Jiang interpreted the traditional virtues in his own way, which he insisted was a new interpretation suited to "the changing times and circumstances." An unbiased reader of the movement's literature will probably agree with Jiang that it owed more to contemporary circumstances than it did to Chinese tradition. His emphasis, for example, on the "military way of life" as a major pillar of rational living and as a manifestation of the four virtues in action probably owes more to his German advisers and his mixed respect for and fear of Japan than it does to Confucius.

The manner in which the New Life Movement was put into practice further illuminates Jiang's conception of how to adapt tradition to modern conditions. It also helps to explain why the government was unable to deal effectively with China's social needs. Lists of rules exhorted people to learn correct posture, button up their clothes, walk on the left side of the street, and take proper care of their fingernails. They were seldom taken seriously. According to one observer, "Uplifting wall slogans were posted in villages where nobody could read, and peasants who could not afford soap were lectured on the duty to wash." Exhortations that might have been taken more seriously—buy Chinese goods rather than foreign ones; kill rats, flies, and mosquitoes— remained little more than exhortations. New Life Movement Promotion Associations, hundreds of which existed on paper, were inactive.

Promotion of the rules was left largely to police, boy scouts, and volunteer groups. Unbelievably, a cardinal rule of operations was that the movement be carried on only in leisure hours or vacation time and not be allowed to interfere with regular duties; it relied heavily on women's auxiliaries and students who gave up their Sunday afternoons to direct traffic or perform other services similarly designed to inculcate the four virtues. Intending to start modestly by improving individual conduct in the most ordinary everyday things and then work its way up to loftier and subtler questions of morality, the movement succeeded only in making itself a laughingstock.

After some trial and error, the movement was oriented more toward patriotic activities, public works, and health and welfare services. But it never recovered from its unfortunate beginnings, and it never reached far beyond the cities where police, students, and other volunteers could work. The movement was administered by a former YMCA secretary who was a favorite of Madame Jiang's and of many Americans, but who had no talent for promoting social reform. Two years after he had initiated the movement, Jiang confessed his disappointment in its results.

To one perceptive observer, "the New Life Movement was a cherished ornament on the government's facade of Western-style progress." Before the war it cleaned up "the surface of life in the big cities" and "had results among those of the small new commercial and industrial upper class who wanted to make China like the West. In the countryside and the smaller provincial towns, however, its work was irrelevant to the point of comedy or tragedy." A scholarly analysis of the movement concludes that it was intended to imitate Japanese, German, and Italian urban practices and that it had little effect on the rural population. The New Life Movement's minimal success only widened the gap between the traditional and the modern and between the Chinese and the Western in China's agonizingly schizophrenic republican government and society.

This schizophrenia increasingly tended to be resolved in favor of the Guomindang's brand of traditionalism. Confucian ethics competed with nationalistic Three People's Principles education even in the early days of the Guomindang government—Confucius's birthday became a national holiday in 1931, a read-the-classics movement was begun, and in many other ways Confucianism enjoyed a vogue in Nanjing. But in 1943, with the publication of Jiang Kaishek's *China's Destiny*, the wobbly balance between Guomindang traditionalism and modernism swung heavily against the modern. By this time the war was turning against Japan, and the Communists were gaining support; Jiang was more than ever preoccupied with the civil war. He set forth a reconstruction program and made an appeal to the Chinese people that dwelled at great length on foreign oppression of China and the glory of Chinese traditional culture. He denounced Western materialism and all who accepted Western ideas, especially Chinese youth, and called for a return to ancient values and old systems of group responsibility. But he also called for industrialization according to the blueprint of Sun Yatsen. In 1943 the Western-oriented elements in China found this new Guomindang mixture shockingly outdated, and even business people found the CCP proposals more attractive than Jiang's.

ECONOMIC DEVELOPMENT

Economic development requires a suitable political and social environment, but what exactly is politically and socially suitable for any particular country's economic development remains difficult to determine. Furthermore, a certain degree of economic development must precede political and social modernization in order for substantial economic development to be possible; it is sometimes argued, for example, that a considerable transportation system must exist before enough political unity can be effected in countries such as China and India to enable them to industrialize. The complexity of these theoretical issues, however, need not obscure two facts about China. One fact, obvious from the preceding discussion, is that political and social conditions were decidedly unfavorable to economic development. The other is that, despite these unfavorable conditions, the economy grew and modernized considerably before 1949, but it did so in an exceedingly unbalanced manner. As a result, China in 1949 still had an essentially traditional or preindustrial economy.

The pattern of pre-1949 economic development resembles the political and social patterns we have observed. The "modern" sector of the economy grew steadily. Railway mileage grew more than twice as rapidly between 1926 and 1937 than it had in the fifteen years before 1926, and most of the increment came between 1935 and 1937. More than 50,000 miles of new highways were opened (to traffic that was largely military). Industrial production in 1936, on the eve of war with Japan, was 90 percent higher than it had been in 1928 when the Guomindang government was founded. The total number of modern banks was raised to 164 with the founding of 128 new banks between 1928 and 1937, with 1,597 branches (concentrated, of course, in the major coastal cities). In addition to such measurable gains, the government scored genuine successes in currency reform, the adoption of modern budgeting techniques, and the development of a modern banking system; and it did much to improve investment and credit mechanisms, rationalize the tax structure, and create a framework of property and contract law within which business could develop. Some of these, notably the credit and tax systems, still possessed basic weaknesses, but the government had clearly gone well beyond its predecessors in a remarkably short time.

Despite this growth, however, modern industry accounted for only about one-fiftieth of China's domestic production and did not lead to the expansion of other crucial sectors of the economy. Handicraft industry produced more than modern industry. Industry as a whole contributed only a small fraction (roughly one-tenth) of China's net domestic product; agriculture contributed about two-thirds and employed about 80 percent of the labor force. The peasants had too little land and produced too little on what they had. Because of inadequate fertilizer, seed, tools, and pest control, China's rice and wheat yields per acre were far below Japan's. Of what they did produce, tenants generally had to give about half to their landlords, and although no one knows exactly how much land was farmed by tenants, it is clear that at least half the peasants in the country suffered from one or another of the ills of tenancy—small plots, insecure tenure, high rents, usurious interest rates on loans, and the near impossibility of improving their lot. Peasants' landholdings shrank until they had barely enough to survive. According to a 1934 survey, one-third of the farms in China were smaller than 1.5 acres, and three-fourths of them were less than 5 acres. Conditions varied greatly in different parts of the country, but in the summer of 1936, according to a field study by China's leading anthropologist, the villagers' income was insufficient to secure the minimum requirements of livelihood. He concluded: "It is the hunger of the people that is the real issue in China." The Guomindang land law of 1930, a model piece of legislation that would have reduced rents and increased peasant landholdings, remained unenforced.

Economic development under the Guomindang government therefore meant stagnation in agriculture, uneven but modest gains in industry, and considerable growth of modern business in some coastal areas. In general, and this is true of rural areas as well as urban, there occurred substantial *commercialization* of the economy, but very little *modernization.* In a brilliant study by G. William Skinner, it has been convincingly argued that in about 90 percent of the agrarian economy true modernization had not yet taken place by 1948. In much of the countryside, the volume of trade had increased, market towns had added additional days to their schedules, and new markets had been formed to take care of the growth in trade. But this merely expanded the old system without changing it. Only about 10 percent of the marketing areas in rural China had broken out of this pattern, become linked to major cities by modern transport facilities, and developed enough modern transportation within the area to destroy old markets.

In the cities business flourished, but industry did not. It was here that government initiative and involvement made itself felt most directly, particularly through its overwhelming control of the country's modern banks. A form of state socialism that has come to be known as "bureaucratic capitalism" permitted an inner circle of party leaders to amass private fortunes and indulge in real estate and bond speculation as well as some legitimate enterprises; other entrepreneurs found it difficult to obtain capital. Those who had capital devoted it to turning a quick profit, and little was available for the risks of investment in industry. The government's own resources went almost entirely into military spending and servicing the national debt, much of which it had inherited from its predecessors. These two items in some years took more than 80 percent of government revenues.

Finally, industry failed to develop because new industrial management and administrative techniques did not materialize. Unlike Japan's modernizers, as Franz Schurmann has aptly pointed out, Chinese entrepreneurs were unable to reconcile modern technical organization with traditional human organization. In Chinese enterprises, there was neither a separate technical organization, as in Japan, nor men who combined policy making with operational leadership.

> Businessmen made decisions on money and rarely on operations. Government, officially or unofficially, provided capital but was ignorant of its use. Managers worked through gang bosses but knew little of how production was going on. Staff workers came from the educated elite; they rarely went down into the plant to observe production.

The Guomindang could not transfer its programs and organizations from the paper they were written on to the lives of Chinese citizens. Land reform, political tutelage, local self-government, constitutionalism, and the New Life Movement remained on a display shelf that the Guomindang might well have labeled "Modernization by Proclamation." One hard-working and widely respected local administrator bitterly summed up his experience as of 1948: "The Nationalist government has been in power for twenty years. During these years they have said all the good words and done all the bad things. Endless talk will result in nothing."

In brief, the Guomindang government compiled a mixed record that left China still on the threshold of modernization. By the time the Guomindang was driven from the mainland in 1949, modernization had proceeded extremely far in some areas of life, but in others it had barely begun. The Guomindang had continued the pattern of highly uneven modernization characteristic of China since the nineteenth century and had demonstrated the same inability of all Chinese governments before 1949 to develop and carry out a systematic program of modernization. In 1948 urban intellectuals still discussed the ideas of the world's great thinkers, bureaucrats drafted plans modeled on America's TVA, publicity men and party workers hurried through the motions of initiating a new era of constitutionalism, and businessmen watched the world market. Nearby, in areas they could see from their rooftops, little had changed. Guangzhou was a city with a population of 1.25 million in 1948, the capital and economic center of Guangdong province, a major meeting point between China and the West (and with a history of foreign contact that reached back more than a millennium), a city that was in the heart of the area in which major modern revolutionary movements had erupted and from which the lion's share of Chinese overseas emigration came. Five miles from Guangzhou, wrote a Chinese sociologist in the 1950s, "despite the increasing pace and degree of social change in the surrounding world, a process now nearly fifty years old, [the village of] Nanching up to the very eve of the victory of Chinese Communism remained essentially fixed in its traditional stable social pattern."

4

THE RISE OF THE CHINESE
COMMUNIST PARTY,
1920–1949

W HEN WESTERN thought made its first deep and lasting impact on Chinese intellectuals, it impressed them with the ideas of struggle and progress. As Yan Fu had remarked, "unity and progress result from diversity and competition." Western devices for securing social cohesion seemed not to interfere with the pursuit of individual interests; national unity, wealth, and power seemed compatible with pluralism. In the early 1900s many Chinese intellectuals believed that representative government and constitutionalism ensured the best combination of unity and diversity, for Western-style democracy created strong, prosperous states and also upheld the ideals of liberty, equality, and fraternity. Hence, even though many prominent Chinese intellectuals paid attention to the Russian revolutionaries, felt some kindship with them, and became superficially acquainted with Marxism, only a few were attracted to Marxist ideas of dialectical materialism and progress by means of class struggle. The Chinese could not yet see any relationship between Marxism and national power.

Between 1912 and 1919 the intellectual and political climate changed. Because many Chinese considered that China's experiment with Western-style constitutional democracy was a dismal failure, their admiration for Western institutions wavered. The precarious balance between envy and resentment of the West tipped once again toward resentment when Westerners and Japanese violated China's territorial integrity at Versailles. Intellectuals still desperately longed for China to be both powerful and democratic, but as the failures of the republic mounted after 1912, and especially after Versailles and May Fourth, Western-style democratic politics lost much of its appeal.

During this disillusionment in China, Russia in 1917 threw off its antiquated autocracy, proclaimed scientific socialism, issued a call for world revolution, and prepared itself for both civil war and resistance to Western and Japanese efforts to crush the new Soviet regime. The Chinese watched these events as closely as they could; a few, such as the Beijing University history professor and chief librarian Li Dazhao (1889–1927), soon commented favorably on the Bolshevik Revolution, but most were not yet touched by the events in Russia. Li began to study Marxism and to discuss it with small groups of students; among the young intellectuals who met in Li's office—which quickly became known as the "Red Chamber," evoking both Li's politics and the title of a famous Chinese novel—was Mao Zedong (1893–1976). Even Li, however, was still uncertain of his ideological convictions and of the prospects for revolution. As late as spring of 1919 the mood of the intellectuals, including the most radical of them, was overwhelmingly one of curiosity, probing, and experimentation. But within a year a few, including Li, Chen Duxiu, and some others who had been prominent in the May Fourth Movement, turned to Marxism-Leninism.

FOUNDING OF THE PARTY

Among the many reasons for this shift, three are particularly relevant to our story. The first was the renewal of political organization and activism fostered by the May Fourth Movement, with its heated anti-imperialist and antiwarlord sentiment. This two-edged nationalism, one slashing at the foreign powers and the other at the warlords who blocked the unification of China, found new meaning in Marxism-Leninism. In 1919 Lenin's writings were just beginning to become readily available to Chinese intellectuals. Works such as *Imperialism, The Highest Stage of Capitalism*, which Lenin had written only a few years before, gave the Chinese appetizing food for thought. The notions that imperialism was a necessary stage in the development of capitalism and an inherent part of capitalism and that imperialism marked the final step in capitalism's growth before it met destruction drew a deep response from the bitterly anti-imperialist intellectuals. The intellectuals' determination to find new political weapons to use against the warlords made Leninist concepts of political organization highly attractive, for the very core of Leninism was the idea of a disciplined, elite party of revolutionary intellectuals. In brief, May Fourth produced among many Chinese intellectuals sentiments that were uniquely receptive to Leninist ideas.

Another reason for the sudden growth of Marxism-Leninism in China was the Soviet Union's timely appeal to Chinese anti-imperialism. In the summer of 1919, the Soviet foreign minister declared that his government was prepared to renounce all privileges obtained from China by previous Russian governments. Later Soviet denials that the renunciation was total and revelations that the Russians were bargaining with the warlord government in Beijing impressed the Chinese much less than the first and unequivocally anti-imperialist pronouncement. Praise for the Russians and salutes to the new era that had dawned in international relations filled the press. Even moderate intellectuals began to investigate Marxism, and Marxist study societies flourished as never before. Some Chinese intellectuals now sensed that Marxism-Leninism resolved one of their most agonizing dilemmas: how to be modern, Western, and scientific in their outlook and at the same time be uncompromisingly anti-imperialist, and therefore nationalist, and therefore Chinese. "Scientific socialism" in Lenin's anti-imperialist state (which was in those very years under attack by Britain, France, the United States, and Japan), offered a combination that earlier foreign objects of Chinese admiration (English liberalism, the French Revolution, United States republicanism, and Japanese modernization) could not match.

Finally, Marxism-Leninism gained impetus from the arrival of agents of the Communist International (Comintern) almost precisely when the Soviet anti-imperialist declaration was made public. With the ground already well prepared, the agents had no difficulty in persuading Chen Duxiu to take the lead in organizing a small Communist group in Shanghai in May 1920. Other groups followed in at least five more Chinese cities, plus Tokyo and Paris. The Shanghai branch soon founded a Sino-Russian news agency, two journals, a youth corps, and a foreign language school, all aimed at recruiting and training cadres. Some cadres were later sent to the Soviet Union for advanced schooling. Only a little more than a year later the Chinese Communist Party (CCP) held its first congress, signifying the formal establishment of the party, with twelve or thirteen delegates representing an estimated fifty-seven members.

The early history of the CCP was marked by Marxist orthodoxy, adherence to a Soviet model, and subservience to outside authority. Having originated largely from the example and with the encouragement of the Soviet Union, the CCP organized itself under the watchful eyes of two Comintern representatives who attended the First Party Congress. According to one participant, the Comintern also sent a Russian worker who represented the Red International of Labor Unions and spoke to the Chinese about its aims and activities. The delegates agreed to learn from the experience and example of the Communist party of the Soviet Union. They also adopted a program that reads, appropriately enough, like a Marxist primer. To show that they meant what they said, the Communists immediately applied themselves to overthrowing "the capitalistic classes" by organizing labor unions and converting the workers into a class-conscious proletariat of which the party members might then be the vanguard. The new party set industriously to work in conventional Marxist fashion.

Perhaps the clearest indication of the CCP's lack of independence was its allegiance to the Comintern. It is likely, though not certain, that a formal affiliation between the CCP and the Comintern took place at the First Party Congress. Formally subservient or not, the CCP felt compelled to accept when the Comintern decided that the time had come to adopt a new strategy. The Comintern insisted on an alliance with the Guomindang in 1923 because it believed that the CCP could in this way isolate its major enemies, the warlords and the imperialist powers; the CCP was too weak to fight alone. The Chinese Communists submitted, even though they despised the Guomindang and were baffled by the Comintern's departure from Marxist orthodoxy. The Guomindang, Moscow explained, did not represent one class, the bourgeoisie; it was a coalition of all classes. Communists could therefore join it and still retain their leadership of the laboring masses. But the CCP knew it had both committed Marxist heresy and strayed from the Bolsheviks' path to power.

What sweetened this bitter pill for at least some members, including Li Dazhao and Mao Zedong, was that the alliance with the Guomindang was aimed at ridding China of imperialism. From this point of view, subservience to the Comintern was in the larger interest of Chinese nationalism. Soon, however, Stalin relegated Chinese nationalism to a lower priority. Not merely Russian or even Comintern interests but those of Stalin himself took first place. Stalin, who was grappling with Trotsky for the right to succeed Lenin, had championed the united front policy against Trotsky's objections. Worrying less about the CCP's fate than his own, Stalin clung to the policy until Trotsky was no longer a threat to him. This, however, was a little too long for the Chinese Communists, many of whom were still clinging to it as they fell before Jiang Kaishek's guns in 1927. Nevertheless, as Lyman P. Van Slyke has neatly put it:

> It can be argued that the disaster of 1927 hid the successes that preceded it. . . . The extent of the defeat may well have been a measure of how much was attempted. . . . The CCP's rapid growth from a membership numbering a few dozen intellectuals to a mass party seriously competing for national pwer was an impressive accomplishment. Perhaps no set of policies could have achieved complete success in so short a time.

To build on its successes and remain a serious competitor for national power, however, the CCP found it necessary to break further with Marxist orthodoxy, Soviet models, and Comintern authority than it was able to do by 1927.

SEEDLINGS OF CCP INDEPENDENCE

Much of Chinese Communist history centers on its transformation from a foreign-dominated movement to an essentially indigenous one. It was a twisting and erratic process in which parts of the scattered movement skidded from one pole to another like iron filings drawn this way and that by a revolving magnet. Indigenous elements were powerfully present in the beginning, and foreign influences persist to this day. But the general trend during the party's sixty-year history has been for the Chinese Communists to shape their movement to their own circumstances, take control of their own destiny, and develop their own brand of Communism.

The Chinese Communist revolution was not simply a peasant revolution; it was also a revolution in which intellectuals who were disposed toward both Western and Chinese values, standards, styles of life, and conceptions of history and social relationships learned they had to bring the two together in a new way. It is not yet clear that they have done this successfully, but it is clear that they have enjoyed more success in dealing with this central problem in modern Chinese history than anyone else who has confronted it since the middle of the nineteenth century. One key to the Communists' success has been their flexibility. They have learned hard lessons and profited from them. They have formulated different types of appeals to different segments of the population and have adjusted the content and delivery of the appeal and their method of organization to changing circumstances in different parts of the country. The creativity of the Communist leadership revealed itself more in this general respect than in specific insights, such as the discovery of the revolutionary potential of the peasantry.

The importance of the peasantry had been recognized by Lenin and was perhaps seen even more clearly by Asian Communists such as the Indian M. N. Roy, who pleaded at the Second Comintern Congress in 1920 for emphasis on "mass struggle" in which peasants as well as workers would be organized by Communist parties. The Comintern itself, although often inconsistent or vague on this point, advised the CCP in May 1923 that the peasantry was "the central problem of our whole policy." In 1925 the Comintern's chief agent in China, Michael Borodin, told the Guomindang that organizing the peasantry for a solution of the land question would determine the success or failure of the revolution. The Comintern usually stressed, however, that the proletariat must take the lead. The question of who made the crucial intellectual breakthrough is unanswerable, but it is beyond dispute that many people realized the potential of the peasantry before anyone did much to translate that realization into political and social action, and that only after years of perseverance did the Chinese intellectuals overcome the deeply ingrained attitudes that walled them off from the Chinese masses. The difficulty of this prolonged effort, which continues even now, has profoundly influenced the Chinese Communist movement.

The work began in the 1920s, when the first serious efforts at mass mobilization were made. By turning to peasants more than to urban workers, a few pioneering Communists blazed a trail toward independence from the Comintern. The first Chinese Communist to devote himself to organizing the peasants was an intellectual who seems to have taken this course of action with little of his colleagues' hesitation. Peng Pai (1896–1929) was the son of a wealthy landlord. He spent three years as a college student in Japan, where he joined a socialist group that devoted itself to agrarian problems. After graduation he returned home, joined the CCP, and soon began organizing peasants. Between May and September 1922 he organized a village peasant union with more than 500 members; four months later he organized a County

Federation of Peasant Unions that claimed 20,000 members. By May 1923 he led a Guangdong Provincial Peasant Union which, after a temporary setback in 1924, grew to an estimated 210,000 or more, covering twenty-two counties. Due partly to Peng's success, the Guomindang (by now allied with the CCP) founded a Peasant Department, in which he became the most prominent individual.

These startling gains received little or no encouragement from the CCP, which was preoccupied with consolidating its alliance with the Guomindang and renewing its emphasis on organizing labor. This preoccupation was not entirely due to Marxist orthodoxy and Comintern instructions, however, for in 1924 and 1925 the labor movement expanded rapidly. There was, in other words, a good practical reason for the CCP to concentrate its efforts on urban workers—the field seemed fertile. The many strikes of 1924 and 1925 testify to the Communist organizers' success.

May Day 1925 coincidentally found both the trade unions and the peasant unions convening in Guangzhou. The Second Labor Congress, however, dwarfed the Peasant Congress, for it represented 166 trade unions that claimed a membership of 540,000. The Peasant Congress acknowledged its subordinate role by adopting a resolution in which it affirmed that "our struggle must be concentrated in the city, because the political center is located in the city; therefore the working class must strive to lead the peasants to participate in this struggle."

By this time the CCP was beginning to take more note of the peasant movement in Guangdong. Party headquarters urged that peasant unions and peasant self-defense corps be organized. Such moves were invariably checked, however, because the alliance with the Guomindang still had top priority, and to keep that alliance the CCP had to avoid offending landlords. Hence the 1925 Peasant Congress did not dare to declare itself in favor of rent reduction. But Peng Pai, who did not attend the Peasant Congress, refused to accept party restraint. A few months later he urged the peasants to take matters into their own hands. They did, and many landlords and others, both innocent and guilty, lost their lives as well as their property. Reforms were at first limited to rent reduction, but soon the tenants in Peng's area abolished rents altogether and took over the landlords' holdings. CCP membership grew from seven hundred in December 1926 to four thousand only three months later, and Communist cells were created in 330 villages. Somewhat ironically, in view of the Russian desire to concentrate on the urban workers and bourgeoisie, Peng Pai's headquarters came to be known as

"Little Moscow." More cruelly ironic was Peng's eventual capture and execution by the Guomindang in Shanghai in 1929.

Earlier, however, the influence of Peng Pai's peasant revolution had spread north to Hunan. Mao Zedong had grown up there on a small farm that he later said had evolved to "middle peasant" range by the time he was ten years old and to "rich peasant" status later on. In 1924 Mao happened to leave his party work temporarily to return to Hunan; there he discovered the revolutionary potential of the peasantry and turned to rural organization work. Thanks mainly to Mao's efforts, Hunanese soon began to pour into Peng Pai's Peasant Movement Training Institute. By the autumn of 1925 Mao himself had become active in the institute, and early in 1926 he was beginning to sort out his own ideas on the relative importance of the workers and peasants. A young, inexperienced, and groping Marxist, Mao was uncusccessful in these early intellectual efforts. His writing shows a deep preoccupation with the peasants' revolutionary power, but he considered them to be only a "semi-proletariat" and held that "the industrial proletariat, though small in number, has become the major force of the national revolutionary movement."

Nevertheless Mao continued to work with the peasants, and from May to October 1926 he served as principal of the Peasant Movement Training Institute. In that capacity he once took the entire student body on a two-week visit to Peng Pai's headquarters to let them see first-hand a rural revolution in the making. Early in 1927 he was back in Hunan, where he witnessed so active a peasant movement that he predicted:

> In a very short time in Central, South, and North China, several hundred million peasants will rise like a mighty storm, a hurricane, a force so swift and violent that no power, however strong, can restrain them. They will break all the shackles that bind them and rush forward along the road of liberation. All imperialists, warlords, corrupt officials, local tyrants, and bad gentry will be sent to their graves by the peasants. All revolutionary parties and comrades will stand before them to be tested and either accepted or rejected as they decide.

Mao then asked rhetorically: "Are we to march at their head and lead them? Or trail behind them, gesticulating and criticizing? Or stand in their way and oppose them?" The growth of the peasant movement in 1926 and 1927 gave Mao and a few others the answer to this question, but the Russians and the CCP leadership saw only a dilemma. To promote the peasant movement was to risk a split with the Guomindang;

to try to check it or to find some compromise was perhaps to miss an opportunity that might not come again. The CCP managed at last to turn toward a peasant emphasis, but the shift came slowly and only at the cost of party unity. The shift was not decisive until the early 1930s, when Moscow's hand was removed and the Chinese were freer to experiment. Until that time the CCP managed to resist any temptation to exploit fully the huge reservoir of rural discontent that Peng Pai and Mao Zedong had revealed.

This important point should not be allowed to obscure the breakthrough that Chinese intellectuals in general, and the Communists in particular, made in the 1920s. Although elementary Marxist ortho- doxy seemed to demand that Communists concentrate on organizing the urban proletariat, it took only a little sophistication in Marxism- Leninism to justify a policy of mobilizing the peasants; and although the Soviet experience and Comintern leadership tended to direct the Chinese to the cities, these guidelines were not fixed, and it was still possible for men like Peng Pai to work in the countryside and make the Comintern reconsider its strategy. The Comintern was aware of the peasants but decided its immediate interests lay more in maintaining the united front with the Guomindang.

The Chinese Communists had to overcome some obstacles that were inherent in Marxism-Leninism, Soviet models, and Comintern discipline, but they also had to address themselves to a central problem that all revolutionaries had to face in China: how to relate rural and urban movements to each other. In this regard their own elitism and, above all, their own inexperience and uncertainty hobbled them as much as outside control. Some, such as Peng Pai, found it easy to go among the peasants; most found it difficult. Mao Zedong himself, after having lived in cities for fifteen years, confessed that he had learned to despise rural life. Communist intellectuals found it easier to go among the workers, perhaps, but probably most of the workers were peasants only recently come from the countryside. The deeper problem was how to go among the masses, urban and rural, and mobilize them for revolution. Opportunity lay on all sides, as the huge growth of labor unions and peasant unions demonstrated. The challenge was to turn the opportunity to the service of the revolution.

In the 1920s the CCP began to meet this challenge, but the party was still too weak and inexperienced to take advantage of the opportu- nity, and Comintern leaderhip was unable to teach what the Chinese needed to know. Perhaps the mass movement was not yet large enough and the Communists' rivals, Jiang Kaishek and the Guomindang, were still stronger than the CCP. Thus the CCP subordinated itself to the Comintern and gave priority to maintaining a united front with the Guomindang, hoping to control the Guomindang and, through it, to carry out a "revolution from above." But in the 1930s the CCP grew more experienced and much stronger. It freed itself of outside direction and once again rose to rival the Guomindang for state power, this time by mobilizing the masses in a "revolution from below."

THE RISE OF MAO ZEDONG

More than a decade after the Communists entered Beijing and made it China's new capital, their foreign minister was to say: "Soviet communism has bloomed a Soviet flower and Chinese communism a Chinese one. Both are equally communism, but their flowers are of different hues." It is not clear precisely when seedlings such as those of Peng Pai and Mao Zedong blossomed fully enough to be identifiable as Chinese, but a trend toward Chinese Communist independence from Moscow is clearly identifiable in the late 1920s and thereafter becomes increasingly plain. CCP independence went hand in hand with the rise of Mao Zedong to leadership of the party.

Mao's rise was erratic, and his ideas as well as his strategy and tactics changed several times. Much as the nineteenth-century reformers, the earlier revolutionaries, and the Guomindang government had shifted their ground, baffled but determined, so Mao probed and backtracked and side-stepped and probed again. One biographer has aptly characterized Mao in the late 1920s as an "apprentice Leninist." Most students of his career would agree that his apprenticeship lasted rather a long time, and hostile critics find little evidence of sophistication in his thinking to this day. But other students of his thought see remarkable growth beginning in the 1930s. A prominent feature of that growth was his departure from Russian models and influence.

In 1927 Jiang Kaishek's coup left the CCP leaders no choice but to seek their own way. Comintern policy was thrown into confusion by Jiang's move, and by the time it recovered the CCP was splintered into many fugitive groups. By the beginning of 1930 there were fifteen Communist bases scattered across half of China. Each had to survive as best it could.

Mao's struggle took him first to Hunan where, in September 1927, he participated in a disastrous defeat that may have been the most valuable learning experience he had yet undergone. In an attempt to regain the initiative from Jiang Kaishek, the CCP decided to attack major cities, including Changsha in Hunan. Mao anticipated optimistically that the fall of Changsha would lead to a successful nationwide revolution like Russia's in 1917. But until the key city fell, Mao thought, there was no point in promoting the rural movement. A shattering reversal at Changsha told him a new strategy was needed.

Limping into the mountains on the border of Hunan and Jiangxi Mao established a base in October 1927 and began to organize it according to what he termed his own "clumsy inventions." For about three years thereafter Mao's inventions were challenged by instructions from the Comintern and the CCP Central Committee. Mao objected more than once. Although in crucial situations he followed orders, he did so only up to a certain point. The best example is a disagreement that matured in 1929 and 1930. By this time Mao's experience had convinced him that the CCP's chief needs were to establish base areas in the countryside, systematically construct a political structure, promote agrarian revolution, and build up the Red Army by slow stages beginning with local militia. He also cautioned against "revolutionary impetuosity" and urged patient but confident preparation; he was beginning to work out the concepts of "despising one's enemy strategically, but respecting him tactically" and of surrounding cities from the countryside. The CCP leadership, however, scoffed at Mao's ideas, and the Comintern still stressed that the vital task of the CCP was to lead the struggles of urban workers. Despite this head-on collision of views, when the order came to march in a major attack on three cities, Mao and his military commander, Zhu De (1886–1976), reluctantly accepted it. But when it was evident to him that the attack was a failure, Mao did not wait for instructions to disengage. He pulled back to the Jiangxi base in September 1930, and from that time forward he developed and followed his own conception of how to carry the revolutionary potential of China's hinterland into its cities.

Alternatives to Mao's conception and challenges to his growing authority in the Communist movement were powerful in the years that followed. Mao was overruled on occasion, and not always to the detriment of the movement; in early 1933 Maoist tactics were abandoned, and a major victory was won by a direct frontal assault on Guomindang troops. Mao was criticized, and some of his adherents were vigorously attacked by the party leadership. Only in January 1935 did

Mao finally move into the inner circle of party leadership and begin to make his policies those of the CCP.

Mao's policies developed in several stages, but the fundamental elements were already present by 1929 and 1930. Perhaps the innermost core of his policies was a belief in mass organization. A leading student of Mao, Stuart Schram, has speculated that in Mao's personality was a natural Leninism, that is, "a certain intuitive understanding of the importance of organization that is one of the reasons for his emergence as the leader of the Chinese Communist Party." Hints of this predilection appear in Mao's writings on labor organization as early as 1920 and emerge more clearly in his 1926 and 1927 writings on the peasantry. On several occasions in the 1920s he also demonstrated a taste and talent for analyzing organizational problems. And in Mao's own account of his efforts in 1929 to build up a base area, he recalled that the "bad tendencies" he had to correct in his followers had included "lack of discipline, exaggerated ideas of democracy, and looseness of organization." Another tendency that had to be fought was " 'vagabondage'—a disinclination to settle down to the serious tasks of government, a love of movement, change, new experience and incident." Mao had little use for spontaneity and improvisation.

Mao's remarks were directed at his troops, but he did not intend them to apply only to military organization. One of the most prominent characteristics of his outlook was the interpenetration of military and political strategy. In 1929, for example, Mao explicitly condemned what he termed "the purely military viewpoint." He explained:

> [The Red Army] is an armed group for carrying out political tasks of a class nature. In order to carry out this task, particularly in present-day China, the Red Army must not merely fight; besides fighting, it should also shoulder such important tasks as agitating among the masses, organizing them, arming them, and helping them to set up political power. When the Red Army fights, it fights not merely for the sake of fighting but exclusively to agitate among the masses, to organize them, to arm them, and to help them establish political power; apart from such objectives, fighting loses its meaning, and the Red Army the reason for its existence.

Mao then went on to explain why "absolute equalitarianism" in the army was essentially the same as "extreme democratization in political matters" and equally reprehensible. In brief, similar principles governed military and political matters, and the purpose of military organizing was to create political organization. The classic and by now the most familiar expression of these concepts is Mao's statement in 1938 that "political power grows out of the barrel of a gun." The statement continues: "Our principle is that the Party commands the gun: the gun shall never be allowed to command the Party. . . . Anything can grow out of the barrel of a gun. . . . As advocates of the abolition of war, we do not desire war; but war can only be abolished through war —in order to get rid of the gun we must first grasp it in hand."

Since Mao was engaged in war almost continually from 1927 to 1953, this experience inevitably molded his thinking and infiltrated his idiom. Mao's stress on military power and his use of military terminology is in no way surprising. More remarkable is the persistent reference to the political context of military affairs. Even during the life-or-death struggle against Japan, Mao said: "Any tendency among the anti-Japanese soldiers to belittle politics, to isolate war from it, and to make war an absolute, is erroneous and must be corrected." Although Mao conceded that "war has its special characteristics and in this sense it is not identical with politics," he insisted they were intimately connected. "Politics," Mao declared, "is war without bloodshed, while war is politics with bloodshed." He concluded:

> such a gigantic national revolutionary war as ours cannot succeed without universal and thoroughly political mobilization. . . . The popular masses are like water, and the army is like a fish. How then can it be said that when there is water, a fish will have difficulty in preserving its existence? An army which fails to maintain good discipline gets into opposition with the popular masses, and thus by its own actions dries up the water. In this case, it naturally cannot continue to exist. All guerrilla units must thoroughly understand this principle.

Thus Mao closed the circle around his core ideas. Base areas were the water in which he would find his fish and from which he would feed them. A revolutionary land program would attract peasant support, and disciplined troops would preserve it. Soldiers recruited from the peasantry would feel they had a stake in protecting the base areas; indeed, a local defense corps would provide a way of initiating peasants into organized activity and solidifying their sense of common purpose.

Mao insisted that *all* people had to be included, even bandits and other unreliable elements, of whom there were many in Mao's original force. Not only were they to be included, they were to be given education and made to feel deeply involved. It was not enough for people to learn of the war by being subjected to enemy action. The people needed the positive message of the Red Army, not merely the negative one of the Japanese. Finally, "with the common people of the whole country mobilized, we shall create a vast sea of humanity in which the enemy will be swallowed up, [we shall] obtain relief for our shortage in arms and other things, and secure the prerequisites to overcome every difficulty in the war."

The actual course of the Chinese Communists' rise to power followed Mao's policies with considerable precision, although deviations were inevitable under the harsh and changing conditions of those years. In Jiangxi in the early 1930s there were also disagreements within the party that interfered with consistency, especially at this early stage in the process of building a base area. But by 1935 the rise of Mao and the rise of Chinese communism had begun to mesh.

YAN'AN COMMUNISM

After the Chinese Communists were forced by Guomindang military pressure to flee the Jiangxi area, they took refuge in the northwest. The relocation required what came to be known as the "Long March," an epic trek of a full year over some six thousand miles of fiercely hostile terrain. Along the way the Communists fought at great loss against pursuing government armies and local warlord forces, but Mao claimed that they had also "sown many seeds in eleven provinces, which will sprout, grow leaves, blossom into flowers, bear fruit and yield a crop in future."

The Long March began the next stage of CCP history, commonly called the "Yan'an period," approximately 1935–1947, although before January 1937 CCP headquarters was near to Yan'an but not in it. During those twelve years the CCP developed a broad range of innovative policies that attracted widespread popular support. In the same period Mao consolidated his power within the party and promoted new ideological emphases on the power of the human will to do the seemingly impossible and on the distinctiveness of the Chinese revolution. These emphases characterize the "Yan'an spirit," to which the Long March is a fitting prologue. The march was an extraordinary test of

The bridge over the Dadu River. Soldiers on the Long March made the crossing under enemy fire. *Eastfoto*

endurance, will power, determination, and self-reliance. It brought the CCP into direct contact with parts of the country that few party members had ever seen and ended by putting the CCP in a position to fight against the invading Japanese, on whom they had declared war in April 1932. Thus the march stimulated patriotic feeling by providing the Communists with a broader knowledge of their country and an opportunity to fight for it. It is entirely possible that the Yan'an spirit was born as a result of the Long March.

The first clear indication of new emphases in Mao's thinking came very shortly after the Long March. In 1936 Mao wrote an essay on China's strategic problems in which he minimized the value of Russian experience as an example for the CCP.

> Although we must value Soviet experience, and even value it somewhat more than experiences in other countries throughout history, because it is the most recent experience of revolutionary war, we must value even more the experience of China's revolutionary war, because there are a great number of conditions special to the Chinese revolution and the Chinese Red Army.

These special conditions determined that the Chinese revolution would be distinctive. First, China was a semicolonial country, controlled by several imperialist powers; Mao refrained from pointing out that Russia, far from being colonized, had been imperialist itself. Second, China was unevenly developed politically and economically. It had only small classes of industrial workers and capitalists but vast numbers of peasants, only a few semimodern industrial and commercial cities, but "boundless expanses of rural districts still stuck in the middle ages." Warlords and warlord armies divided the country, but the Guomindang was strong and gaining in strength. Above all, the Guomindang held "the key positions or lifelines in the politics, economy, communications and culture of China." These conditions compelled the CCP to lead China in a revolutionary war different from the relatively brief civil war in the Soviet Union after the 1917 revolution. China had to plan for a protracted war. Furthermore, the Chinese Red Army had to face two enemies, Japan and the Guomindang, both of whom had armies that were far larger and more modern than the Communists' force. The Red Army could win, Mao said, "because its men have sprung from the agrarian revolution and are fighting for their own interests, and because officers and men are politically united." According to Mao's estimates

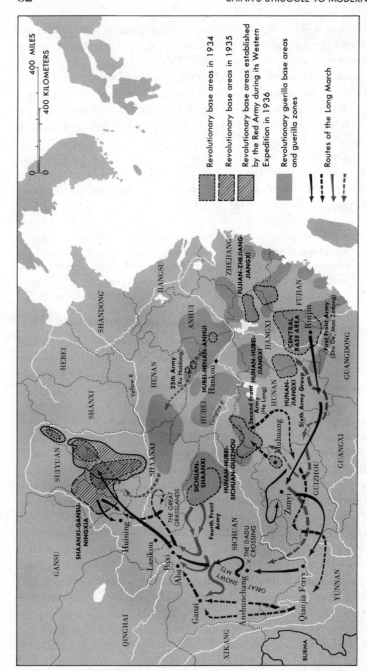

The Long March, October 1934–October 1935

the CCP could win by relying on itself; it needed neither foreign aid nor models. But he stressed that the war would be long and difficult and might even be lost.

Mao reasoned that to fight well, the Red Army had to be a people's army, and to be a people's army it needed a program uniquely suited to Chinese conditions. The conditions Mao outlined were not entirely unique to China; Russia's Red Army, for example, had also faced both foreign and domestic troops that possessed superior numbers and equipment. But China's economy was far less developed than Russia's had been in 1917, and China had a far smaller urban working class. Still more important, the Chinese Communists had failed to gain a foothold in the cities, whereas the Bolsheviks' power was rooted in Moscow, Petrograd, and a few other industrial cities. Finally, and perhaps most important of all, the Bolsheviks gained followers by calling for peace in World War I and surrendering to Germany huge pieces of Russian territory; the Chinese Communists gained followers by calling for resistance to Japan and leading the fight to defend Chinese territory.

In addition to attracting followers by organizing a resistance to Japanese invasion, the CCP carried out extensive social, economic, and political reform that had wide mass appeal. These reforms, which included cooperatives and other innovations that improved the peasants' lives, helped attract recruits to the army. The Chinese Red Army grew from roughly 80,000 to about a million during the war against Japan, and in addition to these regular troops the CCP by 1945 commanded guerrilla forces and militia that amounted to several million more. These huge forces were unlike any soldiers the Chinese masses could remember. The people were accustomed to soldiers who looted and raped. The Red Army became famous for its honesty and discipline. Relying exclusively on volunteers, it became a people's army in the fullest sense of that term. And because its training was at least as much political as military, the Red Army was a school in which countless peasants learned to read, think about national goals, and work for the victory of communism as well as of China.

In 1938 Mao wrote:

A communist is a Marxist internationalist, but Marxism must take on a national form before it can be applied. . . . We must put an end to writing eight-legged essays [old-fashioned essays that have perfect form but no substance] on foreign models; there must be less repeating of empty and abstract refrains; we must discard our dogmatism and replace it by a new and vital Chinese style and manner, pleasing to the eye and to the ear of the Chinese common people.

To reach the eye and ear of the common people in a Chinese manner, the CCP during the Yan'an period adopted a variety of policies that shifted according to time and place. Mao and his followers continued to demonstrate a flexibility that was vital to their success. Where Japanese invaders were the main problem in peoples' lives, the CCP concentrated on organizing the resistance; where the Japanese were absent or distant, the party concentrated on the social, economic, or political problems that were most urgent. In many areas they only reduced rents and interest rates, and they even guaranteed to landlords that rents would be paid and to lenders that loans would be repaid. In some areas they went further, introducing cooperatives and, carefully building on traditional community practices, they developed mutual-aid teams, an early form of socialist agriculture. Elsewhere they focused on reforming local government, introducing a system that resembled, at least in form, parliamentary democracy. These policies helped the CCP to earn a reputation as nationalists and democratic "agrarian reformers." More importantly, they created a vast mass movement under CCP leadership.

To carry out these diverse policies, Mao relied heavily on a single technique, the "mass line." The idea underlying this technique has been summed up most simply by Chalmers Johnson: In order to find out what kind of political program the masses will support, a political leader goes among them and asks them. The concept of the mass line is itself fundamentally simple, but the CCP's efforts to implement it reveal an enormous complexity. The mass-line policy requires CCP members to reconcile what the masses *will* support with what the party in its Marxist-Leninist wisdom thinks they *should* support; once these two rarely matching designs have been stitched together, party members must take the finished products back to the people and, in the words of one leader, "explain and popularize them, and arouse the masses to support these policies *so they will act on them as their own*." Italics have been added to indicate it was in this respect that the CCP did the most to refashion in its own way what is in reality a rather common notion; and, by so doing, the CCP grew by leaps and bounds during the Yan'an period. Through its highly imaginative formulation and skilled execution of a mass-line technique adapted to Chinese conditions, the CCP came to power.

Following the mass-line technique, the CCP sent agents into countless villages. There the agents listened, learned the peasants' grievances, gained their confidence, and tried to explain why the grievances existed and what could be done to erase them. With the party's active encouragement, peasants found the courage to pursue their own interests whether those interests were to regain land they had lost due to usury or high rents, take revenge on a corrupt official, or resist the Japanese occupation. As they corrected old abuses and mobilized to defend their homes, the peasants accepted CCP leadership and organization. Some began to absorb Communist ideas, for the CCP taught many people to read and did so with heavy doses of propaganda that began in the early lessons. Creating new organs of local government, peasant associations, cooperatives, youth and women's organizations, and militia, the Chinese Communists drew unprecedented numbers of the Chinese people into purposeful action.

The CCP was not the only group to perceive patriotism, anti-imperialism, land reform, mass education, and political democracy as desirable ends. Throughout the twentieth century one movement after another had proclaimed these and other laudable goals. But no other group so carefully defined goals with an eye to what the masses of people wanted, and no other group so assiduously cultivated the ability to mobilize the masses in pursuit of those ends. Here is where the Communists are most clearly distinguished from all other political groups in modern Chinese history, for it was the CCP in the Yan'an period that at last, even if only temporarily, bridged the gap between city and country, modern and traditional, Western and Chinese, rulers and ruled. As a result, China made a fresh start in its struggle to modernize.

During the eight years of war against Japan and, concurrently, intermittent fighting against the Guomindang, the CCP's strategy and methods were put to a severe test. Genuine unity still required that Western-oriented modern urban intellectuals come directly to grips with the problems of rural and still largely traditional China. New personnel problems appeared as Communist influence expanded to reach more than 100 million people in 1945, at least one hundred times more people than it reached in 1936. The Communist areas virtually amounted to a huge, sprawling nation. (The population of the United States in 1945 was about 140 million). Numerous Communist enclaves were scattered over vast areas, and it was nearly impossible to maintain contact between them and Yan'an. Local party workers had to be reliable because they often had to work without instructions. The Communists needed more manpower to carry out the mass line; hence party membership grew from 40,000 in 1937 to over 1,200,000 in 1945. According to CCP historians, 90 percent of the new members were from "petty bourgeois" backgrounds, meaning they were intellectuals and peasants. Precisely when the party needed experienced and reliable cadres, it also had to grow rapidly, and it had no choice but to admit untested members and try to train them quickly; both quality and quantity were urgently necessary. A party leader warned that "nonproletarian classes" were influencing the CCP in "ideology, living habits, theory, and action."

By 1940 CCP membership had shot up to about 800,000. Party organization and mobilization of the masses were in danger of being crippled by excessively rapid expansion. Setbacks in 1941 and 1942, due to Japanese offensives and a Guomindang blockade, heightened the sense of urgency and the need for cadres who were dedicated enough to start their work again after a defeat.

The leadership followed two courses. One was to slow down party recruitment, weed out the less desirable members, and indoctrinate intensively those who remained. The other was to simplify administration, develop local leadership, and introduce new social and economic institutions, such as cooperatives, on an unprecedentedly wide scale. The first worked from the top (government) down; the second worked from the bottom (villages) up.

Indoctrination was undertaken on a massive scale from 1942 to 1944, based on a small body of written materials, mostly Mao's, which were widely disseminated, studied, and discussed. One by-product of this campaign was a growing glorification of Mao, which by 1945 reached the proportions of a cult. But the major emphasis lay elsewhere. The central theme was a reaffirmation and strengthening of Mao's 1936 statement that the Chinese revolution posed its own unique and concrete problems and that the Chinese people had to engage those problems in hand-to-hand combat. The bedrock of the entire new movement was Mao's demand, stated in a lecture he gave in 1942, for "a theory in accordance with China's real necessities, a theory which is our own and of a specific nature." Another leader, Liu Shaoqi (1900–1969), explained further the Chinese effort to "make something real of Marxism." The CCP, he said, has passed through many more great events in these twenty-two years [since 1921] than any other Communist Party in the world and has had richer experience in the Chinese revolutionary struggle. If we treat the experience of our Party's struggle in these twenty-two years of great historical change lightly, if we do not diligently learn our lessons from these experiences, but only learn the lessons of the revolutionary experience of comparatively distant foreign countries, we will be turning things upside down and will have to travel many tortuous paths and encounter many more defeats.

Artfully invoking the authority of Stalin, Liu quoted a lengthy statement in which the Russian leader's point was that "true Marxists" are only those who are "guided by methods and procedure in keeping with their environment" and who "do not find their instructions and directives from comparisons and historical analogies," but from "research on surrounding conditions" and from their own "practical experience."

The stress on "practical experience" served to underline the uniquely Chinese emphases of the CCP leaders, and it also honed the blade Mao used to lacerate the intellectuals: "I advise those of you who have only book knowledge and as yet no contact with reality, and those who have had few practical experiences, to realize your own shortcomings and make your attitudes a bit more humble." Humility was taught not only with Mao's advice but also by means of a "to the village" movement that followed the indoctrination. After mastering the selected texts, intellectuals were sent to the countryside, sometimes to work in the fields, sometimes to teach and to aid in local administration. At all times, Mao warned, such "outside cadres" must take care to "cherish, protect, and constantly assist local cadres" and "not ridicule or attack them"; and all cadres "must actually learn from the people."

An excellent example of the CCP's emphasis on practicality and mass initiative can be seen in its educational system. At first, schools in the Communist areas followed familiar Western practices. In the border area of Shaanxi, Gansu, and Ningxia Hui, however, the masses protested that education did not suit their needs. The CCP investigated in order to determine what kind of schools people wanted, and the result was the establishment of "people-managed" schools in which each village decided what should be taught. Problems of many kinds were inevitable — some villages even wanted to stress the Confucian classics, and in such cases the authorities had to persuade the village committee that classical learning was impractical — but the system proved to be so

popular that in 1944 it spread quickly throughout the Communist areas.
Literacy, arithmetic, and vocational subjects predominated, the general
rule being that mass education "should keep to the knowledge needed
by the home and the village." Cadre education, which stressed
leadership in both warfare and production, was conducted by "people
who actually have experience of the armed struggle or production."

This educational system also exemplified the CCP's determination
to dispense with foreign models that did not suit Chinese conditions.
Party directives criticized the Guomindang for copying Western and
Japanese education, referring frequently to the differences between
China and countries that were wealthy, industrialized, capitalist, and at
peace. One crucial difference, for example, was China's extensive adult
illiteracy, which impaired its ability to increase production rapidly and
at the same time carry on a protracted people's war. Since adults had
greater responsibilities than youth, the CCP decided to give adults
priority over children in the mass education campaign.

Chinese peasants in training for the Communists' Eighth Route Army near
Yan'an. *Eastfoto*

The success with which these principles were carried out in the Yan'an period is indicated by the dramatic reversal of the Communist-Guomindang balance. A bedraggled remnant in 1935, the CCP scratched at the barren soil of the northwest and looked out from its caves upon a future as bleak as the land; meanwhile, the resurgent Guomindang seemed capable of destroying its enemy with only another blow. Ten years later the CCP not only was in a position to challenge the Guomindang for power and win, but it had tangible skills and intangible momentum and spirit to carry it into the postrevolutionary era.

The spirit may have developed most of all from the war effort, which was the immediate objective of all other policies. Many of the policies, including mass propaganda and village organization, were implemented through the army, especially in the early years of the war. As trained party workers were produced, they took up more of the burden. But whoever was responsible for the implementation of policy, the spirit was essentially the same. Peasants who had been intimidated by the air power and tanks of Japan's war machine learned to their astonishment that it was possible to fight back by guerrilla methods; at the same time, many learned to read, to command troops, to govern, and to produce more than ever from their land. Mao taught that nothing was impossible for people who combined practical experience, understanding of Marxism-Leninism and the thought of Mao Zedong, and the will to undertake awesome tasks in a spirit of optimism: "So when we see the enemy, whether he is many or few, we must act as though he is bread which can satisfy our hunger, and immediately swallow him." This kind of confidence flourished in the climate of patriotic resistance to invasion. Peasants and intellectuals knew what they were fighting for and became certain they would win. Differences of social class, wealth, and education were outweighed by a new unity of purpose. By 1945 this spirit motivated countless cadre teams like the one in Stone Wall Village. It also welded the dispersed Red areas into a nation within a nation.

As the case of Stone Wall Village demonstrates, the Yan'an spirit developed out of more than anti-Japanese patriotism, and it sometimes went beyond agrarian reformism. Both "peasant nationalism" and a highly varied mix of social-economic-political programs and methods were essential to the CCP's success. The crucial point is that the party brought all of these together in a new and flexible way, and in so doing it raised peasant struggles to a new level of relationship to other national issues. No longer were peasant protests isolated from the protests of

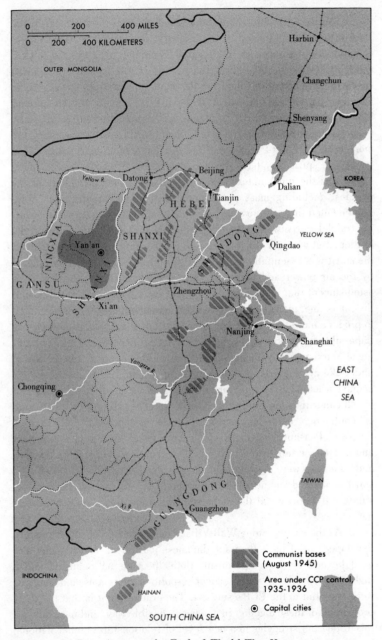

Communist Base Areas at the End of World War II

other social groups. In particular, peasant protests were linked to the demands of urban, Western-oriented intellectuals, and these two vitally important groups developed a new relationship under the guidance of the CCP. Once again a domestic crisis had intersected with an international one. This time it produced a new social and political movement that won a revolution and opened a new era in China's struggle for modernization.

In the civil war of 1946 to 1949, the Chinese Communists won a victory that was even more their own than the victory over Japan. Two stunning military successes against huge mechanized armies vindicated the strategy of people's war. Victory in the civil war also vindicated the Chinese Communists' new independence of the Soviet Union, for they had gone ahead to confront the Guomindang against the advice of Stalin. During the civil war they also promoted a more radical land reform, thereby unleashing a social revolution much like the overturning of Stone Wall Village. As of 1949 the question was: Would the Communists carry the revolution forward in the pattern of the preceding decade? If so, Mao's strategy would undergo its severest test yet, for it would have to adapt the techniques of people's war to the tasks of government.

5

THE PEOPLE'S REPUBLIC OF CHINA, PART ONE: FROM VICTORY AND UNITY TO CRISIS AND STRIFE, 1949–1960

SUCCESSFUL REVOLUTIONARIES face their greatest challenges only when they have succeeded in taking power. The transition from "outsiders" seeking power to "insiders" exercising power is a giant, slippery step into unknown territory. The Chinese Communists were in many ways better equipped than other revolutionaries, including the Russians, to manage this transition. Unlike the Russians when they came to power, the Chinese Communists had had considerable experience in governing large, heavily populated areas and a long history of continuing and coherent leadership. Because of this experience and their belief in the importance of being guided by their own experience, a continuity was to be expected between their policies and methods before and after 1949. In 1945 Mao Zedong said that the Chinese Communists would not follow the Soviet Union's example after they came to power. "Russian history has created the Russian system," he said, but "Chinese history will create the Chinese system." In 1949, however, new circumstances compelled Mao to declare, "the Communist Party of the USSR is our best teacher from whom we must learn."

The new circumstances Mao observed in 1949 were created by the Chinese Communists' rapid conquest of the entire country. Between November 1948 and January 1949 the last decisive battles of the civil war were fought. All of China was soon in Communist hands. In April 1949 the Red Army, which three years earlier had been renamed the

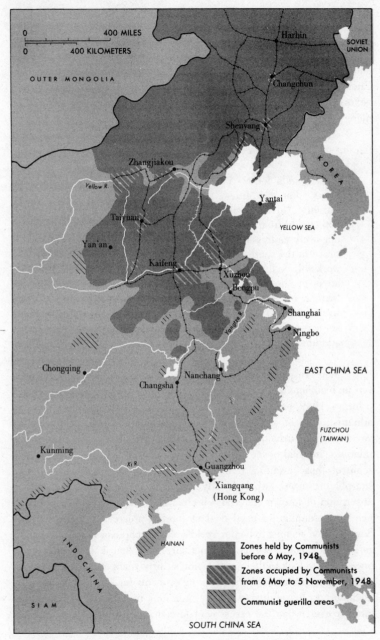

0 400 MILES
0 400 KILOMETERS

OUTER MONGOLIA

SOVIET UNION

Harbin

Changchun

Shenyang

KOREA

Zhangjiakou

Yellow R.

Yantai

Taiyuan

YELLOW SEA

Yan'an

Kaifeng

Xuzhou

Bengpu

Yangze R.

Shanghai

Ningbo

Chongqing

EAST CHINA SEA

Changsha

Nanchang

FUZHOU
(TAIWAN)

Kunming

Xi R.

Guangzhou

Xiangqang
(Hong Kong)

INDOCHINA

HAINAN

Zones held by Communists
before 6 May, 1948

Zones occupied by Communists
from 6 May to 5 November, 1948

Communist guerilla areas

SIAM

SOUTH CHINA SEA

Situation as of 5 November 1948

People's Liberation Army (PLA), crossed the Yangtze River; within another month the PLA swept into major cities of northern and central China, including Xi'an, Wuhan, and Shanghai; and between October and December 1949 the army captured Guangzhou in the southeast and Chengdu in the southwest. In the short space of about two and one-half years of civil war, the CCP took responsibility for governing 400 million more people than it had governed in 1946.

As his troops consolidated their hold on north China and began to fan out to the south in February 1949, Mao told them:

> The formula followed in the past twenty years, "first the rural areas, then the cities," will be reversed and changed to the formula, "first the cities, then the rural areas." . . . In short, you should from now on shoulder all urban problems, with which our army cadres and fighters were unfamiliar in the past. . . . Since in the south all the rural areas will be newly liberated, the work will be fundamentally different from that in the old liberated areas of the north. . . . Therefore, rural work must also be learned afresh. However, as compared with urban work, rural work is easy to learn. Urban work is more difficult and is the main subject you are studying. If our cadres cannot quickly master the administration of cities, we shall encounter extreme difficulties.

Mao realized that the CCP's past experience, though valuable, was an insufficient guide for the new government. The CCP's experience prior to 1949 had been dominated by large-scale warfare and the administration of a dispersed rural population. The CCP had never governed large urban populations or dealt extensively with rural-urban relations and had never confronted economic problems on the gigantic scale of those awaiting it in 1949. Although Mao had years before sharply criticized "wholesale Westernization" and "the mechanical absorption of foreign material," he had also made it plain that "China needs to assimilate a good deal of foreign progressive culture." The Soviet Union seemed to be the world's only example of rapid industrialization in a socialist nation. It is not surprising that in 1949 Mao chose once again to look to the Soviet Union's thirty years of experience as an organized government and developing economy for a model. Rather it is testimony to his ability to assess situations in a rationally calculated manner even when the assessment forced him to unpalatable conclusions.

The conclusions Mao drew in 1949 were unpalatable, first,

because relations between the Russians and the Chinese Communists had been far from smooth for many years. Ever since the 1920s Soviet involvement in CCP affairs had been at best a mixed blessing. Russian aid had been of value, but it had come at the price of Soviet meddling in CCP affairs, involvement in CCP factionalism, and sometimes Soviet domination. Even as the CCP gradually freed itself of Russian control, it saw more Russian aid go to its rivals—the Soviet Union helped the Guomindang resist Japan, especially from 1937 to 1941—than the CCP received. Once the war against Japan ended, the Soviet Union pressured the CCP to negotiate with the Guomindang and minimized the Chinese Communists' success. Although the Soviets gave the CCP some assistance once the civil war broke out, it also took for itself the industrial equipment captured from Japan in northeast China, leaving that huge area stripped of its industrial base. Finally, Moscow preserved its good relations with the Guomindang until the very end, although it switched rapidly and was the first to recognize the People's Republic.

In short, Mao had reason in 1949 not to rush to embrace the Soviet Union. "The Chinese people have stood up," he announced proudly in 1949. "Ours will no longer be a nation subject to insult and humiliation." Although these remarks were aimed mainly at Japan and the Western imperialist powers that had dominated China for the preceding century, they were certainly applicable to the Soviet Union as well. To a China flushed with success, anything less than full equality was insulting. In 1949 Mao anticipated diplomatic relations and trade with all countries, but only "on the basis of equality, mutual benefit, and mutual respect for territorial integrity and sovereignty." "Liberation," as the Chinese still refer to their victory in 1949, meant the end of all forms of "semicolonialism," and Mao was in no mood to exchange one form of subservience for another.

Still, in 1949 Mao saw a world divided into two camps, and he felt there was no choice but to "lean to one side." (It is worth noting, however, that Chinese premier and foreign minister Zhou Enlai had earlier told a top U.S. official that "how far [China leans to one side] depends on you," and in 1949, shortly before Mao's statement, he appealed to the United States to help China follow a more independent course.) Surely Mao knew that by aligning itself with the "socialist bloc" China would obtain only a limited amount of financial aid, since the Soviet Union was not a rich country and was still recovering from the enormous destruction of World War II. But at least there would be technical advice.

A deeper issue was how far to follow the Soviet approach to economic development. The Soviet model gave high priority to nation-wide economic planning, relied heavily on centralized administration, and stressed the use of advanced technology. None of these policies was wholly repugnant to Mao, but some of their implications were distasteful to him. For example, his guerrilla experience had given him a deep distrust of centralization. Guerrilla units in scattered base areas had to rely very much on themselves because communications were too poor and conditions too changeable to permit very much coordination from Yan'an. In 1949 Mao was not optimistic about the possibility of bringing the entire country under a highly centralized direction. Mao knew that the problem of balancing central control and local autonomy figured prominently in Chinese history. China resembles a continent, and her twenty-nine major administrative units are like countries—each of eleven provinces has more people than Poland, and each of ten others has more people than East Germany. Most of these areas had only now come under CCP control, and in many of them lived minority nationali-ties whose customs and languages were unfamiliar to the Communists. South China was also divided by countless mutually unintelligible local dialects. Unity was only a thin membrane covering the countryside, which was still fixed in a traditional decentralized social and political pattern. That "scattered sand" to which Sun Yatsen had likened the Chinese people remained to be cemented into a nation. Could enough centralization be achieved to make the Soviet model work? If it could, how would China train enough administrators and technicians? How would China pay for the advanced technology?

In December 1949 Mao went to Moscow to seek answers to these and many other questions. Two months of bargaining showed that answers were hard to find. In February 1950 the two nations signed a Treaty of Friendship, Alliance, and Mutual Aid, providing among other things for China to receive loans, model industrial units, and technical advisers. It made sense for Russian advisers to teach what they knew best, and they may have demanded Chinese conformity as their price. China's people, weary of war and economic chaos, yearned for peace and stability. Since nearly a century of deep political division had to be overcome, greater centralization was necessary, despite its dangers. Unity was essential if China was to maintain its security and independ-ence, mobilize its resources for industrialization, and advance to socialism and communism.

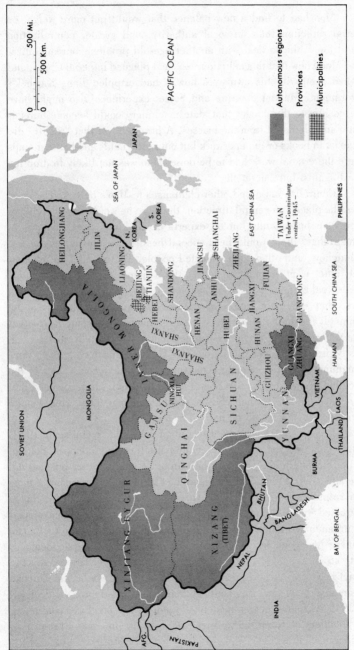

Political Boundaries of China, 1981

Mao had to find a new balance that would put more weight on central direction than on local authority, and greater centralization would force him to deal with another age-old problem, bureaucratization. Mao knew that this affliction, too, had plagued imperial China, and he had seen with his own eyes how it had crippled Jiang Kaishek's government. Marxist doctrine and Soviet experience also might have alerted him to the danger that state machinery could become bureaucratic and alienated from the masses. A firm believer that "reality" did not exist in books or in paperwork but out in the fields and battlegrounds where the crucial work had to be done, Mao was not likely to drop his guard against bureaucratism.

Centralization posed other challenges to Mao's beliefs. The more stress he placed on central direction, the more he would have to rely not merely on bureaucrats but on experts of all kinds. If China was to industrialize, there would be a special need for scientists, engineers, technicians, and other such educated people. The need for an intellectual elite went strongly against Mao's populist, antielitist, anti-intellectual beliefs. It also went against the mystique, built up in Yan'an days, that the mobilization of the masses was the solution to the seemingly insoluble. Mao's distaste for relying heavily on an intellectual elite was reinforced by the knowledge that China's intelligentsia came mostly from bourgeois backgrounds. To him this meant they were contaminated by the acquisitiveness and other bourgeois values of the so-called liberal-democratic West that he detested. He recognized that he needed the intellectuals, but he vowed to change them. Here too the Soviet experience would be helpful to the Chinese.

Thus the new government set out on the road to socialism in 1949, consciously (but not without reservations) following guideposts planted by the Soviet Union. The CCP had turned a sharp corner but had not reversed itself. Although the Chinese had taken power by means of their own resources and, unlike the Russians, had done so by waging a protracted war in the countryside that only after many years enveloped the urban areas, much Russian influence had survived in the CCP. The Chinese had gone far toward developing their own unique ideology, party structure, party-army relations, and mass organizations, but the Soviet heritage was still present. In 1949, in other words, the Chinese Communist movement was not fully Sinified. Furthermore, the decision in 1949 to follow Soviet models did not at all preclude continuing modification of alien borrowings, nor did it preclude a return to deliberate Sinification.

TOWARD SOCIALIST CONSTRUCTION

The Chinese did not move immediately to introduce socialism. In an essay titled "On New Democracy," Mao in 1940 had explained that the Chinese revolution was occurring in two stages: democracy and socialism. These stages were to be reached by means of two different revolutionary processes, he said, and the second could not begin until the first had been completed. In 1949 China was not yet ready to move into socialism. The stage of New Democracy, which Mao had carefully defined as "democracy of the Chinese type, a new and special type," therefore remained to be fulfilled, and Mao had specified that it would exist for "quite a long time." Under New Democracy, large business and industrial enterprises would be owned and managed by the state, but there would be no general confiscation of private property, and not all capitalist production would be discouraged. In the countryside a "rich peasant economy" would be allowed, and only some cooperatives containing "elements of socialism" would be developed. These principles Mao mostly reaffirmed in 1949: "Our present policy is to regulate capitalism, not to destroy it." One important difference from 1940 was that then Mao had called for a joint dictatorship of all revolutionary classes; in 1949, perhaps because of his new orientation toward the cities, Mao stressed the leadership of the industrial working class: "it is only the working class that is most far-sighted, most selfless, and most thoroughly revolutionary."

For about three years after 1949 the Chinese Communist Party stressed consolidation and rehabilitation of China. Conciliatory policies were particularly evident in 1949 and 1950 in the cities, which the CCP thought were so foreign that they had to be "truly Sinified." Runaway inflation was checked, the economy revived on a mixed basis in which the "capitalist" (or private ownership) component was surprisingly prominent, and a new political system gathered in the loose reins of administration. Working primarily through city police forces, which became the first instrument of urban civil administration, the CCP gradually restored order. It then began to organize urban dwellers in their places of employment and residence to publicize its policies, carry out the various tasks of government such as sanitation and fire prevention, and mobilize support for party policies.

Basic to all these measures was a massive campaign to recruit party members and cadres, especially among the urban working class but also among intellectuals and other "bourgeois elements." In 1949 the membership of the CCP was about 4.4 million, of which about 80 percent were peasants, 5 percent intellectuals, and almost none industrial workers. By 1956, when the party had nearly tripled in size, the percentages were 67, 12, and 14, respectively. Since 86 percent of China's population was rural, the peasantry had become underrepresented in the party between 1949 and 1956, while urban workers and intellectuals had made relatively greater gains.

Party policy for at least two years after 1949 was to draw as many urban intellectuals and businessmen as possible into the new regime and to employ their talents to help build it. Even large numbers of Guomindang officials gained employment. Few intellectuals were treated harshly at the very outset. Most were offered a chance to make their peace with the CCP. For many, this chance turned out to be a painful experience in which they were subjected to "ideological remolding" or "thought reform" (sometimes misleadingly called brainwashing), economic penalties, public scorn and mistreatment, and sometimes eventually imprisonment, exile, or death. Nevertheless, many people who had reason to fear merciless treatment by the government managed instead to find places for themselves in it. Thought reform played an important role in this accommodation process.

Thought reform consisted essentially of two parts. The first part was a person's admission that he or she had done wrong in the past and now renounced all such errors. The second was the acquisition of "correct" thinking. Chinese methods of conducting thought reform have evolved over a long period of time and are still changing. For this reason, and because many myths and exaggerated fears have grown up concerning "brainwashing," brief descriptions of it are inadequate. For our purposes it needs to be stressed that the theory and practice of thought reform represent a highly complex mixture of Soviet experience, the Chinese Communists' own experience (especially in the Yan'an period), and some ancient Chinese traditions (although it has also been aimed at destroying some traditional ideas). Two differences between Russian and Chinese practices are striking. One difference is that the Chinese came to regard thought reform as a more important means of effecting intellectual change than the conventional Marxist-Leninist means. Traditionally, Marxists have believed that fundamental intellectual change comes about primarily as a result of economic change; only when a socialist economy is established will people's minds be truly purged of capitalist or bourgeois ideas. Mao, however, came to believe that thought reform can be effective before establishing a socialist economy, and signs of this belief are discernible in his early efforts to remold the ideology of Chinese intellectuals. A second difference is one of relative emphasis: The Chinese have relied much more than the Russians did on thought reform and persuasion and less than they on naked force to effect social and cultural change.

Although thought reform was an uncompromising assault upon old ideas and values, designed to wash away "contaminated" beliefs, some Chinese intellectuals found relief from old doubts and tensions in the new principles it taught. Most important, thought reform gave those who were able to profit from it a new sense of group identity and common purpose and a feeling of participating in a crusade to reform society. Even some who rebelled against thought reform later felt guilty for abandoning the crusade.

For a year or two, Chinese cities enjoyed what one scholar has termed an atmosphere of permissiveness. Moderate and stabilizing policies began to change as early as the autumn of 1950, when China entered the Korean War. Before the end of the year, a "Resist-America –Aid-Korea" campaign was sweeping the Chinese mainland. Designed to mobilize popular support for the war, the campaign began as an intense patriotic movement to recruit volunteers for the army. Gradually it broadened into campaigns to raise money, increase production, suppress counterrevolutionaries, revolutionize the land system, reform the government and party, and wrest control of the urban economy from businessmen. Fears of possible attack by the United States or sabotage and subversion from within played some part, but the campaigns soon went far beyond security needs. By 1951 the authorities had decided to tighten their control over Chinese society and begin to move toward the second stage of revolution, the construction of socialism.

Over a period of about a year, ending in the spring of 1952, three massive political campaigns engulfed China's cities: a thought reform aimed primarily at teachers; the "three-anti" movement aimed at corruption, waste, and bureaucratism among cadres; and a "five-anti" movement directed against bribery, tax evasion, cheating on government contracts, theft of government property, and stealing of state economic secrets by businesspeople and industrialists. During these campaigns the CCP greatly expanded its following among the workers, strengthened discipline among cadres, and reduced the power of the bourgeoisie dramatically. For many, as Kenneth Lieberthal has observed in his careful study of Tianjin, "The revolution came not in 1949 but in early 1952."

These campaigns led to an increasing socialization of industry and commerce. State control of the economy, in turn, permitted the centralized planning needed for a Soviet-style Five-Year Plan. China's first such plan was initiated in 1953. Stressing industry far more than agriculture, heavy industry far more than light, and large enterprises far more than small, the plan faithfully followed the goals and methods of the Soviet Union. Industrial production grew remarkably from 1953 to 1957, and with the success of the first Five-Year Plan, China seemed to have left behind the era of New Democracy that Mao had proclaimed in 1940. In industry, at least, the era of socialist construction had begun.

In the countryside there was a less uniform pattern and a somewhat less faithful adherence to the Soviet example, but there too socialization began to prevail by 1953. The Communists had carried out land reform in some areas of China before they occupied the entire country. After 1949 land reform became a part of the CCP's program of consolidation and rehabilitation. It was a means of making good on old promises, restoring order in the countryside, and establishing a foundation for nursing the shattered economy back to health.

The CCP's first task was to plant itself in every one of China's villages, but China had only one civilian cadre for every two villages. It was clearly impossible to duplicate the Yan'an pattern of sending cadres to penetrate the villages, and for a few years party influence in the rural areas was accordingly quite limited. In most places formal administration reached down only to the township, one level below the county. The government was not yet able to live up to its stated commitment "to forge closer ties between the government and the masses," but its efforts continued and intensified.

From 1950 to 1955, as more cadres graduated from the training institutes, the larger townships were steadily broken up into smaller ones. The general principle was to bring the size of the township, and therefore its government, as close to the village level as the availability of trained, reliable cadres allowed. By 1955 there were a little over 200,000 townships in China, roughly five times the number that had existed in 1949. The average size of the basic unit of administration was about three thousand people.

During the same period, while the political administrative network was stretching down from the county and townships to the masses, another network was beginning to grow up from the villages. Mass organizations of peasants, youth, and women had been created in each village following the entrance of the People's Liberation Army. Usually under the direction of military cadres, these mass organizations were intended to promote popular participation in local affairs, particularly in land reform. As the military cadres were gradually replaced by civil authority, the CCP's shortage of trained personnel compelled it to rely on "outsiders" (nonvillage or urban people) to oversee land reform. One observer gave this report on the cadres sent to a village near Guangzhou:

> The land reform cadres in Nanching, three men and one woman in their late teens or early twenties, were high school graduates, and one seemed from the way he talked to have had one or two years of college. Their manners and conversation revealed an urban bourgeois background which they carefully disguised under dirty gray uniforms and conscious attempts to imitate the peasants' mode of life, occasionally even living in the poor peasants' houses, eating their food, and helping with light farm chores in order to strike up a conversation with them for information about the village.

The eager but inexperienced young cadres made their share of mistakes, such as choosing "middle peasants" instead of poor farmers or agricultural laborers to head the peasant associations responsible for land reform, but land reform was completed nevertheless. Large holdings were broken up, and about 125 million acres of land were redistributed among small owners, former tenants, and farm laborers. Private ownership and "rich peasants" flourished for a time. By the end of 1952 the CCP had completed land reform in most areas.

During the course of completion the party sent in thousands of outside cadres to reinforce its local personnel and weed out recalcitrants. The cadres learned who the activists and potential leaders of the villages were and made a special effort to draw them into party service. New local leadership was thereby created, and the peasant associations became firmly established as centers of village power. The associations excluded rich peasants and former landlords and were headed by local activists chosen by the cadres. Thus the CCP overturned the old village power structure and, through local activists, established its authority in the village.

For the most part, the CCP resorted to violence only in areas where the Guomindang forces or sympathizers contested Communist rule and defended the established order. In some areas the party roused people to violence, but in others the people themselves initiated it and the party stepped in to set limits. Nationwide it is estimated some two million people were executed between 1949 and 1952, and a much larger number was sent to prison or labor camps. Some twenty million people were classified as landlords and the vast majority of them were given small plots of land to cultivate. Estimates of how many landlords died vary widely, but there was less violence than many expected, given the enormity of the land problem. The problem was especially great in southern China, where tenancy was far more widespread than in the north. Whatever the precise level of violence in each area, land reform constituted a vast social revolution that reduced the old rural elite to near impotence. Twelve hundred years of landlordism had come to an end.

By 1952, in addition to the economic and social purposes it served, land reform had also helped to solve a major political problem —the reassertion of central control over outlying regions. By promoting

A people's court, at which peasants "settled accounts" with landlords.
Paul Popper

land reform, the CCP was able to extend its control throughout the countryside. As Ezra Vogel has found for Guangdong province, land reform "transformed a semi-autonomous guerrilla organization into a disciplined local outpost of a strong central administration." In the five provinces of China's central-south region, Vivienne Shue has found, the political and social consequences of land reform were even greater than the economic ones. In that region 40 percent of all land was confiscated and redistributed among 60 percent of the population, making a few people poorer and a great many people somewhat better off. Significant though this was as an economic measure, Shue concludes, it ended the old political order more than it began a new economic order. Land reform laid the foundations both for collectivization and for a unified administrative system.

The first stage of collectivization began soon after peasant associations were formed. Whenever county authorities deemed that enough local leaders were available, the peasants were sufficiently receptive, and other conditions were suitable, they ordered the establishment of mutual aid teams. These were small groups averaging about five families who retained their individual land and possessions but who exchanged labor and shared tools and animals. By 1952 about 40 percent of the peasants were members of mutual aid teams. In February 1953 the CCP ordered this simple and rather informal cooperation expanded into farms called Agricultural Producers Cooperatives (APCs). These averaged about twenty-five families, but there were some with as many as fifty, seventy, or one hundred families. In the APCs, family holdings were pooled, boundary markers destroyed, and the entire holding of all families cultivated as a single farm.

At first the CCP applied only moderate pressure to form cooperatives, and after two years only 13.5 percent of the peasants were in them. To encourage the growth of cooperatives, township officials and local cadres went out to the countryside to explain the advantages and to organize them. By offering the peasants substantial material inducements, the officials and cadres had some success in promoting APCs, and in the process they strengthened their own relationship with the peasants. With each APC that was organized, the township administration established itself a little more firmly among the peasants.

The forging of such links between officialdom and the masses was not smooth. Twice the drives to promote APCs had to be called off; in one area one-third of the nine thousand APCs had to be either dissolved or reduced to mutual aid teams. A central problem was the poor quality of the local cadre leadership; the most common complaint was that excessive use of coercion had alienated the peasants. Many local cadres came from landlord, "rich peasant," or bourgeois backgrounds, or they had friends and relatives who did. Therefore, more nonlocal cadres had to be sent in. But the party did not want to impose outside leadership on the countryside. As the CCP wrestled with the dilemma, mounting peasant resistance slowed collectivization.

Mao Zedong deemed matters so serious that he feared village leadership was about to slip from the party's hands. This was not only a political question; economic growth was at stake. Following the Soviet example, agriculture was supposed to pay for industrialization. But the harvests of 1953 and 1954 were inadequate. Land reform may have been a political success, but the system of small peasant ownership was not sufficiently expanding farm production. With the Five-Year Plan already under way, more agricultural growth was urgently needed. Furthermore, "rich peasants" were gaining too much influence in the countryside to suit many CCP leaders. By the spring of 1955 the party, after a long debate, decided that the pace of collectivization would be quickened in order to assert party control at the village level and to increase production. Recruitment of cadres in the countryside would be vastly intensified; the search for village activists, common in Yan'an and immediate post-1949 days, would be resumed on a much larger scale; and cadres would go from counties and townships not merely to work in the villages but to be based in the village and, in Mao's words, to "become the principal force there." In July Mao announced that within fourteen months the number of households in cooperatives would be doubled, but after five months he announced that the goal had been reached and that a still higher goal was within reach. A "higher stage" of the APC was to be created, in which the semisocialist cooperatives would be replaced by fully socialist collectives; the peasants were to become wage laborers paid according to work points rather than according to the shares they owned in the cooperative. Exultant, Mao declared that socialism's victory over capitalism was almost complete.

Events did not quite fulfill Mao's prediction, despite the promise of early results. The 1955 harvest was good, and many peasants were responding positively to the first stage of collectivization, but others were not. The local cadres in many villages could not obtain the rich peasants' compliance. Higher-level cadres had to step in and back up the local cadres, and more coercion was required than Mao seems to have expected. The Chinese relied much less on force than the Russians had some twenty or more years earlier, and they were more successful than the Russians were, but still the mass-line method of mobilizing the peasants did not suffice to bring about collectivization. The mass-line method of persuasion obtained enough peasant support, participation, and leadership to carry only about one-third of the peasants through the first stages of collectivization by the spring of 1956. Then signs of recalcitrance began to appear, and by autumn many peasants were refusing to go further. Slaughter of livestock, hoarding of grain, refusal to move from lower-stage to higher-stage cooperatives, protests against abolition of private plots and against the failure of income to rise as promised by the party, and substantial migration to the cities were evidence of peasant dismay.

As early as the summer of 1956, therefore, a strong movement developed in the party to slow collectivization. It is likely that outside events helped along this movement in China's internal affairs, for Khrushchev's assault on Stalin's "cult of personality" earlier that year gave Chinese exponents of collective leadership live ammunition to use against Mao. This current in the party won out in time to dominate the Chinese Communist Party Congress in September 1956, where a main theme was the assertion of collective leadership in the party and the consequent downgrading of Mao Zedong. Liu Shaoqi's report to the Congress left the timing of further collectivization flexible, forbade the use of coercion, and stressed that the peasants would have to see the material benefits of collectivization before it could proceed.

In the summer and fall of 1956, then, China's revolution slowed. In seven years China had moved toward socialism in industry and agriculture, but its stress on the Soviet model had resulted in highly unbalanced development. Gains in industry were not matched in agriculture. Poor harvests in 1956 and 1957 forced the government to give food production a higher priority. A period of what is frequently termed relative liberalization or relaxation set in. In September 1957 the government ordered the cooperatives to reduce their size by as much as 40 percent, to use a village of about one hundred families as their basic unit, and to maintain the same size for ten years once it had been fixed. The government also introduced various liberalization measures, including the restoration of private plots and livestock. The heart of the new policy was that APCs would conform roughly to villages. If the villages had less than one hundred families, two or more of them could combine. The government was therefore compromising with traditional patterns, since many village boundaries were left undisturbed.

With these modifications, collectivization was completed in 1956 and 1957. It had not brought about the total abolition of private property in the countryside, but it had furthered this fundamental socialist goal. Although there would have to be further campaigns to socialize agriculture completely, collectivization had put the CCP in a stronger position to conduct such campaigns. A sizable corps of cadres had been created and had taken over village leadership. Each village was an organized unit with a planned economy, and there were now perhaps 800,000 such collectives, averaging six hundred to seven hundred people in each. It remained to be seen whether the bureaucratic apparatus that soon appeared in the villages, together with the peasants' devotion to their remaining private plots and free markets, would create more problems for the CCP than collectivization was thought to have solved.

The most dramatic feature of the period of relaxation in 1956 and 1957 was Mao's encouragement to the people to express themselves freely: "Let a hundred flowers bloom, let a hundred schools of thought contend." This invitation, formally extended in May 1956, found few takers until a year later when, after repeated urging and frequent assurances that candid criticisms were welcome and would not bring retribution, a substantial number of people spoke out. Exactly why the CCP chose to invite criticism at this time is by no means clear. Perhaps the invitation was intended as a safety valve by which malcontents could let off steam harmlessly instead of exploding. Some observers think it was a trap to lure dissidents into the open, and a few believe it was an attempt to show that the intellectuals had been won over and did not have serious criticisms to make. Almost all interpreters agree, however, that the leadership was astonished at the breadth and depth of the criticisms that were finally expressed.

If this interpretation is correct, it helps to explain the liberalization period and Mao's reaction to it. The relaxation was justifiable on the grounds that neither the peasants nor the intellectuals were yet fully prepared for socialism. Mao's populism did not blind him to the Marxist dictum that peasants are potential capitalists. He could not have failed to observe the persistence of such bourgeois values as acquisitiveness and pursuit of self-interest. In 1949 Mao had not been pessimistic about eliminating the bourgeois mentality by following the conventional Marxist principle of altering the economic substructure, supplemented by his own combination of persuasion, inducement, and coercion. Changes in production relations, he thought—especially the removal of big landlords and big capitalists from privileged status, the nationalizing of industry and commerce, and the collectivizing of land—would be enough to inculcate antibourgeois values in nearly everyone. Those who resisted, particularly intellectuals, would undergo thought reform and other forms of "socialist education," and most would join in "socialist construction" as they had in the war against Japan. Only when this proved not to be the case did Mao revise his thinking and adopt more drastic policies.

Mao rejected Liu Shaoqi's view, expressed to the Congress in 1956, that collectivization should be slowed. In February 1957 Mao admitted that "some things did go wrong" and that "some people have stirred up a miniature typhoon" with their criticisms of cooperative farming. But he insisted that what went wrong was not serious and was due to bad weather and other natural causes (which were, in fact, serious) and to cadre errors. Mao dismissed the difficulties with the observation that "new things always have difficulties and ups and downs to get over as they grow." He would be satisfied to finish establishing cooperatives that year and to consolidate them within another five years. Mao agreed with Liu that it was desirable to raise the peasants' incomes year by year, but he countered forcefully that the peasants had gained a great deal in seven years and that if their standard of living was still low the same was true for everyone else. Clearly Mao saw no reason for a policy that would allow collectivization to proceed at the peasants' own pace, as Liu had suggested.

In the same speech that launched his collectivization counterattack, Mao reiterated his Hundred Flowers invitation. In the context of the CCP's internal disagreement about collectivization and political administration, the puzzling Hundred Flowers policy assumes great importance. The full text of Mao's February speech was not published until June, but it was summarized in the Chinese press during March and April. The press explained that Mao wanted to draw particular attention to the bureaucratic tendencies in the party. Bureaucratism, newspaper readers were told, was the main cause of contradictions between leaders and people, and the way to eliminate such contradictions was by criticism and self-criticism. Thus the press presented Mao's unpublished speech as an invitation to criticize the CCP leadership. And in May 1957 this was what intellectuals finally did. Their criticisms ranged widely, but they concentrated on the theme that the party had deteriorated since 1949 and had become elitist, divorced from the masses.

Much of the criticism sounded as if Mao had expressed it himself. Furthermore, when Mao's February speech was published, it was unusually mild in reference to the intellectuals. He even conceded that thought reform had been "carried on in a somewhat rough and ready way" and that "there are bound to be some who are all along reluctant, ideologically, to accept Marxism-Leninism and communism." Mao had often expressed contempt for intellectuals by comparing them to human dung; to say now that "we should not be too exacting in what we expect of them" was remarkably conciliatory. Thus it may not be too far-fetched to interpret the Hundred Flowers policy as Mao's indirect attack on other CCP leaders, although most scholars believe that no CCP leader, including Mao, expected such harsh criticism and that all were shocked. In any case, this attack on the CCP provoked a counterattack by the party.

The CCP had expected a "mild breeze" and "gentle rain" of criticism to bring forth a hundred flowers of fresh ideas. Instead, party leaders complained, a storm had come and left only weeds. Uprooting of the weeds began in June and intensified through the end of 1957. Intellectuals, especially members of some minor political parties that had been allowed to exist, were the first targets. Soon the CCP counterattack became a huge "antirightist" campaign that spread to the government bureaucracy, the army, the countryside, and even the party itself. Among the more than 100,000 "counterrevolutionaries" that the minister of public security claimed to have discovered, about 5,000 were CCP members. Intellectuals were charged with plotting to overthrow socialism and the CCP leadership and to restore capitalism. Army leaders were accused of excessive individualism. And everywhere, even in the countryside, massive campaigns raged against bureaucracy —farmers spoke derisively of "four-armed cadres" who stood in the fields giving orders, jackets slung over their shoulders with the empty sleeves dangling or flapping in the breeze; the sleeves symbolized their nonparticipation in manual labor, much as long fingernails distinguished the traditional gentry from the peasants. The "rightists" had to confess their errors and submit to "reform through labor," which for many meant going to the countryside to work in the fields. Meanwhile CCP leaders convened in September and October 1957 to examine their own errors and achievements and to plan for the future.

TOWARD COMMUNISM

As the first Five-Year Plan drew to a close, ending the period formally designated as the "transition to socialism," the CCP leaders confronted hard decisions. The basic decision was whether the second Five-Year

Plan, scheduled to begin in 1958 and to initiate the "construction of socialism," should follow the pattern of the first. The first had produced highly unbalanced development from 1953 to 1957. Industry had grown enormously, but agriculture had barely kept pace with the increase in population. Without a larger agricultural surplus, there would be insufficient capital to invest in industry. Concessions to the peasants in 1956 had increased the surplus but had also encouraged the reappearance of bourgeois traits in the countryside. Since China's goal was not merely to industrialize but to transform society, an industrialization policy that encouraged capitalist traits was self-defeating. Furthermore, some leaders argued that the plan's emphasis on big factories, which required large amounts of capital, was not as suitable for China as it had been for Russia. China had little capital but many people; many smaller plants that relied mostly on manpower made more sense than a few huge plants that relied mostly on machinery. Smaller plants could be scattered around the country and could reduce the centralized planning and management that made for a top-heavy bureaucracy.

The CCP Central Committee, following this reasoning, decided to adopt a policy that more evenly balanced industry and agriculture, heavy industry and light, and centralized planning and local initiative. For example, although iron and steel production remained a high priority goal, much iron and steel was now to be produced locally in small plants. Furthermore, central government bureaus, such as the one responsible for keeping statistics, were broken up into local agencies. An administrative system was to be created in the countryside that combined all functions, from industry and agriculture to education and self-defense, in a new unit that came to be called the commune. Indeed, the commune can be understood as an effort to break down the barriers between city and countryside by transferring to the rural areas much of the work that had been done in the cities. The commune was the culmination of a sporadic but ever-widening expansion of cooperatives that had been under way from as early as 1950 and that Mao now refused to let slacken in 1957. To assure adequate work at local levels, a purge of local officials was conducted (unlike Stalin's purges, it was not bloody), and heavy emphasis was placed on the participation of the masses.

Early in 1958 this set of policies was ratified by the National People's Congress and soon came to be known as the Great Leap Forward (GLF). The GLF adopted specific national goals, such as surpassing British industrial production within fifteen years, and the "general line" of "going all out, aiming high and achieving greater, faster, better, and more economic results in building socialism." Mao was aiming not only at economic goals, but also at setting in motion "permanent revolution" and driving the country swiftly into full communism.

Huge increases in production were called for beginning in 1958, and targets were steadily raised until the country experienced virtually an epidemic of near-utopian optimism. Even the Association of Chinese Paleontologists vowed that its scientists would cut thirteen years off their twenty-year targets and would reach in seven years a higher level of research than paleontologists in capitalist countries. No one scene better evokes the mass quixotism to which the Great Leap Forward eventually led than that of scores of paleontologists hastening their pursuit of fossils in order that China might leap into the future.

The fundamental idea on which the seemingly impossible dreams of the Great Leap Forward rested was that China's problems were more political than economic or technological. Problems were to be solved primarily by cultivating proper political attitudes and engaging in correct political action. Lethargic agricultural production, for example, could be blamed only in part on shortages of chemical fertilizer, antiquated farming methods and tools, exhausted soil, and other technical barriers; the more fundamental obstacle was the tendency of some peasants to lapse into capitalistic thinking. During the GLF, therefore, "socialist education" was intensively carried on even in the countryside. A national example was made of one poor peasant who was said to have benefited from land reform but then fallen victim to a bourgeois mentality; soon the nation was flooded with stories explaining how he had begun to seek personal profit and to neglect his assignments in the cooperative and how he had been saved by the quick and effective work of good local cadres. Thus economic backwardness was to be overcome by intensified political effort, heightened class consciousness, and unyielding class struggle against bourgeois influences.

The main slogan of the Great Leap Forward was "Politics takes command." In its earliest and simplest form this slogan meant that political authority had to prevail over technical expertise. An alternate slogan was "The Redder, the more expert." This slogan meant that political reliability and even sheer enthusiasm were preferred to what was scorned as "the fetishism of technology." It was thought better, for example, to have enthusiastic peasants attempt to produce steel in numberless, amateurish backyard furnaces than to turn industry over to technical experts and managerial personnel. Experts and managers, together with urban party members, were ordered to engage regularly in manual labor in order to get closer to the masses. Thousands of cadres were "sent down" first to lower levels of the bureaucracy (from province to county or from county to township) and then to production work in cooperatives. The policy was known in Chinese as *xiafang*, the literal meaning of which is "downward transfer." Although *xiafang* was reminiscent of James Yen's *xiaxiang* idea, the CCP's "to the village" movement of the early 1940s, and even earlier CCP practices, its scope was far greater. To demonstrate that *xiafang* was important and applicable to all, high officials such as the first secretaries of province committees went out to plow fields and to carry earth. The mayor of Beijing worked on a road repair gang and pointed out that he was following a tradition established in Yan'an. Indeed, Mao Zedong himself is known to have cultivated a vegetable garden in Yan'an, and in 1958 he participated in the construction of a reservoir.

By February 1958 it was reported that 1.3 million cadres had undergone *xiafang*. Up to this time, a major purpose for *xiafang* was to redistribute cadres within the top-heavy administrative system. It may also have been intended to send trained personnel out to the countryside as part of the general decentralization and to reverse what had become a steady and heavy flow of population into the cities. In the spring *xiafang* was turned into an even broader effort to bridge social gaps. *Xiafang*, purposefully and systematically, was to wipe out the difference between mental and manual labor in all of Chinese society. Not only party cadres and government bureaucrats but all nonmanual workers were to be "sent down." Another million people, mostly urban intellectuals who lacked experience in manual labor, were sent to work in farms and factories for an entire year. In September the party announced that henceforth, "workers of all government organizations, troops, enterprises and industries, except those too old or too sick to take part in physical labor . . . shall spend at least one month a year in physical labor." There could no longer be any doubt that the Chinese revolution was accelerating; bureaucratism and bourgeois values were once again under direct frontal assault.

As the assault got under way during late 1957 and early 1958, the new emphasis on agriculture gave high priority to irrigation and water conservation projects. Following the principle of decentralization, Beijing assigned these projects to the APCs, but many of the projects were too big to be handled by one APC. Individual APCs, therefore, began to join forces. Some groups of APCs then found that their labor could be used more efficiently when several groups worked together. Probably with the permission of top-level CCP leaders, and perhaps even at their instigation, APCs began to amalgamate in order to handle other big projects. As the Great Leap Forward gathered speed in the spring of 1958, the APCs assumed still more tasks, including the establishment of small industries. Amalgamation of APCs increased accordingly, even though party leaders cautiously regarded this expansion as an experiment. In July the combined APCs began officially to be called "people's communes," signifying that the CCP had abandoned its earlier policy of keeping APCs relatively small. In August, when nearly a third of the peasants were already in communes, the CCP adopted the system as national policy. By the end of September the figure had leaped to 98 percent. Within a few months China's countryside had been reorganized into some 24,000 communes, averaging about five thousand families in each.

Mao Zedong hailed the commune movement unreservedly. Much as the peasants had captured his imagination in 1927, the euphoria of the Great Leap Forward now caught him up. Many times in the thirty-one years since he had discovered the peasants' potential, he had been disappointed in them, and on occasion he had pointedly criticized the farmers' attachment to their small holdings, but the rapid amalgamation of the APCs revived his faith. As in Yan'an days, the impossible came to seem possible once the unlimited potential of the masses was tapped. In a now famous metaphor he likened the masses to a blank sheet of paper that "has no blotches, and so the newest and most beautiful words can be written on it, the newest and most beautiful pictures can be painted on it." In September 1958, following a cross-country inspection trip, Mao jubilantly announced: "During this trip I have witnessed the tremendous energy of the masses. On this foundation it is possible to accomplish any task whatsoever."

No doubt Mao hoped that the establishing of the communes would resolve the prolonged debates in the CCP about the proper size and relationship of administrative districts and economic units. The basic principle was simply to integrate them, which was in effect little more than a recognition of what had already occurred under collectivization. This principle, however, left room for communes of different sizes, depending on which level of government the commune absorbed. In most instances the communes were the size of townships, but some communes were the size of counties. As Mao himself later admitted, size became an end in itself. Forced into what G. William Skinner terms a "grotesquely large mold," the communes failed to align themselves with the traditional socioeconomic pattern of rural trade. As a result, the rapid growth of huge communes seriously disrupted the distribution of goods, and further realignments of administrative and economic functions became necessary. These realignments were accomplished only in 1960 and 1961, after the GLF had been abandoned.

Another objective of communization was to reverse the flow of people from rural to urban areas. During the First Five-Year Plan there had been a vast migration of rural people to the cities, where industry was growing, jobs were available, and wages and living standards were thought to be much higher. This trend, which was already visible when the Communists came to power in 1949, became a near avalanche in 1954 due to food shortages. Repeated efforts failed to stem the tide of migrants. In 1956, for example, Shanghai received more than 500,000 peasants. Government leaders complained of an excessive drain on urban food supplies and sent huge numbers of migrants back to the countryside, but more continued to pour into the cities. By the end of 1957 a total of 8 million migrants had been added to the urban populations despite the expulsions. In 1958 the CCP, admitting that something else had to be tried, decided to build small-scale industries in the countryside and, in general, to develop a diversified local economy that would employ the peasants where they lived. This decision became an important aim of the Great Leap Forward and the commune system. Nevertheless, that year another 10 million peasants poured into the cities to find work.

The balance between industry and agriculture had also suffered from a serious decline in rural handicrafts. Toward the end of the First Five-Year Plan, many skilled workers gave up their trades in favor of full-time farm work. A major reason for this was resentment against the hasty manner in which handicraft cooperatives had been founded and, it seems, mismanaged by inexperienced cadres. By the end of 1957 there were nearly 2.5 million fewer skilled workers than three years earlier, a drop of more than 26 percent. Since agricultural production was almost totally dependent on rural handicrafts for many essential farm implements, a continuation of this trend would have been disastrous. During the Great Leap Forward, therefore, an attempt was made to replace the handicraft cooperatives and, most important, to base them in the communes.

The policies of the Great Leap Forward were designed to meet specifically Chinese economic problems. In the First Five-Year Plan the Chinese had followed an essentially Soviet model of central planning, maintaining a distinction (albeit a gradually blurring one) between political administration and economic organization and attempting to substitute capital for labor by investing in heavy industry and mechanizing agriculture. In 1957 and 1958 the Chinese abandoned this Soviet model and began to study their own conditions once again.

China was rich in people but poor in capital and technology. GLF policy, starting from this basic fact, aimed at converting the potential liability of a huge population into an asset. It diagnosed China's problem as one of finding productive employment for people and organizing the population efficiently rather than seeking more labor-saving devices or even limiting population growth. One decision was to end a birth control program that had been in effect for less than two years and return to the traditional stand that more people meant more production. This stand had been shaken slightly in 1953 by China's first census, which revealed that the population was 100 million greater than had been thought, and for the next three years there was some discussion of the issue and a few faltering steps taken toward a birth control policy. But in the first half of 1956 Mao's personal secretary said that China could absorb "at least another 600 million people" (i.e., double the 1956 population) and Premier Zhou Enlai dismissed the need for birth control. A food crisis later that year changed some minds, and in the atmosphere of the Hundred Flowers campaign demographers spoke out strongly for limiting population growth, setting in motion the first nationwide birth control movement in China. In the spring of 1958 it came to an abrupt halt. First Hu Yaobang, who in 1981 was to become chairman of the CCP and in 1958 headed the Communist Youth League, straddled the issue but leaned away from birth control. While "planned parenthood should be promoted," he said, a larger population is not undesirable but good because it "means greater manpower." A month later (May 1958) Liu Shaoqi ridiculed as un-Marxist the arguments of the population experts. The Marxist position, he said, is that "people are first of all producers," and therefore a large population means greater production and more accumulation. Mao then endorsed this view, and the Chinese media proclaimed, "as we see it, the more people the better." Only in 1962 was this view revised and birth control reinstituted.

Population policy is a clear example of how GLF policy was intended to suit Chinese conditions but went awry and had disastrous results. A quite different example that had more mixed results was the effort to develop small-scale rural industry with intermediate rather than high technology, using local resources wherever possible. This strategy proved to be essentially sound and was expanded considerably in the next two decades with highly positive results, but in the 1958–1959 period its more publicized feature was the attempt to manufacture iron and steel.

Mao encouraged the building of countless small blast furnaces, which were made of crude clay and bricks and used all available ore, coal, and household scraps such as old pots and pans for raw materials. The "backyard furnace" campaign was scoffed at by contemporary Western observers and has been acknowledged by economists (including the Chinese themselves) to have produced iron and steel that were often inadequate for modern industrial purposes. The backyard furnaces may well have been an absurdity. Most of them were soon abandoned. On the other hand, Edgar Snow, a well-informed journalist who visited China in 1960, observed that "quite a few, with improved methods, continue to produce iron for locally forged agricultural tools." Snow also learned that the experiment provided a training ground for workers and metallurgists who then built small modern plants which, he argues, may make a great deal of sense "for capital-poor underdeveloped countries with limited transport facilities bent on speedy acquisition of a heavy industry."

The backyard furnace campaign is one of the best illustrations of what the commune system was intended to do. For Mao it had not only tangible potential as a training ground but also the psychological value of involving the masses in new and daring enterprises. "Dare to struggle, dare to win," an old Maoist slogan from guerrilla warfare days against the Japanese war machine, was also an attitude to be cultivated in the production struggle.

However utopian its goals, the Great Leap Forward was inspired by more than blind optimism. It was based on the rational economic choice of refusing to let the central government absorb the surplus that the First Five-Year Plan had produced; instead the surplus was to go to the collectives (or communes) to invest in the development of local resources. Mao's argument, as Jack Gray points out, "was that the peasants would see more point in economic development if they conducted it for themselves as far as possible."

A decentralized economy also made good military sense since it would be much less vulnerable to air attack and to invasion than would an urbanized, concentrated, industrial economy; thus it fitted in with Mao's idea of guerrilla defense and with China's military situation vis-à-vis her major potential military foes. It is questionable whether this was an important consideration at the time the Great Leap Forward was being planned, because Mao was convinced that the launching of the Russian Sputnik in 1957 had given "the Socialist camp" a decisive military lead. However, there are strong indications that Mao was uncertain of Soviet support at this time because of a serious disagreement between the Soviet leadership and himself during his visit to Moscow in November of 1957.

In addition to reasons of economics and military security, the Great Leap Forward in general and the commune system in particular were defensible as programs suited to China's political and social needs. Politically, they attempted to bridge the gap between city and countryside and ease China's eternal tension between centralization and local initiative. Socially, they sought to overcome the distinction between mental and manual labor, a distinction that had been openly sanctioned ever since the great philosopher Mencius explained it in the fourth century B.C.: "Those who labor with their minds rule others; those who labor with their hands are ruled by others."

If there is this much to be said for the rationality of the Great Leap Forward, the obvious question is, Why did it collapse so rapidly and so disastrously? It should be stressed that most scholars do not agree that the Great Leap Forward was a rational program. This is particularly true if rationality is understood to mean the choice of the means that are most appropriate to achieving a desired objective, and if the primary objective of Chinese policy has been economic development in general and industrialization in particular. Economists tend to regard the methods of the Great Leap, particularly the heavy reliance on labor mobilization, as far from the most appropriate means to industrialization. Most probably agree with Ta-Chung Liu: "The Great Leap Forward was based on a sound diagnosis of the basic weakness of the mainland economy but a serious misconception of the proper way to deal with it." The poorly conceived treatment included excessive regimentation of rural life, impossibly long working hours, removal of incentives (such as private plots), unworkable farming and water control techniques, excessive pressure on industrial enterprises to expand production, and "total miscalculation of technical possibilities in introducing the backyard furnaces." He also notes that the Great Leap Forward happened to meet with bad weather conditions, which contributed to the agricultural disaster from 1958 to 1960, and concludes: "The whole economy suffered a serious leap backward from 1958 to 1961."

Of the reasons given for the economic failures of the Great Leap Forward, the one that is most often cited to explain other failures is regimentation. Even those scholars who are least critical of the Great Leap Forward find that the creation of a massive popular militia was among the most striking features of the program and that the "militarization of the peasantry" was the single most distinctive characteristic of the communes. As the CCP journal *Red Flag* explained, rapid development of agriculture required working people to "act faster, in a more disciplined and efficient way, [so] that they can better be shifted around within a broad framework, like the workers in a factory or the soldiers in a military unit."

The crucial step toward militarization of the peasantry came at the very beginning of the Great Leap Forward, when a vast nationwide movement mobilized labor for waterworks and irrigation projects. Although it began as a village-level system in which people who knew each other worked in small groups in their own areas, it soon grew until brigades of irrigation workers were being shifted from place to place. Peasants were forced to be absent from their villages, because they were engaged in irrigation projects elsewhere, when they were needed for spring planting at home. Some cooperatives tried to solve this problem by forming other specialized brigades (following the example of those engaged in water projects) to perform tasks such as wet-rice transplanting, fertilizer accumulating, or well-digging. As a result, instead of peasants doing all or many kinds of work in their own cooperative, they did one kind of work in many. The practice amounted to organizing village work as if villages were factories, and it set a pattern for the communes. It also meant for most Chinese peasants the most wrenching break with the past they had ever known. Schurmann has written:

> The peasant found himself working on strange land, unfamiliar to him. The intimate knowledge of his own land meant nothing to him any longer. Whereas earlier he could cope with the idiosyncrasies of land according to his "particularistic" knowledge, now nothing but the "universalistic" methods of rationally defined work were left to him. Work became mechanistic, and subject to the commands of cadres who undoubtedly had "general" knowledge of farm processes, but could never match the intimate knowledge of the "old peasant."

It seems highly significant that some of the least successful policies of the Great Leap Forward were those that struck at the foundations of traditional rural life and resembled Soviet policies. Although the GLF policies abandoned the Stalinist model of industrialization, some features of communization were similar to Russian collectivization; as an example, the Russians considered the state farm to be "a factory in the field" and, like the Chinese, sought to convert peasants into rural proletarians.

The commune system foundered on such efforts to rechannel some of the deepest currents in Chinese life. Probably the most disastrous of these experiments was the sudden attempt in August 1958 to introduce an entirely new marketing system in the countryside. Virtually overnight the complex structure of traditional periodic markets, about 90 percent of which were still functioning, was to be replaced by a system of supply and marketing departments within each commune. As a result the distribution of goods came to a nearly complete halt. Food, clothing, farm tools, and fertilizer became scarce, while food rotted and other goods piled up at shipping points. Desperate emergency measures and improvisations helped bring rural people through one cold and hungry winter, and then rural markets were reestablished. Some ancient practices, it appears, were best left alone.

The same lesson was learned when cadres attempted to redesign the old marketing systems in order to fit the system of political administration. Cooperatives, which were now roughly equivalent in size to the old villages, were to trade with their county capitals instead of with the old market towns. In many cases this was grossly inefficient and impractical. One cooperative, for example, that had traditionally dealt with a market town which was only two days' travel away, now had to trade with a county capital that was ten days away. Not until 1962 were such unreasoned departures from traditional practices fully abandoned.

Mao Zedong's defense of the GLF was that flaws of this kind were fatal only because China suffered exceptionally unfavorable weather conditions over an extended period of time; the flaws were not inherent in the program but were amenable to correction. Mao felt that the party cadres were at fault. Regimentation was *their* doing; it was cadre "commandism" and a failure to implement the mass line that were responsible. Cadres mistakenly followed a policy of "the bigger the better"; this too was not inherent in communization. The cadres' excessive enthusiasm and incompetence were responsible for false reporting of production that misled planners at higher levels. Uncontrolled desires to overfulfill quotas also led to such incidents as the dismantling of office heaters and other equipment in order to win a scrap collection drive competition, or the circulation of false rumors that rice and clothing were soon to be supplied freely to each person according to need instead of according to work—that is, that full communism was soon to replace socialism. (One Chinese publication of 1958, however, says Mao himself was responsible for initiating this particular rumor.) Thus the argument can indeed be made that the Great Leap Forward was reasonably well conceived but poorly implemented and beset with unfavorable treatment from natural causes.

Mao Zedong's opponents in the party leadership thought that much more was wrong. Many objected to the decentralization concept on which the communes were founded. "Localism," they complained, was already getting out of hand because the APCs were becoming too powerful; the communes made localities even more self-sufficient. Under these conditions, Mao's critics demanded, how was nationwide planning and coordination to be achieved? Some even felt that "local patriotism" might interfere with national unity.

Party cadres, teachers, students, and other urbanites who were "sent down" to the countryside also objected to Mao's policies. They had expected China's progress to bring the blessings of modern urban civilization to deprived rural folk rather than to convert city intellectuals into farm laborers. Progress was supposed to mean less manual labor, not more. Especially to those trained abroad, possession of technical expertise was thought to make a person more valued, not more suspect of having bourgeois leanings.

Others objected to the lower priority given to heavy industry and the new emphasis on handicrafts, light industry, agriculture, and farm-related matters such as water control. Still others objected to the return to a people's militia, some because the militia seemed incompatible with modern military methods, and some because it led to a militarized peasantry and a misplaced confidence in the ability or wisdom of the masses. Finally, there were many who were troubled by the Soviet Union's disapproval of the communes and of Mao's premature claims that China was about to enter the stage of pure communism, particularly since that disapproval led to the withdrawal of Soviet technical advisers and the worsening of Russian-Chinese relations.

Outspoken criticisms of the Great Leap Forward program during most of 1958 forced numerous party conferences to be held. Finally, at the end of the year, a retreat was begun. In December 1958, after only five months of existence, the growth of the communes was checked, and Mao resigned as chairman of the People's Republic of China but not as head of the party. Retrenchment prevailed well into 1959. By late summer, however, Mao had prepared a counterattack. In August, even as the party was admitting catastrophic defeats in the Great Leap and revising downward its production targets for 1959, Mao launched an antirightist campaign. The campaign was directly primarily at those who denied that the masses could handle the tasks of revolutionary construction, who criticized mass movements while failing to participate in them, and who minimized achievements but magnified shortcomings. In brief, the rightists were those opposed to Mao. The campaign continued through October, by which time a second leap was under way, indicating that Mao may have temporarily regained command. Although Mao persevered through 1960, by the end of the year his influence had declined again. The Great Leap Forward was rejected, and in January 1961 liberalization policies were adopted, particularly to stimulate food production. "Experts" who could improve production were now valued over "reds," technical skills over political activism.

The CCP reversed its communization policy, but it maintained the form by subdividing communes into production brigades and teams instead of dismantling them. In effect, the CCP went back, not to traditional administration, but to a system in which the commune conformed roughly to the township. The 24,000 huge communes organized at the peak of the Great Leap Forward were broken up into about 74,000 smaller ones, close to the number of townships that existed in 1958. Commune and township boundaries were remarkably similar. At lower levels, however, the production brigades were not as small as the old villages, and the production teams were not as large as the old villages. The teams, which averaged about forty households, became the basic unit in which important decisions were made. The brigade, which was supposed to include no more than ten teams, had the chief responsibility for annual planning and allocated work to the teams.

Thus power to organize production and distribute income devolved steadily down to the lower levels. Families were allowed small private plots, and even when working in the production team they usually farmed the same land they had always farmed. The communes, made up of one to two dozen brigades, retained a variety of functions much like the old county—such as registry of births, deaths, and marriages, and regulation of civil disputes—and they also were to coordinate brigade plans, manage schools and hospitals, and organize other enterprises that were too large for the brigades. The end of the Great Leap Forward, therefore, found the communes far from moribund. Indeed, they made a valuable contribution in the battle waged against flood and drought in 1959 and 1960. But in the winter of 1960–1961, China was far from communism and deep in crisis.

For the masses of Chinese people, the collapse of the GLF meant "three hard years" (1959–1961), years of hunger and widespread suffering. An army unit in Beijing reported in 1960 that 80 percent of its 193 soldiers received letters from their families telling of disaster in their villages, including death and disease. One soldier said, "The peasants eat only vegetables and sweet potatoes and have no grain." Another: "At present what the peasants eat in the villages is even worse than what dogs ate in the past. At that time dogs ate chaff and grain. Now the people are too hungry to work and pigs are too hungry to stand up. Commune members ask: 'Is Chairman Mao going to allow us to starve to death?'" And another: "In the city there is enough grain, and the grain supplied is fine grain, but in the villages the grain supplied is coarse. . . . Even the sick people at home have to eat sweet potatoes. . . . Why is life in the villages so bad?" The opposite complaint was voiced by a Beijing resident whose family sometimes ate nothing but grain for months at a time: "At least the peasants could grow a few vegetables." Such suffering left scars that were evident twenty years later.

For the leadership, the 1959–1961 disasters meant a thorough reexamination of policy, especially the high priority that had been assigned to developing heavy industry and the relatively low priority that had been assigned to light industry (including consumer goods) and most of all to agriculture. Although it can be argued that overall the agricultural record for the first decade of the People's Republic was highly creditable and that the notable successes in industrialization could not have been achieved without the substantial gains in the countryside, it was plain that agriculture had lagged too far behind industry and that by 1959 food production was becoming a critical issue. Ironically, a party that had come to power on the wings of a surging rural movement and had worried in 1949 about its ability to learn urban and industrial management during its first decade in power had done better in the cities and in industry than in the countryside and in agriculture.

Thus in the middle of 1959, almost precisely ten years after he had first called for shifting the party's attention to urban problems, Mao asked whether the priorities were still correct: "Henceforth we may have to reverse the order. Should it be agriculture, light industry, and heavy industry? . . . We have to solve the problems of clothing, food, housing, utilities and transportation first, for they concern the stable life of 650 million people." The issue had been raised. But its resolution would require years of further struggle.

In 1949, as he proclaimed victory, Mao Zedong announced that China had taken only "the first step in a long march of ten thousand *li*." Ahead lay full emergence from "semifeudalism" and the road to socialism and communism. Even at this high point of a twenty-eight-year struggle, Mao stressed the long road ahead rather than the extraordinary achievement just recorded. Mao was clearly no visionary in 1949, at the moment when he had most reason to think the impossible was possible.

Nor was he utopian five years later when he grumbled that it would take another fifty years, ten five-year plans, to build a great socialist country: "What can we make at present? We can make tables and chairs, teacups and teapots, we can grow grain and grind it into flour, and we can make paper. But we can't make a single motor car, plane, tank or tractor. So we mustn't brag and be cocky." And in January 1956, even as the high tide of collectivization gathered force, Mao ridiculed comrades who called for China to do without foreign help in industrial development: "This is absurd. We are now in a time of cultural revolution, a revolution of techniques, a revolution which attacks ignorance and stupidity; without foreign help, by pretending to rely on our own forces, we will never succeed." He went on to stress the importance of training many more intellectuals and reaching the highest world levels in science and technology. And while he outlined a quite different development strategy only three months later, in his speech "On the Ten Major Relationships," it was a strategy that has since become virtually the touchstone for Chinese "pragmatism." Finally, in 1957 he estimated that it would take "several decades" to make China strong and prosperous.

Clearly something very important and very difficult to explain happened around late 1957 and early 1958, when China suddenly attempted its great leap. The most recent official explanation, issued by the CCP leadership in 1981, stresses that Mao and some others (but mostly Mao) committed "Left errors." Mao became a visionary, impatient for quick results. He ignored "economic laws" and overestimated "the role of man's subjective will and efforts" in bringing about social change. Although it conceded that GLF policies were poorly administered by cadres, sabotaged by the Soviets' withdrawal of aid and advisers, and severely hampered by two years of terrible weather and natural disasters, the official 1981 explanation insisted that Mao's utopianism above all created the crisis of 1959–1961 and, indeed, led to "catastrophe" from 1966 to 1976.

This explanation is remarkably close to what most foreign analysts have said for many years. But more needs to be said about why the GLF was adopted as party policy and about what its failure means.

Mao Zedong was unquestionably the leading advocate of the GLF and, however rational it was in its attempt to modernize in a way suited to Chinese conditions, it unquestionably turned into a utopian experiment. Since we shall see a similar pattern in the Great Proletarian Cultural Revolution, it is a phenomenon that requires careful analysis.

Let us recognize at the outset that despite the practicality and shrewd judgment that characterized Mao Zedong's career, he was a complicated and all too human man who had a visionary side. He could face the harshest facts and accept the most distasteful choices—in 1936–1937 when he agreed to spare Jiang Kaishek's life and ally the CCP once again with the Guomindang, in 1949–1950 when he went to Moscow hat in hand, and many other times before and since—and turn them to his and China's advantage. Much less often, he could misjudge situations and be carried away with excessive enthusiasm. Interestingly enough, even the most glaring examples of this weakness were not so clearly disastrous errors. He was probably wrong about the peasants in 1927, but not all the evidence is on one side. During collectivization in 1955 he became overly optimistic, but in the end he was probably more right than wrong. Still, Mao Zedong clearly had his impetuous side. What we must focus on is the question of when and why he acted impulsively, and how others acted at the same time.

It is highly significant that the major instances of impetuosity on Mao's part were in response to what he regarded, correctly or not, as largely spontaneous mass action. Although he surely knew that the Hunan peasant movement of 1926–1927, the high tide of collectivization in 1955, and the formation of communes in 1958 owed something to the work of party cadres, he viewed each of these movements as evidence of the masses' unlimited potential. When Mao erred on the side of overoptimism, the reason was usually that he expected too much from mass action. In 1927 and 1955 Mao's overoptimism was checked by his comrades. But in 1958 it was not. The reason is not that Mao had greater power to override his comrades in 1958; it is that few of them disagreed with him until late in 1958 and possibly even beyond that. Mao took his share of blame in July 1959:

> I am a complete outsider when it comes to economic construction, and I understand nothing about industrial planning. . . . But comrades, in 1958 and 1959 the main responsibility was mine, and you should take me to task. . . . The chaos caused was on a grand scale and I take responsibility. Comrades, you must all analyze your own responsibility.

While he did not spare himself, he named others and, in the end, few if any leaders emerged unblemished. As he did not have to remind his comrades, in 1956 the party had taken a considered decision to reduce his power and adhere to collective responsibility. All important issues are to be decided collectively, the new party constitution said, and all references to the "thought of Mao Zedong" were erased from it. Although these measures could not so quickly erase Mao's power, they were matched by organizational changes that did reduce his authority. When he proposed the GLF, the party leadership met several times over a period of about four months to discuss and vote on his proposals. No doubt Mao pushed, pressed, and maneuvered to have his policies adopted, but the other party leaders were not political novices. When Liu Shaoqi spoke for the Central Committee in May 1958 to endorse the GLF, which dramatically reversed the policies he had set forth only twenty months earlier, Liu showed no trace of embarrassment or reservation. He merely explained that "many changes of great historic significance" had taken place in those months, and therefore a change in line was perfectly in order.

What were those historic changes? Liu listed many, including internal political shifts and "radical changes in human relations" such as cadres doing manual labor side-by-side with workers and peasants —a bit of self-congratulation, perhaps, since Liu had introduced the idea of *xiafang* back in 1956 in order to combat bureaucratism—but at the top of Liu's list was the world situation: "In extent of popular support, size of populations and rate of development of production, the socialist camp headed by the Soviet Union has long since surpassed the imperialist camp." Now, with the launching of the Soviet intercontinental ballistic missile and earth satellite in 1957, the whole world could see "that in science and technology, too, the Soviet Union has surpassed the United States, the most developed of the capitalist countries." Together with new solidarity in the socialist camp, this signified a major turning point in world affairs, what Mao had termed the East wind shifting to prevail over the West wind.

This remarkable turn of events, combined with their own successes in industrialization (industrial production in 1957 was more than four times what it had been in 1949), contributed to a strong surge of optimism among Chinese leaders. If the Soviet Union could surpass the United States in forty years, why could not China catch up with Britain in fifteen? Even Liu, who in 1956 had called for "step-by-step" industrialization and said it "will take a considerable time" to transform China into an advanced industrial country, in May 1958 criticized "such outmoded ideas as . . . 'it's better to take small steps than to go striding forward.'" With others' help, "and primarily the help of the Soviet Union, economic construction in China will be carried on not slowly but probably at a considerable speed."

In brief, what particularly excited Liu Shaoqi and permitted him to share at least some of Mao's optimism about the Great Leap was the prospect of technological breakthroughs and rapid industrialization. Mao was surely excited by this prospect, too, but he was much more excited by what he saw among the Chinese masses, and he was probably less sanguine than Liu about the future of China's alliance with the Soviet Union.

If there was disagreement among the Chinese leaders at this early stage it was probably here, for Mao was beginning to worry about overreliance on Soviet aid and excessive imitation of Soviet methods. Soviet influence was pervasive in these years. From ballet and acting styles to the structure of education and industry, Chinese life was deeply touched by Russian models. "I couldn't have eggs or chicken soup for three years because an article appeared in the Soviet Union which said that one shouldn't eat them," Mao complained. "We lacked understanding of the whole economic situation, and understood still less the economic differences between the Soviet Union and China. So all we could do was follow blindly. Now [March 1958] the situation has changed." But even this did not become a serious enough issue within the Chinese leadership to divide it until late in 1958. And when party discord sharpened in 1958–1959 Liu and most other key leaders either compromised with Mao or backed him fully. In September 1959, after a bitter debate in the party, Liu spoke out for continuing the Leap, the commune movement, and the general line.

Thus it is plain that whatever utopianism was present in the GLF was widely shared. If Mao's was more pronounced or several steps ahead of others, few hesitated to follow. But there were two kinds of optimism at work, Mao's (based primarily on the potential of the Chinese masses), and Liu's (based primarily on the potential of modern technology). Although matters of emphasis and differences of degree (Mao was not opposed to technology and Liu did not deny the energy of the masses), these were sharply divergent views with serious implications for China's modernization.

In the GLF the attempt to accomplish with the will and energy of millions what might otherwise be done with electricity, turbines, diesel engines, and computers was inconsistent with the priority given to heavy industry and with the attempts to reach standards attained in the most advanced industrial countries (British and U.S. production levels were repeatedly cited during the GLF as China's goals). It clashed too with Chinese leaders' own faith in technology and their desire to spread it widely among the populace. Which was it to be, the energy of the masses or the energy of machines, a broadly but thinly educated population or a concentration on technical expertise? And finally, could China both equal the West in production and surpass it in social and political organization? What happens when the goals of communism—a classless society, self-government by the producers—and the goals of modernization—greater productivity, primarily by means of new industrial technology—absolutely intertwined and inseparable in the GLF, seem to be incompatible?

Looming behind these questions was the issue of China's distinctive path to modernization and the role to be played by foreign models and foreign aid. The GLF began with China still confident that Soviet aid was at hand, even though Soviet experience could no longer be followed as blindly as before. At the very least, Soviet gains in technology were China's inspiration; but more concretely, some 1,400 Soviet experts were to remain in China and the hundreds of projects in which they were cooperating with the Chinese were to continue. When accumulating tensions resulted in the abrupt cancellation of Soviet aid and the sudden withdrawal of Soviet experts in 1960, it did more than cripple the modern sector of the newly developed Chinese economy. It reignited the whole century-old issue of foreign aid versus self-reliance.

A court official had observed in 1867 that if China hires foreign teachers "the cunning barbarians may not teach us their essential techniques." During the next ninety years such suspicions were considerably mitigated, in large part by China's own gains in mastering foreign techniques, but when the Soviets promised in 1957 to share atomic data with China and then two years later (at least according to the Chinese view) reneged on the agreement, old suspicions may well have surfaced again. And when the Soviets pulled out of China so suddenly and completely, they ensured not only that self-reliance would be China's policy for some time to come but that any change in this policy would be powerfully resisted.

Here, then, was the final and perhaps in the long run the most damaging legacy of the GLF: A wide range of issues that went to the very core of China's modernization effort now divided the Chinese leadership to a degree that was unprecedented in the history of the party. There had been major splits before, followed by expulsions and purges and resignations, but each time a working unity was restored that permitted the party to recover. Indeed, the GLF in its origins shows precisely such an ability to heal wounds. In 1956 the party also split on serious issues, including the downgrading of Mao. The chairman did not break with his critics in 1956 (in fact he made some criticism of the "cult of personality"), and they did not break with him when he called on them to switch gears in 1958. By 1960 the unity of the leadership was shattered beyond repair: Mao had broken with his minister of defense, an old comrade with whom he had worked ever since they patched together an army in 1928, in a bitterly personal quarrel that left the exminister humiliated. Liu, another comrade of more than thirty years, soon broke with Mao. From these boulders of anger, dropped into a pond of "three hard years," ripples went out to every corner of the land. Twenty-one years later their effects were still being felt. From the collapse of the GLF on, then, China's struggle to modernize was to be plagued by deep personal animosities and vicious factional quarrels that repeatedly overshadowed the substantial issues that gave them birth.

6

THE PEOPLE'S REPUBLIC OF CHINA, PART TWO: MODERNIZATION AND REVOLUTION, 1961–1981

IT HAD now been fully a century since China's leaders had begun actively and deliberately to cope with the problems posed by the modern world, but the questions asked in 1860 remained to be fully answered: Why were smaller foreign countries so strong and China so weak? How could China become their equal? The strides China had taken by the 1950s were substantial, but in 1960 the Chinese were more impressed by the problems that remained.

As they contemplated the wreckage of the Great Leap Forward, they might well have seen all of those problems in concentrated form. Nature still presented the clearest obstacle to China's development. During the GLF more than 60 percent of China's cultivated areas suffered drought or flood. Typhoons had struck the south and northeast, causing huge damage. Despite the labor of millions of people to solve the problems of irrigation and flood control, solutions were still only partial. Farmland was insufficient and becoming more scarce as towns and industries grew. In China there is one third of an acre of farmland per person; in the United States there are two acres per person. China was trying to feed 23 percent of the world's population with only 7 percent of the world's cultivable land.

The resources with which this unique task might be managed still lay mostly undiscovered, beyond the reach of China's 20,000 miles of railroad (50 percent more than China had ten years earlier but only one

130

tenth of the U.S. mileage, one fourth of the Soviet Union's, and one half of India's). Counting skilled workers, China in 1961 had nearly eight times as many technicians and engineers as it had nine years earlier, but the numbers were still far short of the need. Technology could be the answer to problems of modernization, but how to train the personnel and obtain the money, how to administer it all, and how at the same time to keep moving toward the social and political goals that so many had already died for—a greater measure of equality and dignity, self-government of the producers, a sufficient productivity to distribute to all according to their need? To what extent could a socialist system allow small numbers of people—the better educated, the high cadres, the urban technicians—to attain these goals while the vast majority made little or no progress toward them? Did the achievement of industrialization and a higher standard of living require postponing or modifying socialist goals? Were socialism and modernization achievable together?

In 1961 China was forced to compromise its long-range goals to a considerable extent. Conditions made this unavoidable. Hungry people were stealing food from military farms. Soldiers were robbing and raping. In one notorious case a woman who stole seven cabbages was strung up, beaten, and stripped naked before the other villagers. In another, more than sixty people marched on a school field to pick bananas and vegetables. Stopped by cadres they cursed and shouted: "You have grown fat here, enjoying life, and won't even let us dig a few banana roots!" "You are just as bad as the Guomindang troops."

Gross national product in 1961 had dropped by at least 15 percent and possibly as much as 25 percent from its peak in 1958. Per capita income was down by 32 percent, industrial production by 40 to 45 percent. Per capita production fell back to the level of 1955, a drop of 19 percent. The average person took in only 1,790 calories per day, 19 percent less than in 1958, and 26 percent less protein. Attempts were made at manufacturing artificial food. In one area it was claimed that artificial egg powder had been extracted from a fungus. Others made artificial flour and meat. For the first time since the founding of the new government, China imported grain, buying 6.2 million tons in 1961, mostly from Canada and Australia.

Economists have suggested that China in 1961 faced a depression comparable to the one that struck the United States in 1929. If anything, China's was worse. Therefore, much as the United States resorted to the methods of the "welfare state," compromising its Coolidge-style laissez-faire economics to pull out of its depression, so

China compromised its socialist goals. Since some leaders objected to the compromise, the price of economic recovery was political division that grew into polarization. A split that had first appeared in the GLF reappeared and widened until virtual civil war broke out in 1966. By 1981 China had not yet healed its political wounds enough to permit modernization to go forward smoothly. And yet, go forward it did, awkwardly and disjointedly, throughout two decades of political strife.

ECONOMIC RECOVERY AND ITS POLITICAL COST, 1961–1966

Mao Zedong's rivals in the party did not hesitate to take him at his word and charge him with major responsibility for the failures of the GLF. In a particularly sharp thrust, Liu Shaoqi said that the failures were only 30 percent the fault of nature and 70 percent the fault of man (*which* man did not have to be specified), and he cited as his source for this statistic the peasants of Hunan, Mao's (and Liu's) own province. Under heavy pressure and being treated, as he later complained, like "a dead ancestor," Mao went into semiretirement. He wrote poetry—"I am lost in dreams," went one line—but he also studied intensively a Soviet textbook on political economy, which deepened his concern about the future of socialism. For a time he accepted his demotion with candor ("Why should a person only go up and never down? . . . I think that demotion and transfer, whether justified or not, does good to people") and even some humor ("I myself have had experience in this respect and gained a great deal of benefit. If you do not believe me, why not try it yourselves?"). But the steel showed through, for the benefit of demotion, he said, was to strengthen one's "revolutionary will." Mao had served notice that he would be back. Meanwhile, he left his comrades with his own sharp reminder of China's primary problem when, at a Politburo meeting, he ordered a meal consisting of only one bowl of noodles per person: "Let them eat only half their fill, and they will know how the common people feel when there isn't enough to eat."

Some leaders needed the reminder. In January 1961 a high-level party meeting could arrive only at an ambiguous compromise formula, "take agriculture as the base and industry as the leading factor," for solving the economic crisis. The formula had been put forward nine months earlier and was only a partial retreat from GLF strategy. In practice it meant at first no more than a cutback in industry, a seven-point policy termed "adjustment" and "consolidation," and putting a stop to all but a few capital construction projects already under way and to all expansion or new construction projects.

Within a few months the implications for agriculture were spelled out in a sixty-point document in which the central point was to revise the commune system. Communes were reduced in both size and authority. Not only were more decisions to be made by production teams, the smallest organized unit in the countryside (now reduced to an average of about thirty households), but each household gained wider control over its own affairs. The policy was a fundamental decentralization and loosening of restrictions from above. Peasants now had greater freedom to raise vegetables, fruit, and livestock on private plots of land, to sell their produce in free markets, and to decide production quotas for themselves. Other enterprises such as rural industries, although cut back in order to free labor for food production, were given sole responsibility for their own profits and losses. The communes were not abolished, but the overwhelming weight they had acquired in 1958–1959 was trimmed to fit a new system aimed at "balance," especially in economic decision making.

These changes were spelled out and ratified at a major party conference in September 1962, when an unequivocal "agriculture first" policy was issued. The most concrete expression of the policy was a major shift of state investment into agriculture—to produce, for example, more farm tools, machinery, and chemical fertilizer. At the same time the policy envisioned continued imports of chemical fertilizer and grain. In brief, the single most characteristic emphasis of CCP policy from 1961 to 1966, under the guidance of Liu Shaoqi and his top aide Deng Xiaoping, was to assign first priority to economic growth in general and to food production in particular. Anything that could restore the crippled economy to health would be attempted. As Deng put it, "No matter whether cats are black or white, as long as they can catch mice they are good cats."

It was no accident that Deng expressed his views in color imagery. Everyone in China knew the "three red flags"—the GLF, the communes, and the general line for socialist construction. Everyone knew that during the GLF it became more important to be "red" (socialist-minded) than "expert" (professionally competent). Deng's aphorism could not have been more pointed if he had said red instead of black and had used Mao's name. The policies of economic recovery were also lethal political weapons.

Mao found these policies intolerable. Once again, as in 1956 and 1957, he saw the return of a "rich-peasant mentality" in the countryside and a "bureaucratic mentality" in the CCP. Once again, as he had in 1959, Mao rebounded from demotion and semiretirement. Behind the scenes he cultivated new sources of power, this time in the military. His closest ally became Lin Biao (1907–1971), an old comrade, a famous general, and, since 1959, the minister of defense. Signs of an alliance between Mao and Lin multiplied in 1960: a renewed stress on the importance of militia forces and "people's war," the publication of some long-withheld writings by Mao that stressed the relevance of guerrilla strategy to present and future needs, and a revival with unprecedented intensity of a drive to put "politics in command" in the army. The embryonic alliance between Mao and Lin was insufficient to prevent the party's abandonment of Maoist policies in 1961, but as Liu Shaoqi and his comrades in the CCP leadership led China out of the "three hard years," Mao and Lin prepared to renew the struggle for power. Their efforts consisted first of a nationwide socialist education campaign, especially among soldiers and youth, to propagate Mao's thought.

The campaign was designed to promote Maoist "democracy" among the troops, which meant bringing them closer to the masses. One way to do so was to involve the army in the economy. PLA officers were assigned to business and financial offices, and many economic officials were sent to PLA units for political training. The campaign was also intended to train the young to be the next generation of national revolutionary leaders. Soldiers and revolutionary youth were proclaimed the hope of the future. As the campaign gained momentum in 1963 and 1964, two themes emerged. One theme exposed wrongdoing by party cadres, especially those who were found to have committed "unclean" acts of mismanagement and corruption in the countryside; the other hailed the army as a model for all kinds of work, organization, and behavior. Having profited from more than three years of intensive training in Mao's thought, the army was allegedly immune to the bourgeois germs that were infecting civilian life. The campaign to "Learn from the People's Liberation Army" peaked in 1964, when the press was saturated with stories of selfless heroism and virtuous acts performed by model soldiers and even by entire units.

The contrast between party cadres who were attacked in 1964 because they were "unclean" and soldiers who were lionized because they served the people and gave no thought to personal gain reveals the underlying struggle that led to the Great Proletarian Cultural Revolution

(GPCR). "The party," Jack Gray has written, "is the engine of social change; it cannot just idle, it must pull." If the CCP did not generate social change, Mao feared, China could slip back into what he considered decadent bourgeois democracy. Mao held that precisely such backsliding was occurring in the Soviet Union: The flowering of Soviet "revisionism" was proof that a socialist revolution could be reversed. In the CCP it was apparent, as Michel Oksenberg wrote, that "the zeal for achieving social change has been sapped by a penchant for bureaucratic behavior: the desire to maximize status while minimizing responsibility, the ability to postpone decision and action until the decision or action is no longer required, and the capacity to build an organizational position impregnable to attack." The party was becoming an entrenched elite much like the old gentry—privileged, accustomed to urban comforts, and insensible to the needs and problems of the peasant masses. The entire revolution was at stake.

To underline the contrast between party and army and to provide Mao with support for a new campaign against party bureaucratism, Lin Biao stressed anew that the army would place "continued emphasis on politics" and especially upon the "creative study" of Mao's writings. The most dramatic concrete expression of this renewed emphasis was the decision to abolish ranks, awards, and insignia in the army. During and immediately after the Korean War, which required the Chinese army to depart from its guerrilla methods and organization, numerous Soviet-style changes had been introduced. Although some of these changes had been renounced when the Chinese moved away from Soviet models in the late 1950s, the army kept the elaborate system of ranks, epaulettes, badges, pay differentials, and other such expressions of military hierarchy. Now it was decided to revert to the guerrilla model in which the only distinction was between commanders (officers) and fighters (enlisted men). Furthermore all military personnel would wear the same uniform and simple insignia, a red star on the hat and a red badge on the collar. The Russian-style organization, it was explained, had contributed to "class consciousness and ideas to gain fame and wealth." By learning from the People's Liberation Army, China would learn how to eliminate ranks throughout its government and society; elitist bureaucrats would learn from the masses much as officers learned from the rank and file.

Another major reason for these changes in the army was the war in Vietnam. As United States intervention grew, China's leaders had to consider their country's relationship to the war and, in particular, what to do in case of an American attack. Some army and party leaders wanted a build-up of conventional forces and a rapprochement with the Soviet Union that would allow China to obtain modern weapons from its erstwhile ally. Mao and Lin spurned the idea that weapons were decisive and that China needed to rely on the Soviet Union. They favored a "people's war" strategy, in which the political organization and ideological conviction of Chinese guerrillas would count for more than missiles. This issue, which resembled the "expert versus red" issue that divided China's leaders in matters concerning economic development and party and government operations, came to a head in 1965. Once again, a threat from outside coincided with internal turmoil to produce a dual crisis.

THE GREAT PROLETARIAN CULTURAL REVOLUTION (GPCR), 1965-1969

In January 1965 Mao decided that he had failed to rouse the party to action by means of the socialist education campaign. He accused unnamed leaders of capitalist tendencies and demanded a "cultural revolution"; but he found that the party and its major organs of propaganda and information were not responsive to his wishes or orders. Frustrated, Mao left Beijing and traveled for six months, ending up in Shanghai. Along the way he mobilized support, finding particularly strong sympathy among a group we shall call the "Shanghai radicals." Meanwhile he cultivated allies among student groups and, with Lin Biao's help, within the military. Mao had the army newspaper call for a purge of "anti-socialist" and "right opportunist" elements in the party.

When Mao felt his support was sufficient, he launched a political struggle against the underlings of his opponents in Beijing. When he felt he had weakened them enough, he returned to Beijing and called a meeting of the Central Committee. Amid bitter wrangling Mao pushed through a sixteen-point program for the Great Proletarian Cultural Revolution that was issued as a "Decision of the Central Committee of the CCP." This meant that Mao could now issue directives in the name of the Central Committee; it remained to be seen whether he could enforce them.

Mao's first directive outlined the goals of the new movement. The GPCR was to "use the new ideas, culture, customs, and habits of the proletariat to change the mental outlook of the whole of society" and to

Chinese soldiers, early in the Great Proletarian Cultural Revolution, writing a wall poster in which they pledge to support "our most esteemed and beloved great leader Chairman Mao." *UPI*

"touch people to their very souls." It was to create "new forms of organization . . . to keep our party in close contact with the masses." And it was to revive and expand many of the goals of the Great Leap Forward. All this, Mao hoped, would enable China to overcome the Three Great Differences—the differences (or contradictions) between town and country, industry and agriculture, and mental and manual labor. Once these contradictions were resolved, China would at last be proletarianized, not only in the sense that all Chinese would perform manual labor but in the sense that all would share a new state of mind. To be proletarian now meant to possess no thought of personal advantage and to be totally dedicated to serving one's comrades.

One of Mao's major instruments was the Red Guards. These were organizations of high school and college students that began to form in May 1966. At first they had many names and varied purposes, but they began to gain prominence in June for their sharp public criticism of school and university administrators, "old-fashioned" teachers, and bourgeois students. They put up wall posters denouncing their targets and held mass meetings at which teachers and administrators were forced to criticize themselves and undergo many forms of public humiliation. (A favorite method was to make them wear signboards that said things such as "I am a monster.") By August huge numbers of youth had joined Red Guard organizations and sworn allegiance to Mao's crusade. But the crusade turned into a nightmare for millions.

With Mao Zedong's return to the political fray in the summer of 1966, a critical point was reached. The political divisions that had sharpened in 1958–1959 had been kept within known bounds for the next seven years. Mao had resorted primarily to an ideological campaign; Liu and Deng had countered with one of their own that seemed to support Mao but in fact adroitly checked him. Mao had fumed ("Those of you . . . who do not allow people to speak, who think you are tigers and that nobody will dare to touch your ass, whoever has this attitude will fail. People will talk anyway. You think that nobody will really dare to touch the ass of tigers like you? They damn well will!"), but he had not declared war. Liu had grumbled ("Why is he so attached to calling himself 'Chairman'? 'Chairman Mao.' 'Chairman Mao.' Have you ever heard anyone speak of 'Chairman Lenin'?"), but he held firmly to his belief that "what was done to win the revolutionary war cannot be applied to China's construction." Deng did not go beyond barbs —contrasting the methodical approach of the recovery with the head-long pace of the GLF, he remarked, "a donkey is certainly slow, but at least it rarely has an accident." Mao could complain that from 1959 to 1966 Deng "has never consulted me over anything at all," but until now Mao had merely ridiculed his opponents as insects:

> On this tiny globe
> A few flies dash themselves against the wall,
> Humming without cease,
> Sometimes shrilling,
> Sometimes moaning.
> Ants on the locust tree assume a great-nation swagger
> And mayflies lightly plot to topple the giant tree.

While he had also threatened ("Away with all pests"), until August 1966 he avoided direct conflict. But in that month he wrote his own "big-character poster"—the widely practiced method of airing one's views, especially controversial or dissenting views—and, at a mass rally of Red Guards in Beijing, allowed a Red Guard armband to be pinned to his sleeve. In his big-character poster he accused "some leading comrades from the central down to the local levels" of acting contrary to Marxism-Leninism, of adopting a "bourgeois reactionary stand," and of opposing the working class: "They have stood facts on their head and juggled black and white, . . . imposed a white terror. . . ." With this declaration and his symbolic endorsement of the organization of Red Guards, Mao served notice that the issues between himself and Liu, Deng, et al. had come to a head and would be settled by a test of power. Disputes that had rankled since 1956, sores that had festered, irritated repeatedly for fully a decade, now burst wide open. And China plunged into nearly three years of strife.

Why so serious a conflict, and why then? Surely Mao's deepest beliefs and his most characteristic political methods were fully engaged in 1966. War, he had once said, is politics with bloodshed, while politics is war without bloodshed. Too much of his life had been spent in war for him not to see war and politics as intertwined, but of course this was no less true of Liu and Deng. The difference is that Mao raised the war–politics link to the level of philosophy and that something in his personality and temperament relished combat: "Marxism is a wrangling *ism*, dealing as it does with contradictions and struggles," he wrote. "Contradictions are always present, and where there are contradictions there are struggles." Mao noted an occasion in Moscow when, in a dispute with the Russians, Zhou Enlai "did not stand on ceremony and

During the GPCR, a cult of Mao expressed itself in mass publication of his "sayings," countless buttons and posters, tributes, and giant statues such as this one in Xi'an. © *Marc Riboud*

took them on, and consequently they kicked up a row. This is good, straightening things out face to face." Edgar Snow once asked Mao if he preferred the sedentary life of leader of the People's Republic or the roving life of combat. Mao's reply: "I prefer the military life. My bowels never worked better than during the battle of Changsha."

As both military and political leader, Mao's cardinal principle was to fight at a time and place of his own choosing, to avoid battle when the risks of losing were highest, and to seek battle when the chances of winning were greatest. But it is not at all clear that in 1966 he weighed the risks and chances as coolly and objectively as he had in earlier years of war. His pride had been bruised repeatedly since the party rewrote its constitution in 1956, demoted him in 1958, and sniped at him ever since. A spate of articles mocked and ridiculed him. One prominent writer turned out 153 articles within eighteen months in which he alluded to the GLF as building a castle in the air and told of a victim of mental illness who, if not cured in time, "will become an idiot." The author prescribed full rest, silence, and inaction for the victim. Meanwhile, a pamphlet of Liu's, originally lectures Liu had given in 1938–1939, had been serialized in the party newspaper in 1962 and then republished, selling some fifteen million copies in the next four years. Not only was this a far greater number than any of Mao's writings had sold up to then, but Liu began to be called Chairman and have his portrait hung alongside Mao's. Finally, a play satirizing Mao's dismissal of the defense minister in 1959 reopened that old wound.

In brief, personal grievances, political rivalries, philosophical differences, and sharp disagreements about fundamental matters of economic and social policy fused with international issues to make a deadly brew. Even economic recovery, which by 1965 had shown remarkable results—China was by then self-sufficient in crude oil and petroleum products, and it had increased GNP by 23.6 percent and grain production by 24.3 percent over 1960—may have reassured Mao that he could pursue his political goals without causing an economic catastrophe. The final imponderable element in the mix was the role of Jiang Qing, Mao's wife, who began in these years to be active in politics. Against Mao's wishes—she had been ill, and he warned her that "the struggle's too acute"—she had come to the 1959 meeting where he clashed with the defense minister. Later he began to assign her tasks such as the drafting of policy statements on the arts. By 1961 she was publishing articles of her own, and three years later she started a campaign against old-fashioned plays and operas. In 1964 she also spoke at the biggest opera festival ever held in China and did so at the invitation of Premier Zhou Enlai. All of this put her in a position to settle old scores, and it is plain that she felt she had many to settle. As an American scholar to whom Jiang Qing gave a series of interviews observed, she "sharply remembered . . . her enemies, the cultural commissars who, she was convinced, had thwarted her political career for thirty years." To illustrate the depths to which political rivalries were sinking in the early 1960s, Jiang Qing and Liu Shaoqi's wife even feuded about whose picture received more prominent display in the party newspaper. By this time, in other words, no issue was too small to aggravate what had become a gaping wound in the party's vital organs.

The issue that remains most difficult to pin down is the question of how much the GPCR was provoked by international events. Here we must consider both the presence of rapidly increasing U.S. military power in Vietnam (justified in Washington by ominous statements about the supposed threat to American interests posed by Chinese expansionism and aggressiveness) and Mao's growing preoccupation (it is not too much to say obsession) with the unraveling of socialism in the Soviet Union. However sure or unsure the Chinese were about American intentions (some reports insist that the United States and China came to a quiet but clear understanding that reduced real tension to a minimum), several military engagements did occur between Americans and Chinese. They were less sure about the Russians' intentions (especially because of persistent reports that the Soviets were considering destroying China's nuclear plants), and Mao was most of all concerned that the infection of Soviet revisionism could spread to China. To him, events in Yugoslavia as well as in the Soviet Union proved that a restoration of capitalism was possible in countries that had had successful socialist revolutions, and the economic recovery policies of Liu and Deng were creating the same danger in China. While Mao deeply desired economic development, he had come to feel that the social and political price being paid was too high. To prevent the appearance in China of Soviet-style revisionism was to Mao more than a matter of politics or economics. It was a moral crusade, a purification. This explains the name of his campaign in the early 1960s, the "Four Clean-ups," and the intensity of that campaign—"This war is a nationwide revolutionary movement, and we must make war as we did during the War of Liberation"—and of the GPCR, intended to "touch people to their very souls."

The GPCR is the clearest illustration of how China's quest for modernization was caught up in and, at least temporarily, greatly overshadowed by political power struggles. Some analysts hold that modernization was virtually sidetracked and possibly even derailed by political factionalism, that the GPCR wrecked the Chinese economy and educational system, and that it set back scientific progress by a generation or more. The newly chosen (1981) chairman of the CCP, Hu Yaobang, has called the entire decade of 1966–1976 "a period of catastrophe. There was nothing correct or positive about those ten years. The whole thing was negative." Mao Zedong himself, unquestionably the initiator of the GPCR, traveled the country for three months at the height of it and returned dismayed. "I think this is a civil war," he told Zhou Enlai, and within a few weeks he was ready to call a halt. Indeed, this was not the first time that he tried and failed to slow or stop what he had begun, and his failure tells us much about this enormously complex movement.

The GPCR was much more than a power struggle. Its name is not altogether misleading—in its origins it was a revolutionary movement aimed at creating a "proletarian culture," not only at class struggle. More than three years earlier, in May 1963, Mao had called for *three* great revolutionary movements—struggles for production and scientific experiment as well as class struggle—in order to build "a mighty socialist country." When he recommended in August 1964 that college students, faculty, and administrators spend five months working in factories and five in rural areas, he referred specifically to those in liberal arts and exempted those in the sciences. Two years later his charter for the GPCR called for developing China's production forces and added that "any idea of counterposing the great Cultural Revolution against the development of production is incorrect." His method for increasing productivity was not Liu Shaoqi's, but he was equally serious about doing it. The point was demonstrated in many instances during the GPCR when specialists such as nuclear physicists and oil technicians were generally allowed to remain outside the political arena.

When Mao reentered that arena in 1965–1966 he had not yet decided that the fight would require force: "Four days after my arrival in Beijing [July 18, 1966], I was still inclined to preserve the existing order of things." The GPCR charter, issued three weeks later, called for debates and an effort to "persuade through reasoning," specifically excluding coercion or force and providing for protection of the minority "because sometimes the truth is with the minority." (Having only lately been in the minority, and perhaps not even yet clearly in the majority,

Mao may not have been disinterested here.) Four and one-half months later Mao told his comrades they "must make allowances for other people's mistakes and let them get on with the revolution. . . . We must not get rid of Liu Shaoqi by a stroke of the pen. They [Liu and others] have committed mistakes, but let them correct themselves!" Five months later Mao was almost defending Liu and Deng against what he saw as excessive criticism by his allies, the Shanghai radicals who had given him crucial support in his comeback a year earlier. Finally, in a compromise with his own supporters, Mao agreed to let the political struggle focus on Liu. It ended with Liu expelled from the party in disgrace and, shabbily mistreated, dying in November 1969 after a siege of pneumonia aggravated by diabetes. Deng survived, but he was cast into political oblivion.

The entire movement very quickly outran everyone's control and expectations. "Nobody foresaw this kind of fighting," Mao said in 1968. Originally, he had planned to suspend classes for only half a year, but then the suspension was extended to one, two, and three years. Repeated attempts to get students back to school failed. The genie was out of the bottle. Factions and subfactions multiplied everywhere —among students, workers, even soldiers. Bewildered by the flood of instructions and wall posters, people in schools and workplaces all across the country decided, as one student put it, that "the safest course was to attack the most visible targets." In this case it was teachers, "especially those who had a known bad class background."

From the most visible targets the attacks soon turned to others. Students took "long marches" to drink at the wells of revolutionary heroism such as Yan'an and to carry the message of the GPCR to the distant countryside. Red Guards rampaged through cities and towns on search-and-destroy missions against signs of feudal or bourgeois decadence. Workers mobilized against factory managers and party cadres. Everywhere there were outbursts against established authority. Indeed, what is astonishing and significant about the GPCR is how rapidly and how far it spread and how passionately it erupted. In contrast to the Hundred Flowers campaign of 1956–1957, when it took months of cajoling to bring a relatively small number of intellectuals to speak their minds, the GPCR brought millions into action virtually overnight. What it shows is that Mao had touched a national nerve. So massive a response by so many people can only mean that a great many nerves had become exposed over the years. A great many grievances had accumulated.

Mao saw some of them clearly. As party members, he told his comrades, they had to be out among the people and not confined to their offices. Some eight years earlier he had criticized the Politburo for becoming "a voting machine," like the United Nations. His method against its paper-pushing was "passive resistance. . . . For two years I have not read your documents and I do not expect to read them this year either." In 1966 he elaborated: "Sitting in offices listening to reports is no good. . . . Nobody is willing to go to the lower levels, to go to the trouble spots, to use his own eyes. You will not go and see; you are preoccupied every day by routine business. You have no real understanding. How can you guide anything?" They knew he meant they were too tied to their comforts and privileges: "It doesn't do to live a life of sofas and electric fans," one acknowledged.

Ample testimony of participants in the GPCR reveals popular resentment against elite privileges and their abuse—special shops filled with goods that for the masses were in short supply, special boarding schools (known as "little treasure pagodas") for cadres' children, access to better colleges and job opportunities, avoidance of service in the countryside, abuse of authority. Among students, for example, the outlook on the eve of the GPCR was exceedingly bleak. Many more graduated from middle school (equivalent to American high school) than could be placed in universities. Job opportunities, especially in cities, were scarce and highly competitive. While children of high cadres were placed in universities or good jobs, others in growing numbers were being sent to the countryside and realizing it could be for life. As a result, by 1965 the schools were tinderboxes waiting to be ignited.

This is not to say that the students' complaints received sympathy from the chairman. Their desire for university education or city jobs was precisely, in fact, the kind of bourgeois self-seeking that the GPCR was aimed against. Work as a farmer for a year and then in industry for two, he told a Red Guard: "That's real college education. The real universities are the factories and rural areas." Mao deftly turned the students' discontent against bureaucrats and other elites, appealing to the idealism of the young as well as to their ambition, boredom, and desire for purposeful lives. The Ministry of Public Health ignores the masses of peasants, he said, "so why not change its name to the Ministry of Urban Health, the Ministry of Gentlemen's Health, or even to the Ministry of Urban Gentlemen's Health?" For Mao, it was crucial to narrow the Three Great Differences, and sending trained people to the countryside was half the solution. The other half was to provide more education and health care in the countryside, and to recruit from the less privileged, especially in the rural areas, for advanced training in the cities.

When Mao attacked bureaucracy and bourgeois values he had in mind introducing experiments of this kind, to allow rigid lines between students and workers, peasants and cadres, specialists and manual workers to loosen and finally to disappear. A proletarian culture would be one that broke down hierarchies of all kinds, one in which each person's motive would be to "serve the people," not oneself. Mao had in mind precisely Marx's goals of *The Communist Manifesto*: "Combination of agriculture with manufacturing industries; and gradual abolition of the distinction between town and country. . . . Combination of education with industrial production, etc."

To the dissatisfied in 1965–1966 it was enough to be loosening structures of authority and privilege and to be given the opportunity to strike directly at whatever representatives of authority and privilege were closest to hand. For some, no doubt it was also an opportunity to indulge their "spirit of adventure," as some foreign witnesses observed. Life in China was drab, and the opportunities for travel and excitement few. The GPCR provided some relief. Others surely exploited the situation for short-run personal gain or to avenge real or imagined slights. But so much strife over so long a period is not explicable only in those terms. Deeper dissatisfactions were at work, deep enough to produce more than two years of turmoil that could be brought to a close late in 1968 only after direct intervention by the army and strenuous efforts to restore order by Mao, Zhou Enlai, and other leaders. By then the destruction had been incalculable, the human cost in killings, exile, flight, and suicides still beyond anyone's ability to estimate. The GPCR had touched China to its soul, but not in the way Mao intended.

Not the least of the victims were the CCP and the government. Countless cadres and officials were scattered among reeducation centers and work camps. Morale of those remaining was at an all-time low. Doggedly, the leadership set itself to repair the damage, to rebuild the party and the administrative system. Schools reopened, but on a new basis—now one's class background and political record counted for at least as much as one's academic record. No one could hope to enter college who had not done physical labor and shown the proper political activism. Everywhere there were "revolutionary committees," a new administrative device intended to represent the major groups in Chinese society but, as of 1968–1969, heavily dominated by the military. Brief experiments with institutions modeled on the Paris Commune never were allowed to spread or develop. Mao's populist side very quickly was overtaken by his Leninist side, and the task of rebuilding the shattered party received increasingly high priority. In this unpromising atmosphere the violent phase of the GPCR subsided and its period of experimentation began.

THE GPCR, PHASE TWO, 1969–1976

A former cadre in Beijing, having recounted in detail his harrowing experiences during the GPCR, concluded by asking, "What did it really accomplish? Was it worth it?" In view of what he had just described, and since he had left China and fled to Hong Kong by 1976, one expected a sharply negative answer. Instead, he declared, "Yes, on balance I suppose it was worth it, . . . the Cultural Revolution at our bureau did have its good results, although the cost was high. . . ." The cost was indeed high, and how does one measure if it was worth it?

People who had fought each other bitterly for two years or more now resumed work or studies side by side. Many were bitter: "It turned out that we were all puppets being manipulated by others," said one disillusioned young cadre who surely spoke for vast numbers. "How many of us sit quietly with revenge burning inside our hearts, wanting to settle old scores?" The answer, clearly, was a great many, and before another decade passed some would have a chance to settle those scores. In the meantime work went forward and the country pulled itself together once again, in yet another remarkable recovery.

Once again, too, international troubles coincided with domestic turmoil to bring about a fundamental shift in China's course. In the summer of 1968 the Soviet Union invaded Czechoslovakia, announcing the Brezhnev Doctrine, by which Moscow claimed the right to intervene wherever it considered socialism to be endangered. Since tension and Soviet troop presence along the Chinese-Russian frontier were also increasing, and since the Soviets had long considered that the Chinese were turncoats in the socialist world, there was reason for China to worry. With a huge U.S. army still engaged in Vietnam and Chinese-American relations still icy, China had been at odds with the two major world powers for years. A policy of self-reliance had been unavoidable since 1960, but now that a crisis was brewing China had to gather itself for a possible confrontation. One soon came, as fighting broke out with the Russians along the northeastern frontier in the spring of 1969. After about two weeks talks began between the Russians and Chinese, and they have continued sporadically ever since, with little concrete result except the expansion of trade. The two countries continued to eye each other warily and with deep mutual suspicion. This confrontation made it all the more urgent that China restore internal order, and it reopened debate in China about how to handle its international relations, which had been largely neglected for the preceding three years. From 1969 to 1971 this debate sharpened, with momentous consequences for China's domestic and foreign policies. But in the spring of 1969 China was still giving higher priority to its domestic affairs.

A CCP Congress in 1969, the first to be held since 1956, signaled one paradoxical result of the GPCR—a vast turnover in leadership combined with restoration of the old structure. The new leadership came largely from the army. About 40 percent of the new central committee were military men, and Lin Biao was officially designated as Mao's successor. Although many from peasant and worker as well as military backgrounds were brought into lower levels of the party, its structure and principles and the outlook of its leaders were scarcely changed. Considering how much bad blood had accumulated, this ensured that many of the same political problems that had marred the preceding decade would arise again. Many, but not all. For as the young cadre from Beijing noted (and he spoke for many), work in his office improved during the GPCR, and not only in its technical efficiency: "The top cadres became a little less arrogant, and were more concerned about their relationship to the rest of us working in the bureau." Whether this would last and whether it was a change in substance as well as style were the big questions.

A second paradox has been neatly summarized by Maurice Meisner: Although the GPCR was an overwhelmingly urban movement, the students and workers and intellectuals who were most involved in it got the least out of it. Intellectuals and students suffered exile to physical labor in remote places, while the closing of schools created what has come to be called a "lost generation." Meanwhile, as Meisner says, most of the benefits went to "the masses of poor peasants who had been on the political sidelines." Following a principle he had articulated at least as early as 1927 and practiced many times since, Mao was willing to exceed proper limits in order to right a wrong. The countryside had long lagged behind the cities. The GPCR reforms were now to close the gap.

To some extent they did, but the record is mixed. Education, which for decades had been criticized by reformers for its preoccupation with arts, letters, and remote antiquity and its indifference to problems of food production and other current matters of life and death to millions of people, was for a time delivered almost entirely into the hands of the untrained. As the GPCR wound to an end, schools which had been closed during the height of it reopened under the complete control of workers and poor and lower-middle peasants. In cities, factories ran the schools near them; big factories ran secondary schools, and medium and small factories ran primary schools. In the countryside, peasants ran the schools. These "bare-foot teachers," as they were called, included old farmers, educated youth, and demobilized PLA soldiers. They taught not only the children but also former professional teachers. Those teachers were expected to "be pupils before they become teachers" and were sent to live, labor, learn, and "combat self-interest and repudiate revisionism" under the peasants' tutelage. Schools increasingly became adjunct to factories and farms. Students did part-time work and spent less time than formerly in classrooms and libraries. Those high school graduates who went on to college were expected first to spend three years doing manual labor.

In 1970, as many universities reopened doors that had been closed for more than four years, some concessions were offered to professional teachers, but they were still criticized for old failings. Too many, it was charged, clung to familiar routine, avoided political activity, divorced theory from practice, and "worship things foreign."* To cure these ills universities were reorganized according to a "three-in-one" system that combined teaching, research, and production. At Tsinghua University, which was intended to be a model for others, several factories were established to manufacture goods that were urgently needed by industry and the military, the production of which also met teaching and research needs. Students were recruited from experienced and activist workers, peasants, soldiers, and cadres, whose knowledge of class struggle and production presumably enabled them to teach teachers as well as learn from them.

---

* These worshippers, interestingly enough, were said to be "obsessed with the slavish comprador ideology of trailing behind at a snail's pace." This phrase recalls a famous turning point in Communist history, for in the late 1920s Bukharin opposed Stalin's collectivization scheme with the view that the peasants should "enrich themselves" and the Soviet Union should "creep at a snail's pace" to socialism. Stalin, however, insisted on amalgamating farms in order to reach socialism as quickly as possible.

The new school systems found and developed new talent to an impressive extent. Everywhere in China one now encounters talented people of poor, often rural, background who, as a result of the GPCR, received educational opportunities that they would almost surely not have received otherwise. They moved into jobs that peasant children would not have dreamed of occupying a few years earlier—teaching English at universities, for example. One also encounters intellectuals who admit they profited from experiencing the hard life of the countryside. Against these benefits, to the individuals and families concerned and to the country as a whole, must be weighed the cost of further politicization of the school system and intellectual life, the damage done to older intellectuals in the name of proletarian democracy, the heavy cost to urban schools (and particularly to the "lost generation" that missed four years or more of schooling), and indeed the waste and failures in rural education.

The GPCR school reforms lasted no more than about seven years, hardly enough to provide a fair test for so radical a departure from all preceding education. In a country where funds are lacking and educated people are a scarce and precious resource, educational policy is of crucial importance and inevitably highly controversial. Inevitably too, it became embroiled in politics, and when the political winds shifted again in 1976–1977, so did educational policy. A clear balance sheet cannot be drawn up for so radical and short-lived an experiment. All that can be said is that it surely left a mark on Chinese life by bringing fresh blood into every corner of it but also by adding another dimension to political struggle. GPCR educational experiments also illustrate the persistence of the rural-urban gap in Chinese life and the continuing difficulty of finding an equitable way to close it.

Almost exactly the same things might be said about health care. Experiments such as the training of "barefoot doctors," paramedics assigned to provide basic health care for the most common ailments and injuries, were only one GPCR innovation in medicine. The "bare-foot doctors" in the country and the "workers' doctors" in the city received formal medical training for three months and then divided their time between the practice of relatively easy medicine under the supervision of hospital personnel and their former occupation. They later received advanced medical training for three more months. This training program provided them with enough knowledge to treat routine ailments. More serious medical problems were handled by the commune hospital, and the most difficult by the city hospital. This system was widely praised by foreign observers in the 1970s, but its results cannot be precisely tabulated. Furthermore, health policy did not shift as sharply as educational policy after 1976. "Barefoot doctors" were no longer glorified, but they and the general policy of extending basic health care to the countryside and to neglected groups in the urban population were not totally rejected. On balance it is clear that in this area the GPCR made a lasting contribution, although its weight cannot be measured precisely.

Somewhat more measurable is the economic record, where one GPCR priority, rural industry, is of particular interest and importance. In general, the economy during the GPCR offers a remarkable contrast to political life and to other spheres of major conflict such as education and health care. Continuity and order were maintained to a much higher degree in economic matters. Damage to the economy during the GPCR was vastly less than the damage of 1959–1961. Industrial production, for example, dropped between 13 and 16 percent in 1967 but began to climb again in 1968; in 1969 it rose well beyond the pre-GPCR peak of 1966, then jumped 20 percent in 1970 and substantial amounts every year after that. Even at the height of the GPCR, damage to industrial machinery was slight and capacity continued to expand.

In agriculture the mistakes of 1958–1959 were carefully avoided. Private plots were still allowed, and basic decisions about production and organization of work were left to teams and brigades. Use of chemical fertilizers and machinery continued to expand. Grain production remained well above the previous peak year of 1958 and climbed in every year except 1978. Critics of the GPCR have charged that its agricultural policy put too heavy a stress on grain production, resulting in serious shortages of other farm products. This charge may have merit, but it remains to be proved. Agriculture remained a serious problem —from 1964–1974 the average annual increase in grain production was less than 3 percent and sizable grain imports continued—but the situation was not made significantly worse by the GPCR.

Indeed, farm production was the central concern of GPCR economic policy. Industry was to develop, but in a way that served the agricultural sector. Special attention was paid to such industries as electric power, chemical fertilizer, and farm machinery. "Mechanization," Mao said, "is the fundamental solution in agriculture." But given China's shortages of transportation, fuel, and capital, the solution was more easily described than reached.

One important experiment, with origins going back to the GLF

A small power station in rural Hunan, built in 1959. It powers thirty-one pumping machines that can water nearly 3000 hectares (about 7400 acres) of land. *China Photo Service / Eastfoto*

and which was revived in a much more systematic way during the GPCR, was the development of small-scale industries in rural areas, near or in small cities, and in larger cities. Rural industrialization, which includes small industry in the countryside and also in smaller towns and cities up to about 20,000 population, was part of a broad strategy to promote industrialization without greater urbanization, to diversify industry, and to develop the countryside in an integrated manner. The key was to establish industries that used primarily local materials to meet local demands, thus reducing transportation costs and saving resources. The major rural industries were chemical fertilizer, cement, farm tools and machinery, hydroelectric power, iron and steel, coal, iron ore, limestone and other minerals, food processing, oil pressing, cotton ginning, canning, textile and shoe manufacturing, household goods, and farm machinery repair shops. Some, such as certain chemical fertilizer manufacturing, were developed on an interim basis, pending construction or import of more cost-efficient larger plants. But in most cases the rural industries were envisioned as a long-range and growing part of the Chinese economy. In addition to the advantages already mentioned, rural plants came into production more quickly than larger urban plants, they absorbed surplus labor displaced by farm mechanization, they served as an important training ground for peasants who were learning new skills (administrative and organizational as well as technical) that could later be employed in other areas, and they spread innovations and general technical knowledge more broadly through the country, thereby breaking down the three great differences.

The rural industrial enterprises were established at three levels—county, commune, and brigade. Some of the plants, especially at the county level, were quite large, but even the largest rarely employed more than several hundred workers. Still, since the total number of rural industries was estimated in the mid-1970s to be about a half million or more, total employment in them may have amounted to half of China's employment in manufacturing and mining. In some industries the growth was remarkable. Small cement plants in rural areas grew from 200 in 1965 to 2,800 in 1973, increasing production from about 5 million tons to 19 million, about half of China's total. In 1965 small rural plants were producing 12 percent of China's nitrogen fertilizer; in 1973, 54 percent. Such rural industrialization reflects a basic continuity of policy from the time of the GLF to the present, with continuing experiment, adaptation, and modification. Although the experiment is not unique to China (many developing countries advocate similar policies), numerous rural industries were based on traditional village crafts which, taken together with the unique organizational structures, leadership, and technology that the Chinese brought to the experiment, constituted a unique Chinese success in carrying the policy out. One example the author encountered was the Chinese development of biogas from agricultural wastes, an ingeniously created energy source that was the envy of technicians from other third-world countries.

Rural industrialization suited well the Chinese concern to adapt modernization to their own needs, conditions, and resources and, in a period of minimal foreign contact, to promote national self-reliance. It also complemented the GPCR policies of encouraging local self-sufficiency and reducing centralization in government. To carry out these policies the work force in central ministries was sharply reduced, and many urban cadres were sent to the countryside. Models of self-sufficiency were hailed throughout the country and held up for all to emulate. The most famous were the Dazhai brigade in Shanxi province, the model for agriculture, and Daqing oil field in Heilongjiang, the model for industry. In both cases, it was said, dedicated and selfless people had overcome staggering obstacles to boost production and to move rapidly toward socialism. At the height of the GPCR it was claimed that between 1949 and 1967 Dazhai brigade had raised its yields more than ninefold, creating in the process "a new system of labor management" and a new socialist outlook. Similarly it was claimed that Daqing had developed revolutionary factory management in which workers shared authority with technicians and cadres, the so-called "three-way combination" that also traced its origins to the GLF and, indeed, in principle went back to Yan'an days.

Although the Dazhai model was disavowed and discredited in 1980–1981, the Dazhai emulation campaign remains a vivid example of GPCR spirit applied to agricultural development. This spirit was essentially a high optimism that persistent human effort, guided by correct political ideas, could overcome any obstacles in nature. The campaign also illustrates the oddly contradictory character of the GPCR, which could uphold the Dazhai spirit as a model for all of Chinese agriculture and yet propose that mechanization was the only solution for agricultural backwardness and that rural industrialization suited to each locality's peculiar needs and conditions was a fundamental part of that solution. In 1970 the top party leadership would criticize mechanical imitation of Dazhai, but six years later the campaign to

Farmers in Guangxi, 1965. © Marc Riboud

study Dazhai was continuing and even growing. Only in 1980 was Dazhai denounced.

Daqing, on the other hand, represents an industrial order in which experiment has continued and in which the issues are still lively. Key principles included coordinating food production and sideline occupations with industry to make the oil field self-sufficient, decentralization—Daqing is divided into regions with a central town of about five hundred households and small villages of about one hundred families each—and worker participation in decisions, including election of basic-level cadres. By 1972–1973 the effort to give veteran workers an equal voice in planning production and organizing work was slackening, and the requirement that cadres participate in labor just as workers participate in management was also losing force. The strict division of labor among technicians, cadres, and workers, a major target of GPCR attacks, steadily reappeared. The Daqing model came to include the "four stricts": strict discipline, strict behavior, strict organization, and strict demands. On the Leninist scale of democratic centralism, centralism was gaining weight as democracy lost. But the balance between the two kept changing. The recentralization of the early 1970s swung back to decentralization after 1977 and was again an issue by 1980.

In brief, despite the turmoil in many major cities, economic production escaped major damage during the GPCR. Turbulence was concentrated in the schools and streets and among school populations. Workers also participated, but much more selectively and briefly, and peasants scarcely at all. The GPCR was intense and involved many tens of millions, but it directly and deeply affected only a part and possibly even a minority of China's huge population.

In the early 1970s economic policy once more became embroiled in political factionalism and yet another major political crisis. The most visible expression of the crisis was a bizarre plot organized by Lin Biao and other military leaders in September 1971 to assassinate Mao. It ended with Lin's flight and death in an airplane crash and the arrest or dismissal of more than one hundred generals, thirty-five high party officials in the provinces, fifteen Central Committee members and half the members of the Politburo. Many issues were involved. Lin himself is said to have objected to the steady retreat from original GPCR principles and to Mao's unwillingness to consent to Lin stepping into the position of chief of state, left vacant by Liu Shaoqi's purge. Lin and many of his followers surely objected to erosion of the military's role in government by the rebuilding of the party, especially by the rehabilitation of cadres who had been criticized during the GPCR and the seeming return to pre-GPCR organizational principles and methods. As one GPCR supporter put it, watching the return of pre-1966 practices and personnel, "What did we go through all of that for, to change a few street names?"*

Finally, a central issue emerged in foreign relations. It is likely that China's willingness to begin serious negotiations with the United States (first suggested late in 1970), followed by carefully arranged visits of Americans to China, infuriated Lin and many others. In the spring of 1971 an American Ping-Pong team and accompanying journalists arrived. In the summer, Secretary of State Henry Kissinger came, paving the way for the president of the United States to arrive the following February. Occurring in the midst of the Vietnam War, these visits added betrayal of people's war to betrayal of the GPCR. For Lin it was too much to swallow, no matter how deep his loyalty to Mao.

Thus another decades-old bond dissolved in political warfare, and again factionalism swept China. As had happened in the case of Liu Shaoqi, Lin Biao was soon denounced as a renegade whose crimes went back forty years. For the rest of 1971, all of 1972, and into 1973, a campaign to criticize Lin as an "ultraleftist" was carried out nationwide. Later it was reversed and Lin was attacked together with the "ultra-Right." Even Zhou Enlai joined the chorus and went so far as to link Lin with Liu. Later still Lin was linked with Confucius, a device for indirectly criticizing Zhou (!), and finally with the ultra-Left yet again. Explaining all of this at the regular political discussion meetings in factories, universities, neighborhood associations, and production teams taxed the ingenuity of the most loyal and intellectually nimble party activists.

Rehabilitation of GPCR victims reached a new peak in the spring of 1973, when Deng Xiaoping made his reappearance. (Some GPCR supporters quietly noted that Deng had spent some time in the countryside tending water buffaloes and commented that this was the first real contact he had had with rural society in a long time; they expressed the wish that he had learned something from the experience.) Deng's return was arranged by Zhou Enlai, who was seventy-six, ailing,

---

* A common practice during the GPCR was to change old names of streets, especially those named after foreigners (e.g., Russian scientists) or "feudal" names, to revolutionary names (e.g., "East is Red Street," "Anti-imperialist Road").

and wanted his help. Even Mao acknowledged Deng's ability—"a very clever man and material which should be sought," Mao said, like cotton outside but "like a steel needle inside." To Jiang Qing, however, Deng was "an international capitalist agent and a traitor."

Tension increased rapidly between returning cadres such as Deng and GPCR supporters, headed by the Shanghai radicals such as Jiang Qing. A temporary compromise was reached in time for a party congress to be held, the tenth, in August 1973. It was a shorter and more secret one than usual, notable for the astonishing rise of the youngest leader of the Shanghai radicals, the thirty-six-year-old Wang Hongwen, to the third highest position in the party. GPCR themes were now heard again. New members of the Politburo included the party secretary of Dazhai brigade and a nationally famous model engineer-worker. Just before the congress the party newspaper published a note written by a student who had been in the countryside for five years and had become head of a production team. His note, scribbled on a nearly blank university entrance examination, explained that he had been working too hard to study and that he had "no respect for the bookworms who for many years have been taking it easy and have done nothing useful." Party publications thereupon reopened this most controversial issue of the GPCR, charging that the shift back to academic criteria for college entrance had gone too far and demanding a return to more emphasis on work experience and political commitment. Not coincidentally, veiled criticism of Zhou Enlai and Deng Xiaoping soon appeared, criticism of foreign culture and "slavish" imitation increased, and political campaigns stressed class struggle and the dictatorship of the proletariat.

At the National People's Congress in January 1975 Zhou carefully pointed out that revolution is a "powerful engine" for developing production, implying that political movements were a means to economic objectives. For the economic goals he recalled what he and Mao had said a decade earlier, when they envisioned creating "an independent and relatively comprehensive industrial and economic system" by 1980, and then going on to a second stage, "the comprehensive modernization of agriculture, industry, national defence and science and technology before the end of the century, so that our national economy will be advancing in the front ranks of the world." These modernization goals would be given top priority in another few years, but as of 1975 Zhou had to give at least equal weight to the "struggle between two lines." In so doing he not only praised "the victories of the GPCR" but went so far as to say that China's "primary task is to continue to broaden, deepen and persevere in the movement to criticize Lin Biao and Confucius." This can be interpreted as a form of self-criticism on Zhou's part or as a clever device to disarm or compromise with his opponents. In any case it shows clearly that sharp internal political struggle was being waged throughout this period.

When Zhou died in January 1976 it was widely expected that Deng would succeed him as premier, but instead Mao chose another newly risen (1973) Politburo member, Hua Guofeng. Hua had gained national attention in October 1975 at the First National Conference on Learning from Dazhai in Agriculture. His speech there launched a nationwide campaign to build Dazhai-type counties, and it also earned for Hua impeccable GPCR and "self-reliance" credentials. He then moved swiftly to take maximum advantage of Mao's endorsement (pictures of Hua appeared next to Mao's all across the country in a remarkably short period of time). Deng was promptly attacked again in language almost identical to that used nine years earlier ("the arch unrepentant capitalist-roader in the Party") and was again cast into political limbo. Deng's critics did not pounce directly on his call to put an end to the GPCR (he had adroitly quoted Mao), but he had also been indiscreet enough to say China should import "the latest and the best equipment from foreign countries." Here Deng might also have quoted Mao ("let foreign things serve China") and pointed to the $2.6 billion in foreign industrial purchases that Zhou had engineered between 1972 and 1975, but if he did, it did not help. Perhaps this issue was hotter than the GPCR, and he dared not raise it. Following Deng's advice, said one opponent, would undermine Chinese independence and self-reliance and reduce China to "an appendage" of imperialism. Soon the attack was broadened to include his alleged call to do "everything for modernization." This was denounced as "sinister revisionist junk." Two years later it would be national policy, but in 1975 it was subversive.

Between 1975 and 1977 came a great watershed in Chinese Communist history. In China there is an ancient tradition that unusual phenomena in nature portend momentous events on earth. Was it ominous that a meteorite shower (described in the Chinese press as "something unusual in world history") fell on the northeast on March 8, 1976? And that two strong earthquakes occurred in Yunnan on May 29, and a massive earthquake virtually wiped out the large industrial city of Tanghsan two months later? Six weeks after the Tangshan earthquake, Mao Zedong died. With startling speed the political struggle moved to a new level of intensity. Barely a month after Mao's death Hua arrested

Jiang Qing, Wang Hongwen, and two other Shanghai radicals who were branded a "gang of four" and soon expelled from the party. For reasons that are not clear, although it may be assumed that Hua needed the help of Deng and his supporters to purge the Shanghai radicals, Deng Xiaoping was restored to all of his former posts. With these events the GPCR was officially declared to have ended. Within the first ten months of 1976 both Zhou Enlai and Mao Zedong (and also Zhu De) had died, and another palace coup had occurred. An era had closed.

Not long before these last events, a small group of American visitors and their Chinese hosts huddled around a small kerosene stove in a cold university dormitory room. For the visitors it was a rare opportunity, on their otherwise mostly guided tour, to meet informally with a small group of students and spend an entire evening in freewheeling discussion. The students turned out to be older than the visitors expected, ranging in age from twenty-two to twenty-nine and averaging about twenty-six or twenty-seven. All had done extensive work in farms and factories. One was leader of a production brigade. Most were from peasant or worker families, but there were also some from intellectual and cadre backgrounds. Two were party members. The visitors, who had become accustomed during their tour to hearing many stock phrases and slogans from "responsible persons" who were used to dealing with foreign tourists, were surprised at the freshness and vitality of the students. Heated disagreements broke out among them as they attempted to deal directly with a wide range of questions, often provocative and controversial, posed by the visitors. But the disagreements, however sharp, were friendly and even affectionate. What came through most to the visitors was the liveliness of discussion about China, the wealth of detailed firsthand knowledge the students brought to the discussion of Chinese political and economic affairs, and the candor with which they addressed problems. The visitors, all of whom were politically very active in the United States, a bit older than the Chinese students, and probably better informed on public affairs in the United States than the average American, agreed that they could not have responded to the students' questions about the United States in comparable depth. In any case, this issue did not arise, since the students' questions about the United States were limited almost entirely to its prospects for revolution and to the reasons for the failure of American protest movements in the 1960s to develop into a genuine revolutionary movement. Their knowledge of the United States seemed extremely limited, their interests surprisingly narrow, and their views governed by dogma and a mystique of revolution.

This incident reveals much about the different sides of the GPCR. It brought together people of different backgrounds, but with a heavy emphasis on peasants and workers and practical experience, in a dedicated effort to accelerate social change, to break down hierarchies of many kinds—especially bureaucratic ones but also the old hierarchies in which the conventionally educated dominated those with little or no formal education, older dominated younger, men dominated women, the city dominated the countryside—and to create a new spirit of striving and common purpose comparable to the Yan'an years. Mystiques of the long march, the anti-Japanese struggle, and the social movements that overturned places like Stone Wall Village grew out of hard experience and bitter struggle during the GPCR. Intellectuals suffered hardships that were new to them, but they also gained a firsthand introduction to the lives of the vast majority of the population. For some, the experience meant a new dedication to putting aside self-seeking "bourgeois attitudes," serving the people, giving more opportunities to those who had not received their share, and working to wipe out the old customs ("feudalism") that still blocked China's progress. The key seemed to be once again to "open doors" to the masses, reach out to them, and activate them, to rouse people from passivity and draw on the talent and energy stored in working people.

In attempting to open doors of this kind, however, the GPCR closed others, especially to the outside world. Indeed, its partisans went to absurd lengths, attacking not only individuals who had received education abroad and were thereby judged to be dangerously contaminated but even people who had relatives abroad with whom they had little or no contact. No wisdom could be found abroad. All wisdom was sought in the masses, in work and political struggle, and in the thought of Chairman Mao.

Like most sizable movements in human affairs the GPCR was not an integrated and consistent movement. It went through phases, had many different facets, and was in the end profoundly contradictory. It stood for radical change, especially the elimination of certain "bourgeois" and "feudal" features of Chinese life, but it left virtually untouched the prototypically bourgeois private plots, free markets, and even some material incentive and bonus plans. It stood for activism and the forging of a new mass unity, but it fostered division, class antagonism, and finally even passivity. For it proclaimed its own orthodoxy, which always has a double effect. Orthodoxy, as the history of both religion and politics everywhere in the world shows, leads on the one hand to sectarianism and on the other to silence. It challenges some and cows others.

Much of this was not unique to the GPCR. Continuities between the GPCR and every period of Chinese history are evident, from the orthodoxies and bureaucratism of traditional times to the Mao cult and antibureaucratism of the 1940s, the suspicion of Westernized intellectuals in the 1950s, and the attempt to develop production without sacrificing socialist revolution in the 1960s. The GPCR, rather than constituting a wild and destructive aberration in China's modern quest is best described, first of all, as a movement too vast, too recent, and still too embroiled in partisan politics to be grasped fully, a movement whose character and consequences are still largely unknown to us. Second, it was a many-sided cluster of disparate elements, a constellation of policies and events and struggles that revolved around certain basic problems in the modernization of China. They are the same problems that China has grappled with since 1949 and in some cases for decades or even centuries before that. Given China's size and diversity, where is the most workable balance between centralization and local autonomy? What can be done about the enormous gaps between city and countryside? What relationship should be established between industry and agriculture, heavy industry and light industry, social egalitarianism and the need for highly specialized training and expertise? Between planning and spontaneity, order and freedom, incentives and inner motivation, advanced technology and a simpler one based on local resources? Finally, how does China balance self-reliance against the need for interaction with the outside world and even for some outside help?

If many of these problems sound familiar and universal, it is because they are, but every one of them has a dimension that is entirely unique to China. They all rest on thousands of years of history of the most history-conscious people in the world and in particular on a century of trauma rooted in the dual crisis of the nineteenth century. For China, the issue of self-reliance, for example, goes to the core of Chinese being. It reaches into the deepest recesses of cultural pride and historical experience, and it collides with the checkered history of

Chinese contacts with foreigners, those angels and demons of 1899 who, more than three quarters of a century later, had yet to become merely other human beings of a different kind. No one feature of the GPCR more clearly typifies its contradictory nature than its strident call for national self-reliance and proletarianism on the one hand, resulting in brutal mistreatment of many thousands accused of contacts with foreigners or nonproletarian behavior, and on the other its welcome to an American president well-known for his anti-Communist witch-hunting, a welcome that broke down more than twenty years of hostility between the two countries and opened yet another new era in their relations and in China's struggle for modernization.

TOWARD SOCIALIST MODERNIZATION, 1977–1981

With the announcement at the Eleventh Party Congress, in August 1977, that the GPCR was over and a new era of socialist revolution and construction had begun, China once again directly confronted the question of the relationship between socialism and modernization. At first the party simply called for both. In a remarkable fresh burst of energy, policy statements and directives poured out of Beijing, announcing that there would be more revolutions like the GPCR and also wage increases and bonuses to workers, class struggle and also a higher standard of living, workers' democratic management and also higher production. A Ten-Year Plan for economic development, first formulated in 1975 and debated for the next two years, was finally drafted and approved. Once again attention was focused on raising China to advanced world levels, and the most popular slogan soon became "realization of the four modernizations [agriculture, industry, national defense, and science and technology] by the year 2000," a goal that was written into the 1977 party constitution.

For a year and one-half a near-euphoria surrounded China's new policies, which were in most respects only a relatively modest shift in the balance aimed at during 1972–1977. The policies were new chiefly in the wider opening to the West and Japan and in the accelerated pace. Chinese leaders did not hesitate to say that "a new leap forward" was taking shape. On October 1, 1978, the national press exulted that the four modernizations could be completed even *before* the year 2000. The most visible sign of a new leap was in foreign trade. During 1978, for example, Chinese trade with Japan jumped 46 percent, to over $5 billion. Trade with the United States reached nearly $1.15 billion, more than triple the 1977 figure. China imported mostly items for its chemical, metallurgical, fuel, electric power, transportation, communication, and construction materials industries, including entire chemical fertilizer factories, power stations, and cement plants. A massive iron and steel complex was to be built in Shanghai with the help of a Japanese consortium. A group of British bankers gave China a $1.2-billion line of credit to finance purchases of British industrial equipment. Sino-British trade was to quadruple in seven years. West Germany agreed to build a $15-billion steel complex in Hebei province. U.S. Steel contracted to help China develop its iron-ore mining, and Intercontinental Hotels (a Pan American–World Airways subsidiary) contracted to build and operate a hotel chain. China took its new leap forward, unlike the old, hand in hand with its new foreign friends.

At first the euphoria expanded even more rapidly among foreign bankers and businessmen than among the Chinese. High hopes then collided with some hard economic realities. After a brief dream of one billion customers, foreign traders learned that China had little cash to spend, that it was more interested in selling abroad so as to earn foreign exchange than it was in buying, and that it wanted to learn Western technology more than it wanted to buy Western goods. "They have told us, send engineers, not salesmen," said a disappointed American businessman. One Western diplomat, who had been arguing for years against his government's attending Chinese trade fairs, predicted that "the Chinese will buy only what they cannot make for themselves—and only for as long as it takes them to learn our techniques and copy them."

The Chinese at first counted on their ability to export oil to pay for imports—in 1975 China had exported $740.2 million worth of crude oil, nearly half the value of all exports, to pay for grain and industrial imports—but they soon realized they could not produce enough. They then turned to selling consumer goods such as textiles in Western countries and expanding the opportunities for foreign tourists to visit and spend. China now began to pay attention to packaging and advertising to appeal to Western consumers. In 1974 a Chinese trade official had told a foreign businessman, "I'm afraid you don't understand how we do business, which is different from your way. We don't sell —you buy." In 1977 China began selling.

The internal counterpart of this foreign trade policy was to produce more, especially oil and light industrial goods, and more coal for use in China instead of oil. Still, at least short-term foreign debt could not be avoided. Largely with the aim of increasing production, China also extended certain social and political policies that had already begun to take shape in the early and middle 1970s. To obtain their skills and political support China reached out to its intellectuals, scientists, and, in a newer departure, to its former capitalists and landlords. People whose property and savings had been confiscated during the GPCR were now reimbursed and restored to favor. Intellectuals who had been banished to the countryside or to work camps for "reform through labor" or "reeducation" were recalled and given choice assignments. Instead of being criticized as bourgeois they were pronounced part of the working class. Rehabilitation (or "reversal of verdicts"), already under way since about 1969, was intensified and extended further into the past, before the GPCR. By November 1978 the defense minister Mao had purged in 1959 was posthumously rehabilitated, and it became clear that Liu Shaoqi was next. Such treatment of Mao's opponents inevitably raised questions about a reevaluation of Mao and the GPCR, which until late 1978 were still largely in good repute. Indeed, all the new policies had been bolstered with suitable quotations from Mao's rich and extensive writings, by the leadership's talent for finding suitable items (sometimes "previously unpublished") to quote, and by injunctions to protect the gains of the GPCR. Even criticism of the "cult of personality" had employed statements by Mao to make its point. Now, people in China promptly raised their political antennae a notch, certain that a new struggle was just around the corner. In fact, it had already turned the corner. Less noticed than the sensational rehabilitations were the quieter "struggle meetings" followed by arrests and punishment of GPCR heroes such as famous Red Guard leaders. "Reversal of verdicts" meant not only restoring reputations of dead former leaders; it meant retribution for their opponents and the discrediting of old policies.

Once again, therefore, political factionalism and personal vendettas threatened to undermine unity, stability, and economic development. To hear the leaders tell it, all the evils that had struck China between the onset of the GPCR and the arrest of the Shanghai radicals in October 1976 were the fault of Lin Biao and the "gang of four," and with their arrest an entirely new era had opened. But could so much be explained by the actions of so few? As for the present and future, all could see some important changes, but questions remained. In education, college entrance examinations were revived. Instead of gaining admission chiefly by one's record in work and politics and one's social background and the recommendation of coworkers, performance on nationwide examinations was to be the main criterion. (It was carefully pointed out that Chairman Mao had never been against *all* examinations, only tricky or unfair or otherwise unsuitable examinations; the gang of four had misapplied his instructions.) Instead of a minimum of two years of physical labor before being eligible for college, high school graduates could now go directly on to higher education and fulfill their labor requirements while at college. But as many people noted, this only meant that a different group was being favored, namely the children of intellectuals and cadres (who were better equipped to take such examinations) and those who had graduated from better schools, which were mostly in the larger cities. Some cynics observed that admission to college was in any case gained by "the back door," the Chinese phrase for using one's personal connections and other extralegal means including bribes, an evil that had also been a target of the GPCR but had only grown during that movement. It was sure to grow again. But most important was the basic fact that no matter what college entrance system was used, the vast majority of high school graduates would be assigned to jobs, mostly in the countryside, for China's 460 institutions of higher learning could only admit about 300,000 students, and nearly 6 million took the examinations. Similarly the decision to send several hundred students to Western countries to study, and the expectation that the number would grow to 10,000 within two or three years, touched very few, despite its long-range potential.

Still other changes were being introduced—plans to raise wages, increase commune members' income, improve worker participation in decision making, extend health care, raise the standard of living—but for the most part these involved familiar measures to solve familiar problems, and many questioned when there would indeed be, for example, more pay for more work as promised and wondered how much it would amount to. In December 1978 it was announced that socialist modernization was "a profound and extensive revolution," but the policies announced for the majority of the population were largely a continuation of those already in effect and carefully protected during the GPCR—private plots, sideline occupations, all accounting being done at the level of the production team.

Some promise for the future was indicated by the emphasis on "democratic management and election of cadres" and raising by 20 percent the price paid by the government for grain while reducing by 10 to 15 percent the prices of farm machinery, chemical fertilizer, insecticides, and other manufactured goods needed by farmers. But this last promise was hedged with several qualifications. Peasants would wait and see. Meanwhile, election of local cadres might be a crucial issue, since some 100,000 cadres purged as long ago as 1957 had recently been rehabilitated. The new policies were stressing the transfer of decision-making power down to local levels, allowing many enterprises a much wider range of autonomy than they had previously had. The role of basic-level cadres would therefore be crucial. The appointment of returnees from earlier purges could create serious conflicts with old enemies.

The December 1978 decisions came on the heels of the announcement that relations between China and the United States would be "normalized" as of January 1, 1979. This climaxed many months of highly active diplomacy by China, which included the first suggestion that foreign business might be invited to invest in joint ventures in China and notable trips abroad by Chinese leaders. Deng Xiaoping promptly brought the relationship to a new level with a highly publicized trip to the United States. But scarcely two weeks after he left the United States, China dissipated much of the good will it had won abroad by launching what was described as a "counterattack against provocations by Vietnam." Although China withdrew one month later, on March 17, the incident was costly, and not the least of the cost was the political price to be paid at home. Opposition that had been gathering around domestic policies could now add to its list of complaints a rash and costly step in foreign affairs.

Domestic affairs had moved rapidly following the December 1978 decisions. In some areas production teams were disbanded or preserved in name only while decision making was taken over by households. A wave of concern spread in political circles that private ownership in land was about to return. Criticism of Dazhai was being heard, and its famous leader was reported to be receiving political reeducation because of his links to the gang of four. The combination of a few such punishments of GPCR heroes together with the huge number of rehabilitations and a general political and cultural relaxation encouraged the public expression of grievances. There was widespread talk of a "thaw," in which a rash of new publications was appearing, including a "literature of the wounded" and a "literature of dissent."

One of the earliest dissenting essays, by a leader who was later arrested and sentenced to fifteen years in prison, called for a "fifth modernization"—democracy. A Human Rights League was founded on January 1, 1979, and, calling attention to the beginning of U.S.–China diplomatic relations on the same day, demanded "freedom of thought, freedom of speech," and a wide range of reforms, including legal safeguards. Thousands of peasants came to Beijing to demonstrate. They marched with banners flying: "We don't want hunger." "We don't want to suffer any more." "We want human rights and democracy." A French observer estimated one throng at 34,000. When their leader was arrested they marched again. Many of the urban youth who had been sent to the countryside (a total of at least 12 million in the preceding decade and very likely several million more than that) returned home for the 1979 Spring Festival, the most important holiday in China. In many cities angry students mingled with dissatisfied peasants and unemployed ex-soldiers. Wall posters, which had begun to appear a few weeks before the important December 1978 party meeting and spread rapidly ever since, now proliferated in many parts of Beijing and in other cities. Riots erupted in several places. In Guangzhou rioters looted trains and stoned police. And on March 16 a big demonstration by educated youth demanding the right to return permanently from the countryside drew international attention. The government struck back, first with a newspaper campaign and then, within two weeks, with a wave of arrests followed by restrictions on display of wall posters. Protests were effectively and rapidly checked, at least for the time being. As one intellectual had said a few years earlier, "The leaders may have made political mistakes, . . . but they sure know how to control us."

These protests arose largely from accumulated grievances and were not aimed at the new policies. If anything, they were encouraged by the architect of the new policies, Deng Xiaoping, as a means of mobilizing support for them. An opposition to Deng, centered in those party members (about half the total number) who had joined during the GPCR, was rallying around Hua Guofeng. For a time, therefore, the protests served Deng's interests. But as they spread, and as their spreading coincided with the month-long Chinese war in Vietnam, the protests backfired against Deng. His opposition complained of anarchy and forced not only a crackdown on protesters but also a reevaluation of the December 1978 policies in their entirety.

After three months yet another compromise was effected, and yet another modification of policy was announced. In June 1979 the four modernizations were reaffirmed as "the supreme interest of our country at the present stage," but they would go forward more slowly, under the

Wall posters in Beijing being read by passers-by in January 1979. One poster places the character for "love" in the midst of English words. Another, under "LOVE," says, "We demand broad contact of every kind with the American people." *Rikio Imajo/UPI*

slogans of "readjusting, restructuring, consolidating, and improving the national economy in order to bring it, step by step, on to the path of sustained, proportionate and high-speed development." In short, the new policy was to slow down for a three-year period of "readjustment." A basic change was the decision to concentrate on improving existing enterprises rather than building new ones. China's leaders had decided that too many expensive big new projects had been undertaken simultaneously and would not contribute to production for too long a time. This was a clear setback to the growing economic relations with foreign countries.

The key political statement was that although "capitalists no longer exist as a class" and therefore "large-scale and turbulent class struggle waged by the masses" was unnecessary, there were still "class enemies of all kinds" and therefore class struggle still had to be waged. It was to be waged in such a way as to "serve the central task of socialist modernization." To this end the government would work to strengthen "socialist democracy" and to develop a "socialist legal system" that would provide the stability and unity needed for modernization and put an end to "anarchy."

This compromise initiated a period of economic retrenchment, originally envisaged as three years of readjustment but later extended to "five to ten years" and finally set at ten. It also effected a political truce, but it did not end political strife. Peasants continued to arrive in the capital and squatted in front of the leaders' residence compound, a quiet, dignified, and moving protest by hundreds of people, individuals and families, many of them gaunt and ragged, living on the streets. Suddenly, after about two weeks, they were gone, having obtained a promise that a special investigation of their complaints would be made. Meanwhile, wall posters and underground newspapers continued to appear. The government issued further restrictions on wall posters in December 1979 and four months later eliminated from the nation's constitution a clause permitting the "four bigs"—"speaking out freely, airing views fully, holding great debates and writing big-character posters." At the same time the mass media paid increasing attention to the danger of "ultra-Left ideas," anarchism, and "ultra-individualism," and it began to address directly the question of "leftist errors" made by Mao before and during the GRCR. Liu Shaoqi was fully rehabilitated amid an enormous fanfare of nationwide publicity over a period of weeks, and a major shake-up of party and government leadership culminated in Hua Guofeng's resignation as premier in September 1980. He was replaced by Zhao Ziyang, a protégé of Deng's. Another Deng protégé, Hu Yaobang, was at the same time being groomed to replace Hua as chairman of the party, although Hua and his supporters continued to hold out for another ten months.

The final elements in this latest political struggle were a sensational trial of the gang of four and of Lin Biao's associates in the 1971 plot on Mao's life, and a full-scale reconsideration by the party of its entire history and Mao Zedong's historic role. The theme of both the trial and the historical reevaluation was the disasters that "Left errors" had brought to China. The trial was held between November 20, 1980, and January 25, 1981. Widely publicized by TV, radio and newpapers, it left no doubt that the Deng-Hu-Zhao leadership had arrived at the climax of Deng's twin rehabilitation and retribution policies. Both policies had reached the top of their respective pyramids, with the rehabilitation of Liu Shaoqi and now the convictions of the would-be assassins and the Shanghai radicals. It remained only to pronounce judgment on Mao and the GPCR, which required fifteen months of work, many meetings, and six drafts of a lengthy series of resolutions. A twenty-day meeting of four thousand party officials was held to discuss the first draft, and a later draft was discussed for twelve days by seventy-six of the highest leaders in the country. The final version appeared on the sixtieth anniversary of the founding of the party, midway through 1981.

This extraordinary document, some 20,000 words long in English translation, represented yet another in a countless series of efforts by the CCP to "sum up its experience." The intent of such efforts has always been to present the final word on a controversial issue, to close the subject. It contained the same contradiction as the slogan of the thaw —"emancipate thought" so as to grasp more firmly the "correct" line. An effort to have the last say, it raised more questions than it answered, and therefore defeated its own purpose. Although a classic of its kind, this document illustrated what by 1981 had come to be the central problem in China's struggle for modernization: the party's own credibility and the nature of the leadership it attempted to exercise.

The document, judging Mao's activities as a whole, was attempting to establish that "his contributions to the Chinese revolution far outweigh his mistakes. His merits are primary and his errors secondary." But surely a document of such length was not necessary to establish so modest a thesis. One would have thought this was the least that could be said of Mao. It was clear that the real purpose of the document was to detail his mistakes. Almost every reference to Mao's achievements was made in the context of the party's work and the work of other leaders. References to his errors, however, found him usually alone. In one instance there was the frank statement that both successes and errors were the responsibility of a collective leadership; in the other instances Mao was shown making his errors against the "correct" advice of other leaders. The total effect of the document was to reduce dramatically Mao's stature in the history of the party and to condemn the GPCR ("initiated and led by Comrade Mao Zedong"). Its attempt to distinguish between Mao's erroneous " 'Left' Theses," which were his own responsibility, and "Mao Zedong Thought," which was "a correct theory, a body of correct principles and a summary of the experiences that have been confirmed in the practice of the Chinese revolution, a crystallization of the collective wisdom of the Chinese Communist Party," was in the end an assertion of the correctness and near infallibility of the party.

As this chapter and the two preceding it suggest, the party's 1981 examination of its history, however deftly written as a political document, presented a seriously oversimplified, one-sided, and ultimately self-serving interpretation. Designed to bolster public confidence in its leadership, it could only raise more questions in people's minds about the political future of the country. "We can accomplish the four modernizations," a middle-level cadre said in response to a foreigner's question in 1979, "and maybe even by the year 2000, but only if we're properly led. We'll make the effort and the sacrifices, but only if the leaders lead well." Decades of mass mobilization and attempts to instill activism and initiative had not cancelled out centuries of depending heavily on leaders. The new relationships between leaders and ordinary citizens that were forged in the 1940s have existed ever since in a state of tension with old traditions of paternalistic leadership. Old habits of passivity among the general population frequently overcome the new habits of participation and activism. More than twenty years of almost ceaseless political discord within the highest echelons of leadership had left many people still waiting for the leaders to lead well. As a result, apathy and disillusionment spread in the 1970s—there was a turning away from politics, a growing preoccupation with pursuing self-interest and family interests, and slackening attention to societal goals. More concretely, continued political conflict and settling of old political scores at higher levels fanned the embers of old tensions at lower levels. At best this made coworkers cautious in what they said to each other; at worst it encouraged distance, friction, and the duplication in factories, offices, communes, schools, and neighborhoods of the political discord in the Politburo.

These political conditions had direct effects on the economy. Political struggles absorbed much of the leadership's attention and energy, leading to neglect of other matters. Production, already lagging for many reasons—insufficient raw materials, shortages of electricity and other energy sources, worker malingering—was further disrupted by political campaigns. Western economists, who were divided on the question of whether the draft Ten-Year Plan (1975–1986 but only approved in 1978) set utopian targets or achievable ones, were agreed that the targets could only have a chance of being reached if political stability was maintained. Soon after the plan was scrapped, in September 1980, a ranking Chinese economist attributed China's economic failures to political upheaval. Although he was referring specifically to insufficient improvement in the people's standard of living, which he blamed particularly on "Leftist thinking" that was responsible for "hasty advances" in 1958–1960, 1965, and 1978, it was plain that he and his colleagues agreed that political stability had to be maintained if the economy was to develop. China's solution to the problem in 1981 was another campaign to "clean out 'Left' thought" and to promote "socialist spiritual civilization."

Economic policies in 1981 seemed to be headed in a somewhat different direction than these campaigns suggest. In purely economic terms, China's basic problem could be seen most clearly in one small set of statistics: During the first thirty years of the People's Republic of China (PRC) China's population had doubled, production in heavy industry had grown more than ninetyfold, light industry about twentyfold. Agricultural production had grown 2.4 times. Food production had barely kept ahead of population growth, but light industry had grown ten times as fast as the population and heavy industry forty-five times as fast. This disproportionate growth pattern, in which agriculture lagged behind industry, had originated in the 1950s and was still cited by Chinese economists as the country's number one problem in 1981. Some of the policies already introduced were therefore to be extended still further: Private plots, formerly limited to 5 percent of a commune's acreage, were now allowed to rise to 15 percent; more skilled people were to be sent from metropolitan areas to rural districts; mechanization

Under socialist modernization, city residents have new access to consumer goods *(above)*, and rural people have new opportunities to sell livestock they have raised *(left)*. © *Marc Riboud*

would be increased; more free markets would be allowed for the sale of food; greater diversification of crops would be allowed; and wider decision-making powers would be allotted to production teams and even to households. In general, much more attention would be paid to increasing peasants' income, thus giving them incentive to increase production.

Although authorities recognized that these policies would widen income differentials in the farm population, they defended the policies as "letting some become better off first," adding that this would encourage others and have the effect of stimulating production and, eventually, raising the income of all. To support their view they released results of a survey of more than 10,000 households in 408 counties, showing that average peasant income rose about 20 percent in 1979 over 1978 (to a figure of 160.2 yuan* per person) and that more than one-third of peasant income came from sideline occupations and other sources outside the collective economy. More of the same policies, it was reasoned, would raise peasant incomes still further.

By spring of 1981, however, a difference of degree was turning into a difference in kind. Announcing "an important new policy," the press reported that now "a small number of commune members may devote themselves to household sideline occupations or work on their private plots instead of taking part in collective production." In addition, apart from land under "collective management" (and the reference was to management rather than ownership) "small plots are allocated to individual households for cultivation on a long-term basis." On these plots families would grow what they chose, pay no tax, and either keep the produce or sell it on the open market. The basic structure of collectivized agriculture was beginning to be fundamentally changed.

The nature of the change was further evidenced by other developments. First, along with all these changes came vigorous denials that "a bourgeois policy" was being adopted. These denials, highly defensive in tone, stressed that the essential criterion for socialism is the absence of exploitation; as long as laws forbade speculation, usury, and the hiring of labor, personal income could grow without endangering socialism. Even radio plays were making the point that "getting rich" is not the same as advocating capitalism. The vigor and tone of the denials made it plain that charges were being leveled against the

---

* The Chinese yuan is equivalent to about sixty cents.

leadership by an unidentified opposition that was attacking the leadership for abandoning socialism. To back up its denials, the leadership launched a new campaign against "bourgeois liberalism," making clear especially to artists, writers, and other intellectuals that there were strict limits to the current relaxation of controls. The effect was to dampen hopes for greater political freedom without allaying suspicions that economic policy was moving away from socialism. Second, "readjustment" of the economy was redefined to mean a "strategic shift" and the adoption of "new economic forms." As one economist explained it: "Under the premise of the absolute superiority of socialist public ownership, we are allowing various kinds of economies and methods of management to co-exist." This was clearly a way to leave room for a kind of ownership other than socialist public ownership—in other words, private ownership. Third, the press was full of references to the New Economic Policy (NEP) period in the Soviet Union* as an example of new economic forms in a socialist state and to "feudal vestiges" as a more serious problem than bourgeois remnants. Both these points were justifications for adopting at least semicapitalist policies. Finally, in Sichuan province, following disastrous floods in July 1981, authorities in two districts allowed "decollectivization" to take place as a means of dealing with the natural disaster. It remained to be seen whether this phenomenon would spread, but clearly China had reached a point where the compatibility of socialism and modernization was coming into question. If integration of the two were not achieved, China could once again plunge into political turmoil.

As of mid–1981 China could look back on two decades of political turbulence that overshadowed considerable economic development and social change. The political discord and the persistence of certain doggedly recalcitrant problems—factionalism and bureaucratism in the polity, sluggishness of agricultural development, insufficient supplies of energy and transportation facilities—were magnified by the

---

* From about 1921–1927 the Soviet Union followed the "New Economic Policy," whereby a mixed private and state-owned economy existed for a dual purpose: reviving economic development with the help of private enterprise in the short run and preparing for the socialist sector to gain strength and extend to the whole economy in the long run.

age-old problems of natural disasters and central–local relationships. China in this period was repeatedly struck by floods, droughts, and earthquakes that inflicted enormous damage and suffering. The recurrent problem of balancing centralized coordination with the local decision making so essential in that vast and diverse country bedeviled Communist leaders as it had the emperors. Add to these inflation, unemployment, and foreign debt, and one might wonder whether a unit of 1 billion people, gradually using up its farm land to find living space, could survive, much less modernize itself. "Has China failed?" one analyst asked, in a series of pessimistic articles in 1979. One answer came from an overseas Chinese businessman. Frustrated at his drawn-out negotiations with Beijing counterparts, he scoffed at the idea of the four modernizations: "They'll be lucky to get one modernization by 2000." But two unemployed high school graduates, encountered in a remote inland town, offered another answer: "Wait until the 1980s," they said. "In 1981 the new educational system will produce its first graduates, and the first wave of students who've been to the West will return. Then you'll see what we can do."

By 1981 there was no more talk of the year 2000. Instead there were to be ten years of readjustment. Hua Guofeng's aim of a mechanized agriculture by 1980 had gone the way of Mao Zedong's goal of equaling British industrial production by 1975. But for every such sign of failure there was a sign of success—or at least of hope. One kind of failure had been precisely to aim at hopelessly impossible targets. One kind of success is to learn from such failures, and to find the point at which the positive value of aiming high, the sense of optimism and purpose that aiming high provides, is not canceled out by the disappointment that follows the failure to meet utopian goals. In 1959 Mao Zedong said: "It won't do to build socialism by 'reducing our efforts, striving for the lower reaches, . . .' Now we propose to build a great socialist nation with modern industry, modern agriculture, and modern science and culture in fifteen years. If impossible, then take a little more time! Just what is planned and proportionate development? I hope our comrades will study it."

As the GPCR proves, Mao himself was not always willing to study the question, to take a little more time. But the conclusion to be drawn from such excesses is not simply that he was a misguided visionary, or even that he made serious errors in judgment, although indeed he made them. The more important conclusions may be that the judgment of even the most experienced leaders may fail, especially when extremely weighty decisions must be made under great pressure, and that the ability of any one leader or handful of leaders to control events is severely limited. These conclusions suggest that the pressures under which decisions have had to be made in twentieth-century China have been extremely heavy. So much has been at stake that the judgment of a great many leaders, certainly not only Mao's, has often been warped.

The history of China in 1949–1981, then, and indeed of the entire twentieth century, is a tale of people's successes and failures in trying to cope with immense problems and pressures, but it is at least equally a story of how those problems and pressures took shape and changed shape as people tried to deal with them. A centuries-old bureaucratism has now evolved through feeble experiments in republicanism (1912–1928), then the Guomindang version (1928–1949), and now the PRC variety since 1949. The overseas Chinese businessman who was so frustrated at trying to deal with it was as ready to cut through the red tape as Mao Zedong was in 1966. And yet his frustration, however great the resemblances, was not the same as the frustration felt by British traders in the nineteenth century, American railroad builders in the early twentieth century, or Japanese negotiators in the 1930s. The more important point is that he was in China at all, doing business with socialist traders. For the socialist traders, too, this was a new experience, with a great deal at stake. The overseas businessman, after many days of conferences in a smoke-filled room, was excessively despairing. His judgment was a bit warped too.

Similarly, the two unemployed high school graduates have their predecessors. From the first students who were sent abroad in the 1870s, to the young radicals who flocked to Japan in the early 1900s, the May Fourth (1919) generation and later ones, many waves of Chinese students have gone abroad, and a good number have also returned to do valuable work. Generations of Chinese students have received modern educations in Chinese universities, first under foreign auspices, later with Chinese teachers, many of whom had been trained abroad, or with foreign teachers in China. Much has always been expected of the "returned students" and those who graduated from modern institutions. Perhaps too much was expected. Although they delivered a great deal, they did not provide the answers to all or even most of China's problems. The latest wave will surely be of immense help, but the unemployed high school students' optimism was probably as excessive as the overseas businessman's pessimism.

Has China failed? The answer can only be that China has just begun. The failures of 1959–1981 were glaring. And yet, from the very womb of those failures have come some striking gains, many of which continued right through the successive political crises and twists in political "line." Although serious inequalities remain, especially between city and countryside, most analysts agree that the most glaring inequalities and abuses in Chinese society have been either eliminated or sharply reduced. It remains to be seen whether the new "socialist modernization" policies will reverse this trend, as critics fear they will, or ultimately strengthen it, as supporters claim.

Meanwhile, since 1959 the face of rural China and the character of its relationship to urban China have been significantly changed. Thanks to small-scale industrialization, "rural" China in 1981 contained many more large towns and small cities. The economy of the countryside had been radically transformed. Communes and brigades in 1981 were operating 1.43 million factories employing over 30 million workers, and the value of their production accounted for one-third of the total annual income of the rural collective economy. Chinese planners were carefully studying Yugoslavia's system of agro-industrial complexes and beginning to introduce experiments along those lines, envisioning a sharp reduction in the percentage of rural people directly engaged in agriculture. Correspondingly, some of China's larger cities were organized as "municipalities"; that is, they include enough of the surrounding countryside to produce their own food. The ultimate goal is self-sufficiency, which many municipalities are reaching in vegetables, although not yet in grain and meat. Although this may only convert the urban-rural problem into a municipality-rural problem, it is clear that innovation and experiment are continuing in this sphere and that substantial gains have been recorded.

The same may be said of other areas in Chinese life. Despite the serious economic problems already noted, the overall growth rate was good and forecasts as of 1981 were promising, especially in comparison with other developing countries such as India. The Chinese themselves were beginning to compare their performance with India's rather than with Japan, the United States, and Western Europe, obviously a way of making China look more successful but also a more reasonable comparison to make. Population control was firmly adopted as national policy in 1973, written into the new constitution in 1978, and then implemented with unprecedented vigor. Although two earlier birth control campaigns were allowed to lapse, there is reason to expect that this policy will endure.

All depends on achieving a higher measure of political stability, but doing so in a way that meets the political needs and aspirations of the Chinese people. It is the classic political issue. Here there is less reason to be optimistic. Political losses heavily outweighed political gains between 1959 and 1981, and the roots of factionalism and arbitrariness were scarcely touched by political reform. Old and deep grudges survive. Newer resentments and dissatisfactions continue. Popular complaints and demands remain to be met and satisfied. Carrying out yet another campaign against "erroneous ideas" and introducing a course on "socialist morality" in schools, two recent developments, are not likely to meet demands.

Signs that Chinese intellectuals find promising include some concessions to youth who are sent to the countryside, elections of grass-roots cadres and local governments, some relaxation of restrictions on religion and cultural life—including much wider opportunities to read foreign materials and see foreign movies and TV programs, hear foreign radio programs, and have personal contact with foreigners—and the opportunity to travel, both abroad and within China. But these affect relatively few, they contain seeds of discord, and they are subject to recurrent criticism and to sudden revocation.

At higher levels, it was notable that Hua Guofeng was criticized and demoted but not totally disgraced, that party leaders took at least a modicum of responsibility for mistakes of 1959–1981, and that there has been some self-criticism within the party and some changes in party functioning and in party-government relations. There has also been much talk of workers' democracy, peasants' power to decide things for themselves, and the people being masters of the country. A new marriage law (in effect January 1, 1981) reaffirmed the free choice of marriage partners established in 1950, slightly loosened restrictions on divorce, and added clauses providing for family planning and the duty of children "to support and assist their parents."

Perhaps most fundamental of all, the commune system seemed headed for radical alteration. By late 1981 plans were afoot to separate the political and economic functions of communes and to transfer their role in local administration to township governments. Communes were to retain an economic role, but a lesser one than before—more and more of the communes' economic decision-making powers were being shifted to brigades and teams. Indeed, these smaller units were transferring some of their powers to households and even to individuals. A scholarly analysis by Jürgen Domes concluded that the level of collectivization in

China had returned to about the level of 1953–1954, and that the communes by 1981 existed in name only. In one place the very name commune was abolished and replaced by "Township People's Government," while its enterprises were reorganized into a "united agricultural–industrial–commercial corporation." Some brigades were renamed "administrative villages," and for production teams the old name of "agricultural producers' cooperatives" began to be used. Private plots in some parts of China rose to 25 percent of a commune's arable land, and there were reports that plots were being bought and sold. Although the CCP sharply criticized such exchanges and insisted that China's public ownership system had not been changed, reports persisted that a new constitution to be promulgated in 1982 would officially recognize a limited economic sector of individual ownership.

One can only wait and see whether these and future changes will meet the needs and demands of the Chinese people, and whether their other serious needs—especially for more and better food, housing, health care, and education—are also met. In all these respects the record is mixed and an accurate balance sheet impossible to draw. Above all, it is too early to add up the accounts. If Mao Zedong called the first twenty-eight years only one step in a long march of ten thousand *li*, is it not enough to speak of the next thirty-two years as only another three steps or four? And if so, how can we plot the line of march on the basis of those few paces? Let us merely note that they were shaky but forward steps on a very rocky road and wait to see what the future brings. It is plain that the Chinese people are far from having run out of energy and ideas, and the safest possible prediction is that they have many surprises in store for us—and not only for us, because China's leaders have set out on a path that they themselves are unsure of and that reaches too far over the horizon of time to be seen clearly.

What was unmistakably clear by the end of 1981 was that China's struggle for modernization confronts in a new form the problems that it began to address at least forty years earlier, when cadre teams first entered rural places such as Stone Wall Village. Or earlier still, when James Y. C. Yen took his literacy campaign to the countryside, when Mao Zedong began to build a guerrilla army, and indeed, when the late nineteenth-century reformers and revolutionaries first studied the outside world. China's top leaders, mostly urban-oriented intellectuals, strive to raise China's stature in the world, reach full equivalence with the most advanced nations, and blaze new trails in social organization while maintaining a highly ordered and tightly structured society. The masses of Chinese people, including many urban intellectuals and other city people but most notably the 800 million who live in rural areas, after some thirty years of organized effort largely for national objectives, now begin increasingly to pursue their own varied goals. These goals sometimes coalesce with those of the leaders and sometimes do not, as is to be expected in any large and diverse country. As compared with other countries, however, unity and solidarity are still prized to an exceptional degree in China, and "disorder" is correspondingly abhorred. The CCP has tried repeatedly since 1949, but with highly uneven success, to recreate the social cohesion that it first created in the 1940s. In the 1980s it leads a nation with double the population it had forty years before, a vastly more diverse people in its knowledge and experience, a citizenry that the CCP has done much to awaken and activate. Can a billion people be organized and led so as to integrate the leadership's vision of a modern country with the people's own jumble of ideas about their future? Or must organization and leadership yield more to individual and small group decision making? How will power and authority be distributed?

In brief, once again the classic and universal political questions of relationships between national leaders and the people are central issues in China. By 1981 China was committed to finding answers to many of its problems—industrialization, scientific training, population control, mechanization of agriculture, railway-building—wherever in the world answers might be found. But for some problems, those having to do with social and political organization especially, China still looked mostly within itself. Cautious and selective borrowing from abroad cannot be ruled out, nor can another spasm of intoxication with foreign approaches to society and politics such as occurred in the first quarter of this century and, to a lesser degree, between 1949 and 1956. Indeed, foreign influences are to be found everywhere in Chinese life. Repeatedly, however, China's leaders have found that foreign answers to Chinese social and political problems are at best partial and often unsatisfactory. Repeatedly they have recognized the need to borrow selectively, reject rigorously, and modify and adapt carefully foreign social-political ideas and methods. In so doing they have reached creatively into their own rich storehouse of experience and their own most deeply held values. China's struggle to modernize remains an effort to adapt what it needs from the outside world to its own particular circumstances, a struggle for modernization but not for Westernization.

E PILOGUE

MODERN CHINA AND
WORLD HISTORY

For AT least four thousand years prior to the middle of the nineteenth century, the Chinese people developed their own unique way of life almost entirely in response to their own needs and conditions. Influence by other peoples on Chinese life, although never totally absent, was of distinctly lesser importance. Beginning in the nineteenth century, by contrast, foreign influence forced itself on China to such a degree that today no problem in the study of modern Chinese history is more challenging or more important than the interaction between China and the outside world.

This is a staggering, dazzling fact to a historian of China. It deserves to be recognized as one of the most crucial phenomena in all of human history, for it involves, first of all, nothing less than a radical departure by nearly one-fourth of the human race from a course of development that had dug its own channel for millennia. It involves too a cultural collision of unique magnitude—that is, a collision not simply between China and the West, but between two enormously varied and complex amalgams of cultures, each full of internal contradictions but yet constituting distinct entities vastly different from each other. China in the nineteenth century was ruled by the non-Chinese Manchus and included some sixty other ethnic minorities, as it does today. There were important north-south and urban-rural differences and many other local variations. China was not simply one coherent culture. Still less

184

coherent a culture was "the West" that intruded on China, especially as it came to include Russia and Japan as well as Britain, France, and the United States. And yet there occurred in the nineteenth century, certainly as viewed from a Chinese perspective, an unprecedented confrontation between two worlds—China and the one outside.

Since this confrontation has occupied so tiny a fraction of China's history, it is no wonder that the Chinese took some years to recognize the seriousness and complexity of it. Only when they did recognize it could they begin to grapple with it. Unfortunately for the Chinese people, events in the nineteenth and early twentieth century moved so rapidly that, by the time China came fully to grips with the problem, it had already reached crisis proportions. Therefore, the Chinese have had to deal with it under the pressure of incipient national disaster.

China undertook to modernize itself only reluctantly and defensively. From the outside world it sought at first only military skills. All else it sought within itself. Around the beginning of this century China's effort began to become concentrated and deliberate. Never has the effort been completely free of war or the serious threat of war. Although this threat receded after 1953 it has occasionally returned and is still by no means absent. Rarely in this century has China been free of deep internal strife. And always there has been the pressure of mounting population—China today has more people than lived in the entire world in 1800. Modernization has been smooth and easy nowhere in the world, but in China it has been a struggle of monumental scale and complexity.

For these reasons China's struggle must be seen as a still very young and growing process, with its outcome well in the future and far beyond anyone's ability to envision. At present stage it has produced a disjointed, variegated, hybrid society. The vast majority of the Chinese people are still rural and lead lives much closer to those led by their ancestors than do city people. Families of rural bridegrooms still commonly pay a "bride price," and couples still marry on a day with the number nine in it because the words for "nine" and "long-lasting" are pronounced identically. Rural families build houses in traditional styles, organize their lives in some of the same centuries-old patterns, work the same land their ancestors tilled, go to practitioners of traditional medicine when they are sick, regard sons as the major insurance for their old age, and celebrate traditional festivals. Despite official declarations that the lunar new year is now "spring festival," that couples should have only one child, and that daughters are to be valued as much as sons, in many villages families still celebrate the new year and paste up signs that say "may sons and grandsons fill the hall."

Side by side with such traditional elements, however, a revolution has been taking place in rural China. Marrying couples make more of their own decisions, meet before agreeing to marry, and sometimes live apart from the groom's parents. Apartment houses and growing towns with small industries and schools dot the countryside. Landlords, rents, and usury no longer exist, and land is owned in common. Modern medical care is spreading, many old diseases have been wiped out, infant mortality is one-sixth what it was in 1949 (and one-fifth the rate in India), and life expectancy is now 67 for men and 69.5 for women, nearly double what it was in 1949 (and 27 percent higher than in India). Traditional festivals are celebrated with less of the old ritual, and new holidays such as International Women's Day are also observed. Electricity now serves nearly all rural communities, which means not only light and radios but the automatic pumping of water that not long ago was done by human muscle. Rapidly increasing numbers of rural people have bicycles, wristwatches, sewing machines, and transistor radios; television is becoming available. Farmers now use more modern tools, seed, and irrigation methods as well as insect sprays, chemical fertilizer, and tractors and other machinery. Above all, the Chinese masses have a new range of opportunities and an unprecedented degree of security. Almost none of these changes had occurred before 1949. Directly affecting the daily lives of some 800 million people, these changes represent as vast a transformation as has ever occurred in human history.

Even this gigantic revolution, however, has been highly uneven. Not only do traditional and modern elements coexist in uneasy and sometimes clashing patterns, but their proportions and relationship vary sharply from one rural community to another. Remote areas in the southwest differ radically from the Guangzhou delta and the north China plain. Life in ethnic minority communities has its own distinct character. The largest gap remains that between urban and rural, but here too there are important differences. Life in the countryside surrounding big cities in many ways resembles urban life as much as it does life in the remote hinterland. Cities are also different from each other. Goods that are available in Beijing, Shanghai, and Guangzhou are often not available elsewhere. In those cities and some others, instead of Maoist slogans on billboards there are now advertisements for foreign products.

English-speaking students seek out foreign tourists to practice conversation while countless others study English by listening to Voice of America broadcasts. Western music is played in concert halls, Western movies and TV programs are shown, some Western styles in clothing and hairdos can be seen. In Beijing around 7,000 Chinese Catholics attended Easter Sunday High Mass in 1981. From religion and politics to management practices, high technology, and the formula for Coca-Cola, curiosity about all things Western seems to overflow in China's biggest cities.

So avid is the recent desire to know more of the outside world, after three decades of strictly limited contact, that the Chinese press has issued a steady stream of reports to remind its audience that not all is rosy in Western societies, a sure sign that many in China think it is. Such reports, together with the observations of Chinese travelers abroad, have had some effect. Widespread admiration for Western technology, material inventiveness, cultural life, and high material standard of living is to some degree balanced by shock at the shabby treatment of the aged in many parts of the West, and at divorce, unemployment, crime, drugs, pornography, casual sex, political corruption, racial conflict, and what is commonly viewed as the rampant materialism and near anarchy of Western society in general and the decay of family life in particular. Especially in urban China, therefore, people hold a jumble of mixed impressions about the outside world, and since they assimilate what they know in a variety of ways, a new range of attitudes has been developing, from those who seek almost desperately for foreign things in any form to those who shun nearly all things foreign and cling more tightly to China's familiar social cohesion and the security of an essentially traditional family life.

China has reached, then, a new stage in the century-long effort to reconcile preservation of its own core values with its deep determination to reach full equivalence with the outside world. The question posed by the scholar in 1860 has been partly answered. China's stature in the world is now vastly different from what it was then. But the attainment of world standards in all spheres of life remains a struggle for the future. To accomplish this while assimilating many foreign things and yet retaining the essence of its own culture remains an issue in China's struggle for modernization. It is a goal that nearly all who have charted China's course since 1860 have shared. This book has attempted to show the vitally important differences among the nineteenth-century reformers, late Qing reform, Yan Fu, Liang Qichao, Sun Yatsen, Jiang Kaishek, Mao Zedong, and Deng Xiaoping, but all in their own way wanted to preserve a core of solid Chinese identity as well as to introduce basic changes from abroad. Liang Qichao's "new people" were not to erase their entire heritage; Jiang Kaishek's "new citizen" was to be created by a New Life Movement rooted in updated Confucian values; and the "socialist spiritual civilization" called for in 1981 evokes moral themes that echo traditional ones.

Even Jiang and Mao, bitterly opposed though they were, could occasionally find common ground. Partly it was on matters of short-run political convenience that only temporarily overshadowed the crucial differences between Mao's revolutionary vision of a classless society and Jiang's counterrevolutionary notion of "revival." But when Jiang called for a moral regeneration, "public morality," and a national salvation movement so that China would "not again suffer from the aggression and oppression of foreign countries or receive disdain and insults," the words could as easily have been Mao's. The differences underlying those words are clear, as we have shown; civil wars and the continuing division of China testify to the seriousness of those differences. But Beijing and Taibei share more than nationalist political interests and a devotion to Sun Yatsen. They share a sense of Chinese identity grounded in millennia of history. Their race to attain equivalence with the rest of the world is spurred no less by that deep sense of cultural pride than it is by nationalist politics.

It may well turn out, therefore, that the impact of Western culture on China has been in some ways comparable to the impact of the outside world on late medieval and early Renaissance Europe. "Europe itself," Professor R. R. Palmer pointed out,

> has always received much from others—from the calendar and Christianity to the use of cotton and potatoes. Europe itself, moreover, became "modernized" by the effects upon it of its growing contacts with the earth as a whole, especially after the discovery of America and the ocean trade routes in the days of Columbus.

Thus Europe, after a long history of borrowing from abroad, came to a point in its history when foreign contact stimulated it to pursue new directions; those directions are perhaps best symbolized by the idea of people's unlimited potential and their Faustian striving. Europeans' striving did not produce uniformly rapid results. Copernicus was only a generation later than Columbus, but Galileo did not appear for another century and Darwin two centuries more; James Watt's steam engine and the Declaration of the Rights of Man and Citizen both appeared about two hundred years ago, but we are still waiting for more than a small fraction of the human race to enjoy the fruits of steam power and human rights. China, sometimes regarded as a "failure" in comparison with Western Europe and Japan, has barely begun its struggle to modernize. If it has accomplished no "miracles" comparable to those achieved by Japan's samurai and industrialists, neither has it visited upon the world anything like the destruction and suffering caused by Japan's militarists, to say nothing of this century's European wars. At this early stage it is enough that, like Europe, China has now been stimulated to pursue new directions and that it is irrevocably committed to the pursuit. Outside stimulation aroused Europe and contributed to a cultural (scientific) revolution, but it did not tear Europe loose from all its roots. Perhaps outside stimulation has similarly revitalized China. If so, it suggests that whatever changes they effect, great revolutions depend precisely on the tradition they renew by altering.

B IBLIOGRAPHY

F OLLOWING IS a short list of basic sources, most of which have been heavily drawn upon for this book. Beginning students are advised to refer to these sources.

The standard general texts on modern China are John K. Fairbank, *The United States and China*, 4th ed. (Cambridge, Mass.: Harvard University Press, 1979), and Immanuel C. Y. Hsü, *The Rise of Modern China*, 2nd ed. (New York: Oxford University Press, 1975). Both contain extensive lists of recommended readings.

The entire range of Chinese history is being treated in *The Cambridge History of China* under the general editorship of Denis Twitchett and John K. Fairbank. Volumes 10 and 11, dealing with China from 1800 to about 1912, have already been published (Cambridge University Press, 1978 and 1980). Subsequent volumes will deal with the period from 1912 to the present.

Other outstanding general works on modern China include the following: Jonathan Spence, *To Change China* (New York: Penguin Books, 1980); James E. Sheridan, *China in Disintegration: The Republican Era in Chinese History*, 1912–1949 (New York: Free Press, 1975); Lucien Bianco, *Origins of the Chinese Revolution, 1915–1949* (Stanford, Calif.: Stanford University Press, 1971); and *China's Modern Economy in Historical Perspective*, edited by Dwight H. Perkins (Stanford, Calif.: Stanford University Press, 1975). Among others that touch on a wide range of issues, one of the most stimulating is *China in Crisis*, edited by Ping-ti Ho and Tang Tsou, 2 vols. (Chicago: University of Chicago Press, 1968).

Beginning students now have access to a number of excellent collections that combine translations of original Chinese sources and Chinese scholarly writings, original Western-language sources, Western scholarly writings, journalists' accounts, and authoritative editorial commentary: *The China Reader*, edited by Franz Schurmann and Orville Schell, 4 vols. (New York: Vintage Books, 1967–1974); *The Awakening of China, 1793–1949*, edited by Roger Pelissier (New York: Capricorn Books, 1970); *Sources of Chinese Tradition*, compiled by W. T. deBary, Wing-tsit Chan, and Chester Tan (New York: Columbia University Press, 1960; in the two-volume paperback edition, Volume 2 deals with modern times); *China's Response to the West, A Documentary Survey, 1839–1923*, edited by Ssu-yu Teng and John K. Fairbank (Cambridge, Mass.: Harvard University Press, 1954; New York: Atheneum, 1963); *China in Revolution*, edited by Vera Simone (New York: Fawcett Books, 1968); and *Changing China: Readings in the History of China from the Opium War to the Present*, edited by J. Mason Gentzler (New York: Praeger, 1977).

On the history of Chinese Communism the standard references are James Pinckney Harrison, *The Long March to Power: A History of the Chinese Communist Party, 1921–1972* (New York: Praeger, 1972), and Donald Klein and Anne B. Clark, *Biographic Dictionary of Chinese Communism, 1921–1965*, 2 vols. (Harvard University Press, 1971). Two important new biographies of Mao Zedong are *The People's Emperor* by Dick Wilson (Garden City, N.Y.: Doubleday, 1979), and Ross Terrill, *Mao* (New York: Harper & Row, 1980).

Other general works include Jacques Guillermaz, *A History of the Chinese Communist Party 1921–1949* (New York: Random House, 1972), and the same author's *The Chinese Communist Party in Power 1949–1976* (Boulder, Colo.: Westview Press, 1976), both translated by Anne Destenay; Bill Brugger, *Contemporary China* (London: Croom Helm, 1977); Alain Roux, *Le casse-tête chinois: Trente ans de chine socialiste vus par un communiste français* (Paris: Editions Sociales, 1980); Maurice Meisner, *Mao's China: A History of the People's Republic* (New York: Free Press, 1977); and *The People's Republic of China: A Documentary History of Revolutionary Change*, edited and

* Available in paperback.

with an introduction by Mark Selden (New York and London: Monthly Review Press, 1979). An indispensable original source is the *Selected Works of Mao Tse-tung [Mao Zedong]*, 5 vols. (Beijing: Foreign Languages Press, 1967–1977).

More specialized works on the People's Republic that do not fit the chapter headings include Roxane Witke, *Comrade Chiang Ch'ing* (Boston and Toronto: Little, Brown, 1977); Lowell Dittmer, *Liu Shao-ch'i [Liu Shaoqi] and the Chinese Cultural Revolution: The Politics of Mass Criticism* (Berkeley and Los Angeles: University of California Press, 1974); Martin King Whyte, *Small Groups and Political Rituals in China* (Berkeley and Los Angeles: University of California Press, 1974); Christopher Howe, *China's Economy: A Basic Guide* (New York: Basic Books, 1978); Alexander Eckstein, *China's Economic Revolution* (Cambridge University Press, 1977); John Wong, *Land Reform in The People's Republic of China: Institutional Transformation in Agriculture* (New York: Praeger, 1973); Stephen Andors, *China's Industrial Revolution: Politics, Planning and Management, 1949 to the Present* (New York: Pantheon Books, 1977); Thomas P. Bernstein, *Up to the Mountains and Down to the Villages: The Transfer of Youth from Urban to Rural China* (New Haven and London: Yale University Press, 1977); Jon Sigurdson, *Rural Industrialization in China* (Cambridge, Mass.: Harvard University Press, 1977); American Rural Small-scale Industry Delegation, *Rural Small-scale Industries in the People's Republic of China* (Berkeley: University of California Press, 1977); Peggy Printz and Paul Steinle, *Commune: Life in Rural China* (New York: Dodd, Mead, 1977); Leo A. Orleans, *Every Fifth Child: The Population of China* (Stanford, Calif.: Stanford University Press, 1972); *Authority, Participation, and Cultural Change in China*, edited and with an introduction by Stuart R. Schram (Cambridge University Press, 1973); *Chairman Mao Talks to the People: Talks and Letters: 1956–1971*, edited and with an introduction by Stuart Schram, translated by John Chinnery and Tieyun (New York: Pantheon, 1974); Delia Davin, *Woman-Work: Women and the Party in Revolutionary China* (Oxford: Clarendon, 1976); Franz Schurmann, *Ideology and Organization in Communist China*, 2nd ed., enlarged (Berkeley and Los Angeles: University of California Press, 1968); A. Doak Barnett, *Cadres, Bureaucracy, and Political Power in Communist China* (New York: Columbia University Press, 1967); A. Doak Barnett (ed.), *Chinese Communist Politics in Action* (Seattle: University of Washington Press, 1969); John Gittings, *The Role of the Chinese Army* (London: Oxford

University Press, 1967); James R. Townsend, *Political Participation in Communist China* (Berkeley and Los Angeles: University of California Press, 1967) and *Politics in China*, 2nd ed. (Little, Brown, 1980); and Ezra Vogel, *Canton under Communism* (Cambridge, Mass.: Harvard University Press, 1969).

The leading scholarly journal devoted entirely to modern China is *The China Quarterly* (London, 1960–   ), which includes a regular chronicle and documentation section as well as valuable articles, reports, notes, and book reviews. Other valuable journals are *Modern China: An International Quarterly* (Beverly Hills, 1975–   ) and Chinese periodicals such as *Beijing Review*, *China Reconstructs*, *China Pictorial*, and *Chinese Literature*.

There are several books that deal with a considerable portion of modern Chinese history and do not fit the chapter listings that follow: Y. C. Wang, *Chinese Intellectuals and the West, 1872–1949*, (Chapel Hill: University of North Carolina Press, 1966); *Biographical Dictionary of Republican China*, edited by Howard L. Boorman and Richard C. Howard, 4 vols. (New York: Columbia University Press, 1967–1970); Joseph R. Levenson, *Confucian China and Its Modern Fate: A Trilogy* (Berkeley: University of California Press, 1968); Guy Alitto, *The Last Confucian* (Berkeley: University of California Press, 1979); and Rhoads Murphey, *The Outsiders: The Western Experience in India and China* (Ann Arbor: University of Michigan Press, 1977).

Finally, among the titles on "modernization," a good starting place is Cyril E. Black, *The Dynamics of Modernization* (New York: Harper & Row, 1966). Other titles include David E. Apter, *The Politics of Modernization* (Chicago: University of Chicago Press, 1965); J. A. Coleman and G. A. Almond, *The Politics of the Developing Areas* (Englewood Cliffs, N.J.: Prentice-Hall, 1960); A. R. Desai, ed., *Essays on Modernization of Underdeveloped Societies*, 2 vols. (New York: Humanities Press, 1971); three books by S. N. Eisenstadt, *Modernization: Protest and Change* (Englewood Cliffs, N.J.: Prentice-Hall, 1966), *Readings in Social Evolution and Development* (New York: Oxford University Press, 1970), and *Tradition, Change and Modernity* (New York: John Wiley, 1973); Irving Louis Horowitz, *Three Worlds of Development* (New York: Oxford University Press, 1966); Alex Inkeles and David H. Smith, *Becoming Modern* (Cambridge, Mass.: Harvard University Press, 1974); John H. Kautsky, *The Political Consequences of Modernization* (New York: John Wiley, 1972); Albert Lauterbach, *Psychological Challenges to Modernization* (New York: Elsevier Scien-

tific Publishing Co., 1974); Daniel Lerner, James S. Coleman, and
Ronald P. Dove, "Modernization," in *International Encyclopedia of the
Social Sciences*, edited by David L. Schils, Vol. 10 (New York:
MacMillan, 1968, pp. 386–409); Daniel Lerner, *The Passing of
Traditional Society* (Glencoe, Ill.: Free Press, 1963); Marion J. Levy,
Jr., *Modernization and The Structure of Societies*, 2 vols. (Princeton,
N.J.: Princeton University Press, 1970); Immanuel Wallerstein, *The
Modern World System* (New York: Academic Press, 1974); Myron
Weiner, ed., *Modernization: The Dynamics of Growth* (New York: Basic
Books, 1966). A Chinese scholar's perspective is presented in Frank
Wen-hui Tsai, *Essays on the Study of Chinese Modernization* (Taipei:
Orient Cultural Service, 1976). A new book, Gilbert Rozman, ed., *The
Modernization of China*, The Free Press, 1981, was received too late to
be evaluated here, but its authors are distinguished students of this
subject.

1   THE MODERN WORLD AND NINETEENTH-CENTURY CHINA

Banno, Masataka. *China and the West, 1858–1861*. Cambridge, Mass.:
    Harvard University Press, 1964.
* Chung-li Chang. *The Chinese Gentry*. Seattle: University of Washing-
    ton Press, 1955.
Cohen, Paul A., and John Schrecker, eds. *Reform in Nineteenth-
    Century China*. Cambridge, Mass.: Harvard University Press,
    1976.
* Fairbank, John K. *Trade and Diplomacy on the China Coast*.
    Cambridge, Mass.: Harvard University Press, 1953.
Hsiao Kung-chüan. *A Modern China and a New World: K'ang Yu-wei
    [Kang Youwei], Reformer and Utopian, 1858–1927*. Seattle:
    University of Washington Press, 1975.
————. *Rural China*. Rev. ed. Seattle: University of Washington
    Press, 1967.
* Hucker, Charles O. *The Traditional Chinese State in Ming Times*.
    Tucson: University of Arizona Press, 1961.
Kuhn, Philip A. *Rebellion and Its Enemies in Late Imperial China:
    Militarization and Social Structure, 1796–1864*. Cambridge,
    Mass.: Harvard University Press, 1970.
Michael, Franz, and Chung-li Chang. *The Taiping Rebellion*. 3 vols.
    Seattle: University of Washington Press, 1966–1970.

Naquin, Susan. *Millenarian Rebellion in China: The Eight Trigrams Uprising of 1813.* New Haven: Yale University Press, 1976.

Overmyer, Daniel L. *Folk Buddhist Religion: Dissenting Sects in Late Traditional China.* Cambridge, Mass.: Harvard University Press, 1976.

Palmer, R. R., and Joel Colton. *A History of the Modern World.* 3rd ed. New York: Knopf, 1961.

* Tung-tsu Ch'ü. *Local Government in China under the Ch'ing.* Cambridge, Mass.: Harvard University Press, 1962.

* Wright, Mary C. *The Last Stand of Chinese Conservatism.* Palo Alto, Calif.: Stanford University Press, 1957.

2 THE SWING TOWARD WESTERNIZATION, 1900–1928

Cameron, Meribeth E. *The Reform Movement in China, 1898–1912.* Palo Alto, Calif.: Stanford University Press, 1931.

* Chow, Tse-tsung. *The May Fourth Movement.* Cambridge, Mass.: Harvard University Press, 1960.

Gasster, Michael. *Chinese Intellectuals and the Revolution of 1911.* Seattle: University of Washington Press, 1969.

Grieder, Jerome B. *Hu Shih [Hu Shi] and The Chinese Renaissance: Liberalism in the Chinese Revolution, 1917–1937.* Cambridge, Mass.: Harvard University Press, 1970.

Kapp, Robert A. *Szechwan [Sichuan] and The Chinese Republic: Provincial Militarism and Central Power, 1911–1938.* New Haven: Yale University Press, 1973.

* Levenson, Joseph R. *Liang Ch'i-ch'ao [Liang Qichao] and the Mind of Modern China.* Cambridge, Mass.: Harvard University Press, 1953.

McCormack, Gavan. *Chang Tso-lin [Zhang Zuolin] in Northeast China, 1911–1928: China, Japan, and The Manchurian Idea.* Stanford, Calif.: Stanford University Press, 1978.

McDonald, Angus W., Jr. *The Urban Origins of Rural Revolution: Elites and The Masses in Hunan Province, China, 1911–1927.* Stanford, Calif.: University of California Press, 1978.

Schiffrin, Harold Z. *Sun Yat-sen [Sun Yatsen]: Reluctant Revolutionary.* Boston: Little, Brown, 1980.

* ———. *Sun Yat-sen and the Origins of the Chinese Revolution.* Berkeley: University of California Press, 1969.

Schwartz, Benjamin. *In Search of Wealth and Power: Yen Fu [Yan Fu] and the West*. Cambridge, Mass.: Harvard University Press, 1964.

Sheridan, James E. *Chinese Warlord: The Career of Feng Yü-hsiang [Feng Yuxiang]*. Stanford, Calif.: Stanford University Press, 1966.

Sutton, Donald S. *Provincial Militarism and The Chinese Republic: The Yunnan Army, 1905–25*. Ann Arbor: University of Michigan Press, 1980.

Tretiakov, S. M. *A Chinese Testament*. New York: Simon & Schuster, 1934.

* Wright, Mary C., ed. *China in Revolution: The First Phase, 1900–1913*. New Haven: Yale University Press, 1968.

Young, Ernest P. *The Presidency of Yüan Shih-k'ai: Liberalism and Dictatorship in Early Republican China*. Ann Arbor: University of Michigan Press, 1977.

3 MODERNIZATION UNDER THE GUOMINDANG GOVERNMENT, 1928–1949

* Barnett, A. Doak. *China on the Eve of Communist Takeover*. New York: Praeger, 1963.

Chang, John K. "Industrial Development of China, 1912–1949," *Journal of Economic History*, 28 (March 1967): 56–81.

———. *Industrial Development in Pre-Communist China*. Chicago: Aldine, 1969.

* Ch'ien, Tuan-sheng. *The Government and Politics of China*. Cambridge, Mass.: Harvard University Press, 1950.

Chu, Samuel C. "The New Life Movement, 1934–1937." In John E. Lane, ed., *Researches in the Social Sciences on China*. New York: East Asian Institute, Columbia University, 1957.

Dirlik, Arif. "The Ideological Foundations of The New Life Movement: A Study in Counterrevolution," *Journal of Asian Studies*, 34 (August 1975): 945–980.

Eastman, Lloyd E. *The Abortive Revolution: China Under Nationalist Rule, 1927–1937*. Cambridge, Mass.: Harvard University Press, 1974.

* Feuerwerker, Albert. *The Chinese Economy, 1912–1949*. Ann Arbor: Center for Chinese Studies, University of Michigan, 1968.

Liu, F. F. [Liu Chih-pu]. *A Military History of Modern China, 1924–1949*. Princeton, N.J.: Princeton University Press, 1956.

Liu, Ta-chung, and Kung-chia Yeh. *The Economy of the Chinese Mainland: National Income and Economic Development, 1933–1959*. Princeton, N.J.: Princeton University Press, 1965.

* North, Robert C. *Kuomintang and Chinese Communist Elites*. Stanford, Calif.: Stanford University Press, 1952.

* Peck, Graham. *Two Kinds of Time*. Boston: Houghton Mifflin, 1950.

Skinner, G. William. "Marketing and Social Structure in Rural China, Part II," *Journal of Asian Studies*, 24 (February 1965): 195–228.

Sun Yat-sen. *San Min Chu I, The Three Principles of the People*. Frank W. Price, trans. Shanghai: The Commercial Press, 1927.

Tien, Hung-mao. *Government and Politics in Kuomintang China, 1927–1937*. Stanford, Calif.: Stanford University Press, 1972.

Tung W. L. *Political Institutions of Modern China*. New York: International Publications Service, 1964.

4 THE RISE OF THE CHINESE COMMUNIST PARTY, 1920–1949

* Barnett, A. Doak, ed. *Chinese Communist Politics in Action*. Seattle: University of Washington Press, 1969. See Part One, articles by Roy Hofheinz, Jr., Ilpyong J. Kim, and Mark Selden.

* Belden, Jack. *China Shakes the World*. New York: Monthly Review Press, 1970.

* Chen, Jerome. *Mao and the Chinese Revolution*. New York: Oxford University Press, 1967.

Chesneaux, Jean. *The Chinese Labor Movement, 1919–1927*. Stanford, Calif.: Stanford University Press, 1968.

* Compton, Boyd. *Mao's China: Party Reform Documents, 1942–44*. Seattle: University of Washington Press, 1952.

Eto, Shinkichi. "Hai-lu-feng: The First Chinese Soviet Government," *China Quarterly*, 8 (October–December 1961): 161–183 and No. 9 (January–March 1962): 149–181.

* Hinton, William. *Fanshen: A Documentary of Revolution in a Chinese Village*, New York: Vintage Books, 1968.

Hofheinz, Roy, Jr. *The Broken Wave: The Chinese Communist Peasant Movement, 1922–1928*. Cambridge, Mass.: Harvard University Press, 1977.

* Johnson, Chalmers A. *Peasant Nationalism and Communist Power:*

The Emergence of Revolutionary China, 1937–1945. Stanford, Calif.: Stanford University Press, 1962.

Kataoka, Tetsuya. *Resistance and Revolution in China: The Communists and the Second United Front.* Berkeley and Los Angeles: University of California Press, 1974.

Kim, Ilpyong J. *The Politics of Chinese Communism: Kiangsi [Jiangxi] under the Soviets.* Berkeley and Los Angeles: University of California Press, 1973.

* Mao Tse-tung [Mao Zedong]. *Selected Military Writings, 1928–1949.* Peking [Beijing]: Foreign Languages Press, 1963.

Pepper, Suzanne. *Civil War in China: The Political Struggle, 1945–1949.* Berkeley and Los Angeles: University of California Press, 1978.

Rue, John E. *Mao Tse-tung in Opposition, 1927–1935.* Stanford, Calif.: Stanford University Press, 1966.

* Schram, Stuart R. *Mao Tse-tung.* New York: Simon & Schuster, 1967.

* ———. *The Political Thought of Mao Tse-tung.* Rev. ed., enlarged. New York: Praeger, 1969.

Schran, Peter. *Guerrilla Economy: The Development of the Shensi-Kansu-Ningshia [Shaanxi-Gansu-Ningxia] Border Region, 1937–1945.* State University of New York Press, 1976.

* Selden, Mark. *The Yenan [Yan'an] Way in Revolutionary China.* Cambridge, Mass.: Harvard University Press, 1971.

* Snow, Edgar. *Red Star Over China.* New York: Random House, 1938.

Swarup, Shanti. *A Study of the Chinese Communist Movement, 1927–1934.* Oxford: Clarendon, 1966.

Van Slyke, Lyman P. *Enemies and Friends: The United Front in Chinese Communist History.* Stanford, Calif.: Stanford University Press, 1967.

* Whiting, Allen S. *Soviet Policies in China, 1917–1924.* New York: Columbia University Press, 1954.

* Wilson, Dick. *The Long March, 1935: The Epic of Chinese Communism's Survival.* New York: Viking Press, 1972.

5   THE PEOPLE'S REPUBLIC OF CHINA, PART ONE: FROM VICTORY AND UNITY TO CRISIS AND STRIFE, 1949–1960

Barnett, A. Doak. *Cadres, Bureaucracy, and Political Power in Communist China.* New York: Columbia University Press, 1967.

* ———. *Chinese Communist Politics in Action*. Seattle: University of Washington Press, 1969.

* Bowie, Robert R., and John K. Fairbank. *Communist China 1955–59, Policy Documents with Analysis*. Cambridge, Mass.: Harvard University Press, 1962.

Cheng, J. Chester, ed. *The Politics of The Chinese Red Army: A Translation of the Bulletin of Activities of The People's Liberation Army*. Stanford, Calif.: Hoover Institution on War, Revolution, and Peace, 1966.

Hofheinz, Roy. "Rural Administration in Communist China," *China Quarterly*, 11 (July–September 1962): 140–159.

Lieberthal, Kenneth G. *Revolution and Tradition in Tientsin [Tianjin], 1949–52*. Stanford: Stanford University Press, 1980.

Lippit, Victor D. "The Great Leap Forward Reconsidered," *Modern China*, 1 (January 1975): pp. 92–115.

MacFarquhar, Roderick. *The Origins of The Cultural Revolution: 1. Contradictions among the People, 1956–1957*. New York: Columbia University Press, 1974.

* Schwartz, Benjamin. *Chinese Communism and the Rise of Mao*. Cambridge, Mass.: Harvard University Press, 1951.

Shue, Vivienne. *Peasant China in Transition: The Dynamics of Development Toward Socialism, 1949–1956*. Berkeley and Los Angeles: University of California Press, 1980.

Skinner, G. William. "Marketing and Social Structure in Rural China, Part III," *Journal of Asian Studies*, 24 (May 1965): 363–399.

Snow, Edgar. *The Other Side of the River*. New York: Random House, 1962.

* Yang, C. K. *A Chinese Village in Early Communist Transition*. Cambridge, Mass.: Technology Press, 1959.

6 THE PEOPLE'S REPUBLIC OF CHINA, PART TWO:
MODERNIZATION AND REVOLUTION, 1961–1981

Brugger, Bill, ed. *China: The Impact of the Cultural Revolution*. London: Croom Helm, 1978.

A Chinese Biogas Manual. Ed., Ariane van Buren; technical ed., Leo Pyle; trans., Michael Crook; from the original by the Office of the Leading Group for the Propagation of Marshgas, Sichuan Province. London: Intermediate Technology Publications, 1979.

China: A Reassessment of the Economy. A Compendium of Papers Submitted to the Joint Economic Committee, Congress of the

United States. Washington, D.C.: U.S. Government Printing Office, 1975.

Chinese Economy Post-Mao. A Compendium of Papers Submitted to the Joint Economic Committee, Congress of the United States. Volume 1. Policy and Performance. Washington, D.C.: U.S. Government Printing Office, 1978.

Dittmer, Lowell. "Death and Transfiguration: Liu Shaoqi's Rehabilitation and Contemporary Chinese Politics," *Journal of Asian Studies,* 40 (May 1981): 455–479.

Domes, Jürgen. "New Policies in the Communes: Notes on Rural Societal Structures in China, 1976-1981," *Journal of Asian Studies,* 41 (February 1982): 253–267.

An Economic Profile of Mainland China. Studies Prepared for the Joint Economic Committee, Congress of the United States. 2 vols. Washington, D.C.: U.S. Government Printing Office, 1967.

* Frolic, B. Michael. *Mao's People: Sixteen Portraits of Life in Revolutionary China.* Cambridge, Mass.: Harvard University Press, 1980.

Gray, Jack, and Patrick Cavendish. *Chinese Communism in Crisis: Maoism and the Cultural Revolution.* New York: Praeger, 1968.

Lee, Hong Yung. *The Politics of the Chinese Cultural Revolution.* Berkeley and Los Angeles: University of California Press, 1978.

Murphey, Rhoads. *The Fading of the Maoist Vision: City and Country in China's Development.* New York: Methuen, 1980.

Oksenberg, Michel. "Communist China: A Quiet Crisis in Revolution," *Asian Survey,* 6 (January 1966): 3–11.

Parish, William L., and Martin King Whyte. *Village and Family in Contemporary China.* Chicago: University of Chicago Press, 1978.

People's Republic of China: An Economic Assessment. A Compendium of Papers Submitted to the Joint Economic Committee, Congress of the United States. Washington, D.C.: U.S. Government Printing Office, 1972.

Seymour, James D., ed. *The Fifth Modernization: China's Human Rights Movement, 1978–1979.* Stanfordville, N.Y.: Human Rights Publishing Group, 1980.

Skinner, G. William. "Vegetable Supply and Marketing in Chinese Cities," *China Quarterly,* 76 (December 1978): 733–793.

Terrill, Ross., ed. *The China Difference.* New York: Harper & Row, 1979.

CHRONOLOGY

1839–1860	Period of "opium wars" and "unequal treaties"
1850–1864	Taiping Rebellion
1884–1885	China defeated in war with France
1894–1895	China defeated in war with Japan
1897–1898	Foreign powers' rush for colonies in China
1898	Hundred Days' reform, led by Kang Youwei
1900	Boxer Uprising
1905	Abolition of China's traditional civil service examination system; founding of Revolutionary Alliance, led by Sun Yatsen
OCTOBER 1911	Outbreak of republican revolution
1912	Abdication of Manchus and establishment of Republic of China
MAY 1915	Japan presents Twenty-one Demands to China
1919	May Fourth Movement
JULY 1921	First congress of Chinese Communist Party
JANUARY 1923	Joint statement by Sun Yatsen and Adolph Joffe; beginning of cooperation between Guomindang and CCP (first united front)

1925	May Thirtieth Movement against foreigners in Shanghai
MARCH 1926	Coup by Jiang Kaishek against Communists in Guangzhou
JULY 1926	Beginning of Northern Expedition
APRIL 1927	Jiang Kaishek breaks with Guomindang left and Communists
OCTOBER 1927	Mao Zedong sets up Hunan-Jiangxi Border Area regime
OCTOBER 1928	Founding of Nationalist government; Jiang Kaishek president
SEPTEMBER 1931	Japan invades Manchuria
NOVEMBER 1931	Founding of the Chinese Soviet Republic in Jiangxi province
OCTOBER 1934	Beginning of the Long March
OCTOBER 1935	CCP headquarters established in Shaanxi province, near Yan'an
JULY 1937	Beginning of Sino-Japanese War; second Guomindang–CCP united front
DECEMBER 1938	Fighting resumes between Guomindang and CCP forces
APRIL–JUNE 1945	Seventh CCP Congress. Recognition of Mao's leadership
AUGUST 1945	War with Japan ends; CCP and Guomindang negotiations begin
JULY 1946	Beginning of civil war
JANUARY 1949	End of battle of Huaihai, last major military engagement of civil war; Communists take Beijing
OCTOBER 1949	Establishment of People's Republic of China
FEBRUARY 1950	Sino-Soviet Pact of Friendship and Alliance, and trade agreement between China and Soviet Union
JUNE 1950	Adoption of land reform law
DECEMBER 1952	Announcement of First Five-Year Plan to begin in 1953
SUMMER–FALL 1955	Drive to fulfill targets of Five-Year Plan and promote agricultural cooperatives

SEPTEMBER 1956	Eighth CCP Congress: Collective leadership, Mao downgraded
MAY 1957	Hundred Flowers period; three weeks of free expression
JUNE 1957	Beginning of antirightist campaign
AUGUST 1957	Beginning of *xiafang*; cadres sent to work in factories and villages
FALL 1957	Beginning of decentralization
MAY 1958	Great Leap Forward policies stated
DECEMBER 1958	Retreat from Great Leap Forward; Mao resigns as chairman of government
1960 TO JANUARY 1961	A second Great Leap Forward
1962–1965	Socialist Education Movement
1963–1964	Campaign to "Learn from the People's Liberation Army"
NOVEMBER 1965	First signs of Great Proletarian Cultural Revolution
MAY 1966	GPCR begins in universities
AUGUST 1966	GPCR fully under way; Red Guards officially recognized
APRIL 1967	Campaign against Liu Shaoqi officially begins
1968	China governed by "revolutionary committees"
APRIL 1969	Ninth CCP Congress, Lin Biao named Mao's successor
DECEMBER 1970 TO AUGUST 1971	Party committees established in all provinces, replace revolutionary committees
SEPTEMBER 1971	Lin Biao plot to assassinate Mao fails; death of Lin
OCTOBER 1971	People's Republic of China accepts Chinese seat in United Nations
1972–1973	Rehabilitation of GPCR victims; Deng Xiaoping returns, April 1973
AUGUST 1973	Tenth CCP Congress; power of military reduced
1973–1974	Revival of GPCR themes, especially continuing class struggle

APRIL 1974	Deng addresses United Nations, says socialist camp no longer exists, China belongs to Third World
SUMMER 1975	Ten-Year Plan for economic development formulated
JANUARY 1976	Death of Zhou Enlai, Hua Guofeng named acting premier
APRIL 1976	Tiananmen incident: pro-Zhou Enlai mass demonstration suppressed in Beijing, Deng Xiaoping dismissed from posts
JULY 1976	Death of Zhu De; Tangshan earthquake
SEPTEMBER 1976	Death of Mao Zedong
OCTOBER 1976	Arrest of four radical leaders including Jiang Qing, "gang of four" accused of conspiracy; Hua Guofeng succeeds Mao as CCP Chairman
DECEMBER 1976	Hua proclaims criticism of "gang of four" to be China's first task; party building, learning from Dazhai and Daqing also stressed; tributes to Mao Zedong continue
JULY 1977	CCP restores Deng Xiaoping to all posts and expels "gang of four"
AUGUST 1977	Eleventh CCP Congress, GPCR declared victoriously ended, "three great revolutionary movements" to continue; Hua confirmed as premier
FEBRUARY 1978	Ten-year draft economic plan approved, stress on closing gap between China and "advanced world levels," "four modernizations"
MARCH 1978	Concessions made to former capitalists and landlords
NOVEMBER 1978	Tienanmen incident declared "completely revolutionary," Deng exonerated; more GPCR victims rehabilitated; "thaw" begins
DECEMBER 1978	CCP declares "socialist modernization" to be central task, new emphasis on agricultural development and on foreign trade and investment
JANUARY–MARCH 1979	Political thaw becomes protest movement, authorities crack down
MARCH–APRIL 1979	Reevaluation of new modernization policies, sharp debate

JUNE 1979	Modernization policies checked, "readjustment" proclaimed
SEPTEMBER 1979	Reevaluation of Mao and GPCR begins, emphasis on order and stability
DECEMBER 1979	"Democracy wall" closed
FEBRUARY 1980	Liu Shaoqi posthumously rehabilitated; Hu Yaobang named general secretary of CCP; 1950 treaty with Soviet Union expires
APRIL 1980	Constitution revised, "four bigs" amendment rescinded
AUGUST–SEPTEMBER 1980	Joint ventures with foreign investors permitted; new marriage law; Hua resigns as premier, replaced by Zhao Ziyang; ten-year economic plan dropped
NOVEMBER 1980–JANUARY 1981	Trial of "gang of four"
APRIL–JUNE 1981	Reevaluation of Mao discussed publicly
JUNE–JULY 1981	Party resolutions downgrade Mao and condemn GPCR

INDEX

Agricultural Producers Cooperatives (APCs), 105–6, 113–14, 121, 182
Agriculture, 63, 64, 84, 111, 113, 115, 123, 130–31, 133, 151, 154–55, 173, 180
   reform of, 76, 81, 84, 105–6, 112

Belden, Jack, 3
Birth control, 116
Borodin, Michael, 71
Buddhism, 6
Bureaucratism, 8, 98, 101, 109, 113, 127, 135, 146, 179

Cadres, 2, 86–89, 101–3, 105–6, 108–10, 113, 120, 134, 145, 166
Capitalism, 43, 64, 67, 106, 110, 176
Chen Duxiu (Ch'en Tu-hsiu), 35, 40, 67–68
Chinese Communist party (CCP)
   Central Committee, 76, 111, 126, 136
   criticism invited, 108–10
   factionalism and internal dissension, 128, 132, 136, 138–39, 141, 143–44, 156–57, 165, 171
   founding of, 67–70
   guerrilla tactics of, 89, 118, 134
   and Guomindang, 41–42, 44–45, 48, 51, 59, 69, 76, 103–4, 125
   membership, 85–86, 100
   organization and expansion, 40–41, 66–91, 99–111
   party congresses, 69, 107, 148, 158, 163
   v. Russian communism, 41, 75, 81, 92, 95–96, 98, 106–7, 149
   Yan'an period, 79–88
Chinese people
   bourgeois ideology, 100, 102, 108, 112–13, 146, 161, 176–77
   family system, 4, 7, 9, 11, 35, 54–55
   prejudices against, 19–20
   secret societies, 23, 30–31
   social classes, 8–9, 11, 54

206

ABOUT THE AUTHOR

MICHAEL GASSTER has been teaching Chinese history at Rutgers University since 1970. Before going to Rutgers he taught at Princeton, The George Washington University, and the University of Washington. He received his education in the New York City public schools and at City College of New York, Columbia University, and the University of Washington. As a student he spent two years in Taiwan (1957–1959) studying the Chinese language and doing research for his doctoral dissertation. In 1979–1980 he was in the People's Republic of China as a research scholar sponsored by the National Academy of Sciences. He made shorter visits to Taiwan in 1970 and 1975 and to the People's Republic of China in 1976 and 1981. In addition to this book he is the author of *Chinese Intellectuals and The Revolution of 1911: The Birth of Modern Chinese Radicalism* (Seattle: University of Washington Press, 1969) and articles and book reviews on modern Chinese history.

A Note on the Type

This book was set on the Linotron in Bodoni Book, named after Giambattista Bodoni (1740–1813), son of a printer of Piedmont. After gaining experience and fame as a superintendent of the Press of the Propaganda in Rome, in 1768 Bodoni became the head of the ducal printing house at Parma, which he soon made the foremost of its kind in Europe. His *Manuale Tipografico*, completed by his widow in 1818, contains 279 pages of type specimens, including alphabets of about thirty languages. His editions of Greek, Latin, Italian, and French classics are celebrated for their typography. In type designing he was a innovator, making his new faces rounder, wider, and lighter, with greater openness and delicacy, and with sharper contrast between the thick and thin lines.